$15.00

201

Breaking the Chain
Women, Theory, and French Realist Fiction

GENDER AND CULTURE
Carolyn G. Heilbrun and Nancy K. Miller, Editors

BREAKING THE CHAIN

Women, Theory, and
French Realist Fiction

NAOMI SCHOR

New York   COLUMBIA UNIVERSITY PRESS

*The Andrew W. Mellon Foundation, through a special grant,
has assisted the Press in publishing this volume.*

Library of Congress Cataloging in Publication Data

Schor, Naomi.
Breaking the chain.

(Gender and culture)
Bibliography: p.
Includes index.
1. French fiction—19th century—History and
criticism. 2. Women in literature. 3. French
fiction—Men authors—History and criticism.
4. Feminism and literature. 5. Psychoanalysis and
literature. 6. Realism in literature. 7. Naturalism
in literature. I. Title. II. Series.
PQ653.S3 1985   843'.009'9287   84-23697

ISBN 0-231-05874-8
ISBN 0-231-05875-6   (pa.)

COLUMBIA UNIVERSITY PRESS
NEW YORK   GUILFORD, SURREY
COPYRIGHT © 1985 COLUMBIA UNIVERSITY PRESS

For
Nancy

Gender and Culture
A series of Columbia University Press

Edited by
Carolyn G. Heilbrun and Nancy Miller

Contents

Preface

The writing of *Breaking the Chain* spans eight years (1975–1983) which witnessed a number of significant developments in the fields of literary theory and criticism, notably the passing of structuralism and the rise in its wake of two equally powerful movements: feminism and deconstruction. These essays are the product of this age of transition and liberation and in preparing them for publication in book form, I have resisted the impulse to idealization through the erasure of all marks of time. Nor could I erase them if I wanted to. My debt to structuralism and its poetics is immense and woven into the very fabric of my texts: it is most apparent in my overriding and abiding concern with what is known in structuralese as the "literariness" of the text, that is, in this instance, with what is *specifically literary* about the representation of woman in nineteenth-century French fiction, with the *poetics of representation* of the female protagonist in the realist novel. If, however, structuralism provided me with invaluable tools for studying the functioning of the feminocentric text, it also placed in my path (and not only mine, of course) sizable stumbling blocks which made it impossible, indeed unthinkable, for me to write *as a woman* until the critique of structuralism undertaken by those theoreticians known loosely as post-structuralists, Jacques Derrida in particular, was well under way.

It is difficult but I think important—if only to "bear witness"—to communicate to younger critics, especially the feminist, who have come of age in the relatively permissive intellectual climate of post-structuralism, the subtle oppression exercised by structuralism at its least self-critical and most doctrinaire on a reader who bridled at bracketing herself, who felt stifled in a conceptual universe organized into the neat paradigms of binary logic, and who ultimately found it impossible to accept the claims to universality of models of intelligibility elaborated without taking gender into account. It was not then until Derrida began to deconstruct the

ix

major paradigms/hierarchies of Western metaphysics at their linguistic foundations that feminist criticism became possible in the context of departments of *French* in American universities. The fact that, as is becoming increasingly obvious, the relationship of deconstruction and feminism is complex and fraught with controversy, should not obscure the immense significance of early Derrida for French neo-feminisms and, by the same token, their American spin-offs: when the writings of such influential figures as Hélène Cixous and Luce Irigaray were imported to the United States, they brought along with them Derrida's critique of phallogocentrism, as well as deconstructive reading strategies.

Because deconstruction can intersect with feminism at different levels—now enhancing difference, now interrogating the very categories of gender—caution dictates that one define as clearly as possible how one views that articulation. I see it as double: there is first and foremost deconstruction's undoing of the man/woman hierarchy with its concomitant valorization of the previously devalorized term. So far as my own reading practice is concerned, however, the uses of deconstruction for feminism are not limited to the still timely inversion of the paradigm of sexual difference, they consist also in the homologous inversion of what I would call the paradigm of significance: essential/accessory. In other words, these essays are written in the space opened up by the valorization of woman *and* the detail deconstruction entails. This is not to say that I believe that woman as writer or reader possesses an inborn affinity for details, an essentialist argument I regard as dangerous for the elaboration of both a feminist poetics and aesthetics. What I do believe is that a pronounced attention to details has traditionally been connoted as feminine and hence devalorized. And, further, that it is in textual details either overlooked or misprized by male critics that something crucial about woman's stake in representation is to be found. These details refer to the female body, in particular the synecdochic axis so highly prized by the fetishist linking woman's sexual organs to her foot. *Refetishizing the fetish* may well be a necessary step in understanding the function of the female protagonist in realism, for finally my concern is not so much with the *representation of woman* as with the relationship between *woman and representation*.

Feminist criticism has amply demonstrated the remarkable consistency with which representational fiction has from its origins figured the particularly inexorable repression to which female desire is subject under bourgeois patriarchy. *Breaking the Chain* can be seen as part of a series of critical studies concerned with mapping the strategies deployed in representation to contain female libido, works that have often resorted to striking spatial metaphors to lend a sensory immediacy to the fate of the female protagonist: the attic (Gilbert and Gubar) and, at the other end of the vertical axis, the crypt (Kamuf). Implicit in my readings of some of the major as well as "minor" novels written in France in the nineteenth century is the conviction I share with Nina Auerbach—who in *Woman and the Demon* has shown that the familiar images of mutilated and infantilized womanhood so widespread in Victorian literature are the obverse side of a vision of woman as a demonic figure of terrifying power and irrepressible mobility—that the apparent victimage of nineteenth-century female protagonists testifies to a perception of femininity as anything but passive and pathetic. The French tradition cannot, of course, be simply assimilated to the English, not only because it is caught up in a different intertextual network and embedded in a different historical context, but also because our access to these national traditions, our constructions and reconstructions are filtered through a different set of lenses: where Auerbach sees a Demon, I see a figure in the image of my own "continental" preoccupations, woman as orgasmic mother (Kristeva) and possessor of the Logos (Cixous). Ultimately for me the question becomes not how but why. What function, if any, is served by the repression of female libido within the economy of the realist text? By focusing on the detail of the foot, chained and/or unchained, I am led to conclude that the binding of female energy is one of (if not) the enabling conditions of the forward movement of the "classical text." Realism is that paradoxical moment in Western literature when representation can neither accommodate the Otherness of Woman nor exist without it.

With the sole exception of the final essay, which serves as a general theoretical statement, I have left the essays in the order in which they were written, an order which quite obviously violates the chronology of literary history, but is consonant with another logic, that of the unconscious. The five essays I have grouped together under the rubric, "Reading (for) the Feminine" mime the process referred to in psychoanalytic terms as "working through." Working through is the long haul of the psychoanalytic treatment during which resistance is slowly overcome. At stake in these essays is the female critic's insertion into patriarchal theoretical discourse. This process has often—aptly I think—been described in playful terms, as a form of either playacting (Irigaray's "mimeticism") or playing around (Kolodny's "playful pluralism"). Because the discourse woman mimes or appropriates is almost always the father's, I prefer to call this process *patriody*, a term I have borrowed from Joyce to translate my French coinage, "pèrodie." Patriody names a linguistic act of repetition and difference which hovers between parody and parricide. What I have in mind here is neither Gilbert and Gubar's feminization of Bloomian "anxiety of influence," nor Gallop's allegorization of feminism's relationship to psychoanalysis as the mutual seduction of father and daughter. In the first instance the recoded oedipal scenario concerns the relationship of women writers to their *female* predecessors, in the second, it involves the relationship of the daughter to a *single* body of patriarchal theory: psychoanalysis. Patriody as it is practiced in "Reading (for) the Feminine" links woman as theorist to a number of symbolic fathers through language. My use of the word *patriody*, which may irritate some readers, is meant to body forth the inherently linguistic nature of woman's playful relationship to paternal theoretical discourse.

Nowhere in this volume is the transition between structuralism—with its emphasis on literary texts as allegories of structural linguistics—and poststructuralism—with its deconstruction of the basic dichotomies of structuralist linguistics—more tangible than in "For a Restricted Thematics: Writing, Speech, and Difference in *Madame Bovary*." As long as Emma is apprehended within the confines of the binary logic that opposes speech to writing, the longheld masculinist view of her as a "foolish woman" (Lubbock) prevails. As soon as one becomes aware of the split within writing itself, on the other hand, another aspect of Emma comes into view: she appears as the figure of a writer whose relationship to writing approximates Flaubert's and is opposed to that of Homais, that representative of representation. The difference *within* writing is then coextensive with the difference *between* the sexes, as it is bodied forth by the Emma/Homais couple.

In "Smiles of the Sphinx: Zola and the Riddle of Femininity," another structuralist paradigm is deconstructed in the light of sexual difference. My concern here is with one of the most celebrated models of intelligibility proposed by Roland Barthes, the Hermeneutic Code. Applying this code to two novels by Zola and one by Balzac, I show that the implicit claims to universality made for this code are shattered when it is brought to bear on feminocentric texts grounded in the representation of woman

as enigma. Unlike the oedipal text Barthes takes as his model, the preoedipal text is marked by the nonsynchronicity of closure and the exhaustion of the riddle. The smiles of the Sphinx allegorizes by its insistent plural the feminocentric text's, but also the female reader's resistance
to closure and resolution.

The essay on Maupassant, which while centered on *Une Vie* takes into
account his entire fictional oeuvre, examines the validity for feminocentric texts of another supposedly universal law: the primordial role of the
paternal signifier in the formation of the speaking subject according to
Jacques Lacan. Read with the heightened attention to the signifier and
its insistence Lacanism requires, Maupassant's texts appear to be informed by the anagrammatization of the name not of his father but of
his mother.

René Girard's sacrificial scenario—yet another genderless cultural model
with sweeping claims to universality—is the focus of the essay on Barbey
d'Aurevilly's *L'Ensorcelée*. Reading Girard against himself, I look at the
ways the sacrificial syntax misfires in a novel whose female protagonist is
"scandalized."

In the last essay in this section, *"Eugénie Grandet:* Mirrors and Melancholia," I return to Lacan, more specifically to some of the uses to which
his notions of the Imaginary and the Symbolic have been put by male
critics working on phallocentric texts. These applications are doubly
problematic: they implicitly devalorize the Imaginary as the realm of the
maternal, while glossing over what Luce Irigaray has shown to be the
phallocentrism built in to the very notion of the mirror stage. The feminist revalorization of the Imaginary is inseparable from its critique.

What emerges at the end of "Reading (for) the Feminine" is a developmental model at odds with the one derived from Lacan, which calls
for the mediation of the mother-child dyad by the paternal instance: in
order for the feminist critic to break her illusory mirror relationship with
her symbolic father or fathers, the intervention of a maternal instance is
necessary. Thus, in "Salammbô Bound," two contrasting and even conflicting accounts of Freud's essay on fetishism, Derrida's and Kristeva's,
are brought into play to read a novel in which the chain that impedes
woman's progress in nineteenth-century French fiction is explicitly thematized and fleetingly broken. By focusing on the detail of the chain and
its vicissitudes in masculinist readings of Flaubert's *Salammbô*, I want to
propose a poetics of reading which not only takes over details referring

to woman's body, but also breaks the linearity of the signifying chain, in order to privilege what Roman Jakobson calls "concurrence" over "concatenation."

Throughout "Breaking the Chain" my concern is with the function of woman in some of the dominant modes of representation in the latter half of nineteenth-century France: realism, naturalism, and the decadent style I prefer to call ornamentalism. "Naturalizing Woman: *Germinie Lacerteux*" examines the process whereby woman is inducted into naturalism in the light of a minor passage in Barthes' *S/Z*, while in "Unwriting *Lamiel*," I consider the implications for the relationship of woman and realism of Stendhal's unwriting of one of the most remarkable feminocentric texts of the nineteenth century.

The heterogeneity of these texts is flagrant: some were originally written in French, others in English; some are quite long, others very brief; some make use of the metalanguages of structuralism, others eschew metalanguage altogether. I hope that these differences in tone and texture will be regarded as adding to rather than detracting from the volume's interest.

I am pleased to thank those who helped me bring this manuscript into being: first and foremost my friend and colleague Karen Newman, who initiated me into the wonders of the computer, and Tracy Clark, Ann Murphy, and Ted Hopton who helped input large sections of the manuscript with cheerful expertise. I owe a special debt of gratitude to Elisabeth Weed who kindly accepted to read my manuscript and most of whose helpful suggestions have been incorporated in the final text.

Though largely unthematized, the mother-daughter relationship features prominently in several of these texts; it seems only fitting then for me to express my deepest gratitude for her unwavering support to my mother, Resia Schor, maker and breaker of chains.

I
READING (FOR) THE FEMININE

I

For a Restricted Thematics: Writing, Speech, and Difference in *Madame Bovary*

It is time to say out loud what has been whispered for some time: thematic criticism, which was given a first-class funeral a few years ago, is not dead. Like a repressed desire that insists on returning to consciousness, like a guilty pleasure that resists all threat of castration, thematic criticism is coming out from the shadows. This new thematic criticism is not, however, a nostalgic textual practice, a "retro" criticism, a regression to the styles (of reading) of the 1950s. Just as hyperrealism in painting is a return to the figurative passed through a minimalist grid, neothematism is a thematism passed through the filter of structuralist criticism. One could even argue that a certain structuralism, namely structural semantics, was in fact never anything but a recuperation of thematism, a structuralist neothematism.

But it is not our purpose to study the persistence of thematics; the point is not, within the narrow framework of our study, to anticipate a history of contemporary criticism which is yet to be written.[1] Rather it is a question of opening an inquiry into the continuity that links thematics, structural semantics, and even "poststructuralism." This very undertaking, this implicit valorization of continuity, is precisely what to our eyes constitutes thematics' characteristic, distinctive feature: I shall term thematic all textual practices that suffer from what might be called, in the manner of Bachelard, an Ariadne complex, all readings that cling to the Ariadne's thread ("fil conducteur"), whether it be the "synonymic chains" of Barthes, the "chain of supplements" of Derrida, or the "series" of Deleuze.[2] Be it

3

vertical, horizontal, or transversal, the Ariadne's thread haunts the texts of Barthes, Derrida, and Deleuze, not in the typically structuralist form—that is, metalinguistic—of the Greimasian isotope, but in a poetic form: the thread ("fil") has become an extended metaphor. As Deleuze's "spider web," Barthes' "braid," and Derrida's texture indicate,[3] the relationship between the "textural" and the textile is on its way to becoming one of the obsessive metaphors of current criticism.[4] How are we to explain this obsession common to thinkers otherwise so different? One seductive hypothesis is that they all draw from the same source, namely Proust's metaphoric repertory. The following quotations from Richard (on Proust), Derrida (on Plato), and Barthes (on the pleasure of the text) substantiate this notion:

> Thematization thus clearly resembles weaving. The interweaving of all thematic series assumes in the Proustian daydream the form of a net in which the matter of the work is caught, or that of a network, both innervational and cybernetic, that enables us to circulate in it from link to link, knot to knot, "star" to "star" with the utmost freedom; because "between the least significant point in our past and all the others there exists a rich network of memories offering a plethora of communications."[5]

> The dissimulation of the woven texture can in any case take centuries to undo its web: a web that envelops a web, undoing the web for centuries; reconstituting it too as an organism, indefinitely regenerating its own tissue behind the cutting trace, the decision of each reading. There is always a surprise in store for the anatomy or physiology of a critique that might think it had mastered the game, surveyed all the threads at once, a critique that deludes itself too, in wanting to look at the text without touching it, without laying a hand on the "object," without risking—which is the sole chance of entering into the game by getting a few fingers caught—the addition of some new thread. Adding, here, is nothing other than giving to read. One must manage to think this out: that it is not a question of embroidering upon a text, unless one considers that to know how to embroider is still to take heed to follow the given thread. That is, if you follow me, the hidden thread.[6]

While taking the opposite view from Derrida insofar as hidden meaning is concerned, Barthes adopts his textile metaphor; Derrida's *istos* becomes Barthes' *hyphos:*

4

> *Text* means *Tissue;* but whereas hitherto we have always taken
> this tissue as a product, a ready-made veil, behind which lies,
> more or less hidden, meaning (truth) we are now emphasizing,
> in the tissue, the generative idea that the text is made, is worked
> out in a perpetual interweaving; lost in this tissue—this tex-
> ture—the subject unmakes himself, like a spider dissolving in the
> constructive secretions of its web. Were we fond of neologisms,
> we might define the theory of the text as an *hyphology (hyphos* is
> the tissue and the spider's web).[7]

The metaphors that these authors weave again and again are extremely
significant, since according to Freud the only contribution of women "to
the discoveries and inventions in the history of civilization" is a "technique," "that of plaiting and weaving."[8] The thread unraveled by Ariadne, cut by the Fates, woven by Penelope, is a peculiarly feminine attribute, a metonym for femininity. There is thus cause to speculate about
the relations (necessarily hypothetical at the current stage of our knowledge) between a thematic reading and a feminine reading, by which I
certainly do not mean that reading practiced uniquely by women. If my
hypothesis concerning the femininity of thematism were justified, this
would explain its culpabilization on the one hand and, paradoxically, its
masculine recuperation on the other. This hypothesis presupposes a
question: does reading have a sex? And this question in turn brings up
another: does writing have a sex? It is, as we will attempt to demonstrate,
precisely this question of the sex of writing that underlies *Madame Bovary.* We can no longer read *Madame Bovary* outside of the "sexual problematic" that Sartre analyzed in its author,[9] but we must no longer separate the sexual problematic from the scriptural problematic, as did
Baudelaire, who was the first to qualify Emma Bovary as a "strange an-
drogynous creature."[10]

Let us note at the close, in order to weave the many threads of our
introduction, that there exists in *Madame Bovary* the description of an object
which can be readily inscribed in the line of thought that we have just
evoked. I am referring to the green silk cigar case that Charles picks up
when leaving la Vaubyessard and that Emma so preciously keeps. Read,
or reread, in light of the preceding remarks, this passage seems to assume
a new meaning: the green silk cigar case becomes the emblem of the imbrication of weaving, the text, and feminity. *Madame Bovary* thus con-

tains not only an objective correlative of its production, but a protocol for its interpretation as well:

> It had been embroidered on some rosewood frame, a pretty piece of furniture, hidden from all eyes, that had occupied many hours, and over which had fallen the soft curls of the pensive worker. A breath of love had passed over the stitches on the canvas; each prick of the needle had fixed there a hope or a memory, and all those interwoven threads of silk were but the continued extension of the same silent passion.[11]

> On avait brodé cela sur quelque métier de palissandre, meuble mignon que l'on cachait à tous les yeux, qui avait occupé bien des heures et où s'étaient penchées les boucles molles de la travailleuse pensive. Un souffle d'amour avait passé parmi les mailles du canevas; chaque coup d'aiguille avait fixé là une espérance ou un souvenir, et tous ces fils de soie entrelacés n'étaient que la continuité de la même passion silencieuse.[12]

To conclude these prolegomena, I would like to put to the test a new thematics that I propose to call a "restricted thematics" because, if the definition of the field of possible themes must henceforth answer to the call for literary specificity, the reciprocal play of speech and writing will replace the time/space paradigm privileged since Proust, with speech occupying the field of time, and writing inscribed in that of space. Unlike the "general" thematic reading which always tends toward "an infinite reading,"[13] which exists, that is, in an anamorphic relationship with the text, restricted thematics would be the equivalent of an anastomosis, sectioning the text in order to bring together binary opposites (on the semantic plane), doubles (on the actantial plane), and repeated sequences (on the evenemential plane).

> En somme, cette femme est vraiment grande, elle est surtout pitoyable, et malgré la dureté systématique de l'auteur, qui a fait tous ses efforts pour être absent de son œuvre et pour jouer la fonction d'un montreur de marionnettes, toutes les femmes *intellectuelles* lui sauront gré d'avoir élevé la femelle à une si haute puissance, si loin de l'animal pur et si près de l'homme idéal.
>   Baudelaire

As a starting-point for our reflection, let us recall René Girard's statement concerning Flaubert's "grotesque antitheses": "As Flaubert's novelistic genius ripens his oppositions become more futile; the identity of the contraries is drawn more clearly."[14] If—as we are firmly convinced— this breakdown of opposites is manifest at all levels of the Flaubertian text and along its entire diachronic course, how does it apply to the writing/speech opposition, explicitly thematized by Flaubert in *L'Education sentimentale* during a conversation between Frédéric and Madame Arnoux: "She admired orators; he preferred a writer's fame."[15] Does this orators/writers opposition also participate in the obsessional tyranny of the identity of the contraries, in this system of growing in-differentiation?

The speech axis permits a first division of the characters in *Madame Bovary* into two large categories: those who are adept at speaking, such as Rodolphe and Homais, and those who are not, such as Charles and Emma. But the insufficiency of this first distribution is instantly apparent since certain characters adept at speaking are not good listeners. The speech axis must be subordinated to the communication axis, a bipolar axis with at one end an encoder/emitter, at the other a decoder/receiver. Depending on whether or not a character exhibits the aptitudes for encoding and decoding, we can foresee four combinations:

$$(1)\ encoding\ +\quad (2)\ encoding\ -\quad (3)\ encoding\ +\quad (4)\ encoding\ -$$
$$decoding\ +\qquad decoding\ -\qquad decoding\ -\qquad decoding\ +$$

If we examine the characters named above in light of these *roles*,[16] certain aspects of the speech problematic in *Madame Bovary* emerge. From his first appearance, Charles reveals himself to be an impotent speaker:

> The new boy then took a supreme resolution, opened an inordinately large mouth, and shouted at the top of his voice as if calling some one, the word "Charbovari."

> Le *nouveau*, prenant alors une résolution extrême, ouvrit une bouche démesurée et lança à pleins poumons, comme pour appeler quelqu'un, ce mot: *Charbovari*. (p. 3/38)

Incapable of articulating the syllables of his name, Charles can but repeat the words of others:

> Charles' conversation was commonplace as a street pavement, and every one's ideas trooped through it in their everyday garb, without exciting emotion, laughter, or thought.

7

Reading (for) the Feminine

La conversation de Charles était plate comme un trottoir de rue, et les idées de tout le monde y défilaient, dans leur costume ordinaire, sans exciter d'émotion, de rire ou de rêverie. (p. 29/76)

What distinguishes Charles' conversation from that of the glib speaker is not so much its painful banality, but its neutrality. His is an inefficient speech, lacking resonance, a speech in which nothing is transmitted from the enunciator to his interlocutor. Nevertheless, it must be noted that this "zero" on the encoding plane will have a great word, his last:

He even made a phrase, the only one he'd ever made:
"Fate willed it this way."
Il ajouta même un grand mot, le seul qu'il ait jamais dit:
—C'est la faute de la fatalité. (pp. 254–255/366)

The effect of this grandiloquent sentence is, however, doubly subverted by its receptor, Rodolphe:

Rodolphe, who had been the agent of this fate, thought him very meek for a man in his situation, comic even and slightly despicable.
Rodolphe, qui avait conduit cette fatalité, le trouva bien débonnaire pour un homme dans sa situation, comique même, et un peu vil. *(Ibid.)*

First irony: the receptor is, in fact, the encoder. It is Rodolphe who was the first to put the word "fate" into circulation in the novel when he composed his letter breaking with Emma:

Why were you so beautiful? Is it my fault? God, no! only fate is to blame!
"That's a word that always helps," he said to himself.
Pourquoi étiez-vous si belle? Est-ce ma faute? O mon Dieu! non, non, n'en accusez que la fatalité!
—Voilà un mot qui fait toujours de l'effet, se dit-il. (p. 146/230)

And Charles reads this letter (pp. 249–50/360). As we will see below, once launched, this word will continually reappear. In using it in talking to Rodolphe, Charles only completes the series, closes the circuit: Ro-

8

dolphe → Emma → Charles → Rodolphe. Second irony: the original encoder (the "voluntary deceiver"),[17] presents himself as judge and condemns his imitator (his involuntary dupe). Flaubert thus puts the parrot
and the hypocrite back to back.

With Charles the inability to encode goes along with an inability to
decode which makes him unable to understand Emma. For Emma,
speaking to Charles is a last resort:

> At other times, she told him what she had been reading . . .
> for, after all, Charles was someone to talk to, an ever-open ear,
> an ever-ready approbation. She even confided many a thing to
> her greyhound! She would have done so to the logs in the fire-
> place or to the pendulum of the clock.

> Quelquefois aussi, elle lui parlait des choses qu'elle avait lues . . .
> car, enfin, Charles était quelqu'un, une oreille toujours ouverte,
> une approbation toujours prête. Elle faisait bien des confidences
> à sa levrette! Elle en eût fait aux bûches de la cheminée et au
> balancier de la pendule. (p. 44/96)

Charles' qualifications as a listener are minimal; they can be reduced to
the possession of an ear and the promise of his ever-identical reaction.
The equivalence established among Charles, the greyhound, the logs, and
the pendulum says a great deal about his inability to decode, for the progression from the animate to the inanimate, the choice of the logs and
the pendulum in the domestic code, with their semes of hardness (hence
the figurative meaning of "bûche" [log]: "stupid person") and mechan-
icity, confirms Charles' nullity: he actualizes combination #2, which is
doubly negative.

Initially, Rodolphe seems gifted with all the faculties that Charles lacks.
This is not to say that his discourse is more "original" than Charles', but
that he draws from the same dictionary of received ideas as Emma: he
speaks her language. The juxtaposition in the oft-commented-upon chapter of the agricultural fair of Rodolphe's conventional seduction of Emma
and the functionaries' set speech serves only to underscore the parallelism
of the two discourses: opposed on the spatial (vertical) axis, Rodolphe
and the two orators echo each other on the speech axis, as the intersection of the two discourses indicates. The only difference between Rodolphe's speech and that of Charles is that Rodolphe's acts upon Emma;
it evokes dreams, it becomes action, love.

Reading (for) the Feminine

A clever encoder, Rodolphe is also a cunning decoder of corporeal semiology; he is a diagnostician of great talent:

> Monsieur Rodolphe Boulanger was thirty-four; he combined brutality of temperament with a shrewd judgment, having had much experience with women and being something of a connoisseur. This one had seemed pretty to him; so he kept dreaming about her and her husband.
> "I think he is very stupid. She must be tired of him, no doubt. *He has dirty nails, and hasn't shaved for three days.*"
>
> M. Rodolphe Boulanger avait trente-quatre ans; il était de tempérament brutal et d'intelligence perspicace, ayant d'ailleurs beaucoup fréquenté les femmes et s'y connaissant bien. Celle-là lui avait paru jolie: il y rêvait donc, et à son mari.
> —Je le crois très bête. Elle en est fatiguée sans doute. *Il porte des ongles sales et une barbe de trois jours* . . . (p. 93/161; emphasis mine)

But it is precisely that which enables him to decode this *clue*, namely his experience, that prevents him from decoding Emma's oral messages. Having spent his life repeating, indeed perfecting an invariable scenario whose only variant is the partner, Rodolphe cannot go beyond clichés, ready-made formulas. Everything happens as if Rodolphe's decoding mechanism were programmed to function only with information that has already been received. We find in Rodolphe the same "linguistic deafness" that Genette analyzes in certain Proustian characters who, he remarks, only hear what they can or want to hear,[18] that is in the extreme, what they can or want to say. Rodolphe's decoding of Charles' speech (see above) exemplifies this form of listening by projection. Emma's case is, however, far more complex:

> He had so often heard these things said that they did not strike *him* as original. Emma was like all his mistresses; and the charm of novelty, gradually falling away like a garment, laid bare the eternal monotony of passion, that has always the same shape and the same language. He was unable to see, this man so full of experience, the variety of feelings hidden within the same expressions. Since libertine or venal lips had murmured similar phrases, he only faintly believed in the candor of Emma's; he thought one should beware of exaggerated declarations which

only serve to cloak a tepid love; *as though* the abundance of one's soul did not sometimes overflow with empty metaphors, since no one ever has been able to give the exact measure of his needs, his concepts, or his sorrows. The human tongue is like a cracked cauldron on which we beat out tunes to set a bear dancing when we would make the stars weep with our melodies.

Il s'était tant de fois entendu dire ces choses, qu'elles n'avaient *pour lui* rien d'original. Emma ressemblait à toutes les maîtresses; et le charme de la nouveauté, peu à peu tombant comme un vêtement, laissait voir à nu l'éternelle monotonie de la passion, qui a toujours les mêmes formes et le même langage. Il ne distinguait pas, cet homme si plein de pratique, la dissemblance des sentiments sous la parité des expressions. Parce que des lèvres libertines ou vénales lui avaient murmuré des phrases pareilles, il ne croyait que faiblement à la candeur de celles-là; on en devait rabattre, pensait-il, les discours exagérés cachant les affections médiocres; *comme si* la plénitude de l'âme ne débordait pas quelquefois par les métaphores les plus vides, puisque personne, jamais, ne peut donner l'exacte mesure de ses besoins, ni de ses conceptions, ni de ses douleurs, et que la parole humaine est comme un chaudron fêlé où nous battons des mélodies à faire danser les ours, quand on voudrait attendrir les étoiles. (p. 138/219; emphasis mine)

The increased intervention of the narrator from the "him" of disassociation (indirect intervention) to the "as though" of judgment (direct intervention) translates the importance that Flaubert attaches to this passage, in which he puts forth his speech problematic. In effect, this passage does no more than reiterate an invariant opposition: unique feelings vs. common speech. In other words: how does one communicate difference by means of sameness, how does one give an individual charge to words used by all? With Flaubert the renewal of the cliché is not so much a matter of style as metaphysics, for, on a purely linguistic plane, there is in his work as a constant inspiration by the cliché, an aspiration by the received idea. Thus in *L'Education sentimentale* the cliché favors more than it prevents the communication of passionate feelings: "he . . . poured out his love more freely through the medium of commonplaces" (p. 197). But what the cliché cannot communicate is unicity. Two presuppositions underlie this passage: first, there is a "dissimilarity of feelings," original feel-

II

ings, unique essence; second, in an ideal system of speech there is a total adequation of the word and the psychic signified. Flaubert's oral ideal is, to use Genette's expression, nothing but a new "avatar of Cratylism,"[19] which is hardly surprising in this avowed Platonist.

Madame Bovary tests the romantic notions of exceptionality and ineffability, for the destiny of the romantic hero is bound up with a theory of speech.[20] The "double intervention" noted above translates the doubling of the narrative sequence;[21] we could adopt here the writer/novelist distinction proposed by Marcel Muller to account for two of the seven voices in *A la Recherche du temps perdu*,[22] attributing to the "writer" Rodolphe's point of view, and to the "novelist" Emma's. To assign Rodolphe's decoding a minus sign—Rodolphe would actualize combination #3—amounts to espousing the cause of the novelist, who supports Emma's essential superiority/difference, betrayed not only by the inferiority of those who surround her, but also by speech, which is not up to her level. Girard, it should be noted here, adopts the point of view of the writer, indirectly justifying Rodolphe: "the opposition between Emma and Charles, and between Emma and the citizens of Yonville is essential only in Emma's mind."[23]

If, however, we follow the thread of the thematic paradigm speech/writing, we find that the structuring opposition of the novel is neither Emma vs. Rodolphe nor Emma vs. Charles (nor is it the commonplace of traditional criticism, Homais vs. Bournisien); the privileged doublet is none other than Emma vs. Homais, a fundamental opposition half-expressed, half-concealed by their names, which should be read "Femm(a) vs. Hom(ais)"—*Femme* (Woman) vs. *Homme* (Man). This reading consists of remedying Emma's lack by restoring her truncated "F" to her, and of cutting off Homais' supplement by putting his adjunctive suffix in parentheses. How can one fail to see in the operations to which Flaubert subjected the terms of sexual opposition to generate the characters' names, the equivalent of castration on the plane of the signifier? We could thus term the castration axis the arch-axis, the principal axis that subordinates all the other semantic axes of the novel.

Opposed to Emma's inability to find the words necessary to express her thoughts (one of the corollaries of the Cratylian theory being that thoughts/feelings *precede* speech), is the always reiterated adequation of the pharmacist's thoughts and words:

Perhaps she would have liked to confide all these things to some one. But how tell an undefinable uneasiness, changing as the clouds, unstable as the winds? Words failed her and, by the same token, the opportunity, the courage.

Peut-être aurait-elle souhaité faire à quelqu'un la confidence de toutes ces choses. Mais comment dire un insaisissable malaise, qui change d'aspect comme les nuées, qui tourbillonne comme le vent? Les mots lui manquaient donc, l'occasion, la hardiesse. (p. 29/75)

"What a dreadful catastrophe!" exclaimed the pharmacist, who always found expressions that filled all imaginable circumstances.

—Quelle épouvantable catastrophe! s'écria l'apothicaire, qui avait toujours des expressions congruentes à toutes les situations imaginables. (p. 96/166)

Emma's incapacity, let us note, is intermittent; her cyclothymia is also a pathology of speech:

On certain days she chattered with feverish profusion, and this overexcitement was suddenly followed by a state of torpor, in which she remained without speaking, without moving.

En de certains jours, elle bavardait avec une abondance fébrile; à ces exaltations succédaient tout à coup des torpeurs où elle restait sans parler, sans bouger. (p. 48/100)

This alternate encoding can be represented as follows:

Emma: encoding $+ / -$

Nevertheless, on the speech-encoding plane, Homais is the undisputed winner. Of all the characters in the novel, he is the only one to work tirelessly at his expression. For him talking is both a delight *(jouissance)*—"for the pharmacist much enjoyed pronouncing the word 'doctor,' as if addressing another by it reflected on himself some of the grandeur of the title" ("car le pharmacien se plaisait beaucoup à prononcer ce mot *docteur*, comme si, en l'adressant à un autre, il eût fait rejaillir sur lui-même quelque chose de la pompe qu'il y trouvait" [p. 120/195])—

and an art—"Homais had meditated at length over his speech; he had rounded, polished it, given it the proper cadence; it was a masterpiece of prudence and transitions, of subtle turns and delicacy" ("Il avait médité sa phrase, il l'avait arrondie, polie, rythmée; c'était un chef-d'œuvre de prudence et de transition, de tournures fines et de délicatesse" [p. 181/275]). Unlike Rodolphe, Homais does not speak a stilted language, but takes pleasure in hearing and reproducing new thoughts, stylish expressions. Thus we see him, in the course of a conversation with Léon, reveal his extraordinary mimetic gifts, speaking "Parislang":

> he even used slang to impress [. . .] the "bourgeois," saying "flip," "cool," "sweet," "neat-o" and "I must break it up," for "I must leave."
>
> il parlait argot afin d'éblouir [. . .] les bourgeois, disant *turne, bazar, chicard, chicandard, Breda-street,* et *Je me la casse,* pour: Je m'en vais. (p. 202/301)

If Rodolphe is a smooth talker, if he dexterously manages the code of the vile seducer, Homais has a gift for *languages* (Latin, English, slang) that he handles with the love of a savant, an expert in transcoding.

But if on the communication axis Homais wins out over Emma, who, it must be remembered, does not shine as a decoder, allowing herself to be easily duped by the clichés that Rodolphe reels off to her both before and after their affair—"It was the first time that Emma had heard such words addressed to her, and her pride unfolded languidly in the warmth of this language, like someone stretching in a hot bath" ("C'était la première fois qu'Emma s'entendait dire ces choses; et son orgueil, comme quelqu'un qui se délasse dans une étuve, s'étirait mollement et tout entier à la chaleur de ce langage" [p. 112/185]); "She yielded to his words" ("Elle se laissa prendre à ses paroles" [p. 226/330]), when one turns to that delayed communication which is writing, the balance of forces is equalized. Certain readers, unaware of Emma's scriptural activities, will perhaps be surprised at this affirmation. It is, however, in the area of writing that the Emma/Homais rivalry turns out to be the most violent; it is to the extent that they practice two different forms of writing that their sexual opposition becomes significant.

The medal that motivates Homais and whose reception closes the novel—"He has just been given the cross of the Legion of Honor" ("Il vient de recevoir la croix d'honneur" [p. 255/366])—is destined to crown his writings, which are numerous. He is the classic pedant scribbler, having published " 'at my expense, various works of public usefulness, such as' (and he recalled his pamphlet entitled, *On Cider, its Manufacture and Effects,* besides observations on the wooly aphis that he had sent to the Academy; his volume of statistics, and down to his pharmaceutical thesis)" ("à mes frais, différents ouvrages d'utilité publique tels que [et il rappelait son mémoire intitulé: *Du cidre, de sa fabrication et de ses effets;* plus, des observations sur le puceron laniger, envoyées à l'Académie; son volume de statistique, et jusqu'à sa thèse de pharmacien]"—p. 253/364). Compared to this journalistic logorrhea, what has Emma published? Nothing, but she does write. What, to my knowledge, has escaped critical notice is the thematic and structural relationship between *Madame Bovary* and the first *Education:* the Emma/Homais couple is a new avatar of the Jules/Henry couple. Even those who have taken literally the famous exclamation *"Madame Bovary, c'est moi"* have bypassed the essential, the too evident, in their concern for the anecdotal similarities between Emma and Gustave. Emma is also the portrait of an artist, but the artist as a young woman, and it is this difference, this bold representation of the writer as a woman which disconcerts, which misleads, and which, for these reasons, must be examined.

Emma's search for love's passion is doubly motivated by literature. First there is "external mediation,"[24] the desire to transform the (dead) letters that she has read into lived experience, to coincide with literary models:

> And Emma tried to find out what one meant exactly in life by the words *bliss, passion, ecstasy,* that had seemed to her so beautiful in books.
>
> Et Emma cherchait à savoir ce que l'on entendait au juste dans la vie par les mots de *félicité,* de *passion* et d'*ivresse,* qui lui avaient paru si beaux dans les livres. (p. 24/69)

When she becomes Rodolphe's mistress, this much longed-for identification seems to be realized; Emma progresses from the passive status of a reader to the active status of a heroine:

> Then she recalled the heroines of the books that she had read.
> . . . She became herself, as it were, an actual part of these lyr-

ical imaginings; at long last, as she saw herself among those lovers she had so envied, she fulfilled the love-dream of her youth.

> Alors elle se rappela les héroïnes des livres qu'elle avait lus . . . Elle devenait elle-même comme une partie véritable de ces imaginations et réalisait la longue rêverie de sa jeunesse, en se considérant dans ce type d'amoureuse qu'elle avait tant envié. (p. 117/191)

Finally, with Léon she attains her goal: from a heroine-for-herself she is transformed into a heroine-for-others: "She was the mistress of all the novels, the heroine of all the dramas, the vague 'she' of all the volumes of verse" ("Elle était l'amoureuse de tous les romans, l'héroïne de tous les drames, le vague *elle* de tous les volumes de vers" [p. 192/289]).

But this first love-letters link conceals another of prime importance to our study: Emma seeks a lover not only to become a novelistic character, but especially to become an author. When, in the early stage of her marriage, Emma settles in to wait for "something to happen," she outfits herself in advance with a writer's tools:

> She had bought herself a blotter, writing-case, pen-holder, and envelopes although *she had no one to write to* . . . .
>
> Elle s'était acheté un buvard, une papeterie, un porte-plume et des enveloppes, quoiqu'*elle n'eût personne à qui écrire* . . . (p. 43/94; emphasis mine)

What Emma lacks is not a lover, but a receiver ("destinataire"), and what she desires through this receiver-pretext for writing is literary fame. To convince oneself of this, one need only compare the above quotation with another seemingly innocent remark which follows one page later. Emma wants Charles to become a great doctor because:

> She would have wished this name of Bovary, which was hers, to be illustrious, to see it displayed at the booksellers', repeated in the newspapers, known to all France.
>
> Elle aurait voulu que ce nom de Bovary, qui était le sien, fût illustre, le voir étalé chez les libraires, répété dans les journaux, connu par toute la France. (p. 44/95)

By bringing together these two segments of the same sentence, of the same phantasm, we witness the emergence of Emma's profound ambi-

16

tion: to be a famous novelist. Why then is this wish expressed on the one hand by an intermediary, projected onto Charles, and on the other hand occulted by the separation of the means (writing instruments) from the end (to be famous)? This repression, this censure, results from Emma's sex. What she envies in a man is not so much the possibility of traveling, but the possibility of writing; what she lacks in order to write are neither words nor pen, but a phallus.[25]

Imbued with eighteenth-century literature, Emma cannot conceive of a literary production other than a novel by letters, and the taking of a lover is the necessary condition for this form of writing. Once she becomes Rodolphe's mistress, Emma begins her epistolary novel. Rodolphe serves as both her initiator and her receiver:

> From that day on they wrote to one another regularly every evening. Emma placed her letter at the end of the garden, by the river, in a crack of the wall. Rodolphe came to fetch it, and put another in its place that she always accused of being too short.

> A partir de ce jour-là, ils s'écrivirent régulièrement tous les soirs. Emma portait sa lettre au bout du jardin près de la rivière, dans une fissure de la terrasse. Rodolphe venait l'y chercher et en plaçait une autre, qu'elle accusait toujours d'être trop courte. (p. 117/191)

This little game of hide-and-seek inaugurates Emma's apprenticeship, which will go through three stages, the first of which is marked by the persistence of the illusion of communication. Rather than renounce this illusion, Emma brings to correspondence all those desires unsatisfied by conversation, continuing to valorize *exchange,* clinging to the double role of sender/receiver that defines the interlocutor. Thus Emma complains of the brevity of Rodolphe's letters; thus she demands verses from Léon:

> She asked him for some verses—some verses "for herself," a "love poem" in honor of her.

> Elle demanda des vers, des vers pour elle, *une pièce d'amour* en son honneur . . . (p. 201/300)

If initially Emma writes to receive letters, to take pleasure in the communication forbidden, impossible on the speech plane, writing subsequently becomes the adjuvant of a "waning passion" in the manner of an aphrodisiac:

> in the letters that Emma wrote him she spoke of flowers, po-
> etry, the moon and the stars, naïve resources of a waning pas-
> sion striving to keep itself alive by all external aids.
>
> dans les lettres qu'Emma lui envoyait, il était question de fleurs,
> de vers, de la lune et des étoiles, ressources naïves d'une passion
> affaiblie, qui essayait de s'aviver à tous les secours extérieurs. (p.
> 205/304)

It is only during the third stage when the receiver-lover has been demystified, unmasked as the double of her husband—"Emma found again in adultery all the platitudes of marriage" ("Emma retrouvait dans l'adultère toutes les platitudes du mariage" [p. 211/311-312; an excellent example of the identity of opposites!])—that Emma must yield to the evidence: she no longer loves Léon, but she continues more and more to love to write. It is only at this stage that Emma fully assumes her role as writer:

> She blamed Léon for her disappointed hopes, as if he had be-
> trayed her. . . .
> She none the less went on writing him love letters, in keep-
> ing with the notion that a woman must write to her lover.
> But while writing to him, it was another man she saw, a
> phantom fashioned out of her most ardent memories, of her fa-
> vorite books, her strongest desires, and at last he became so real,
> so tangible, that her heart beat wildly in awe and admiration,
> though unable to see him distinctly, for, like a god, he was hid-
> den beneath the abundance of his attributes. . . . She felt him
> near her; he was coming and would ravish her entire being in a
> kiss. Then she would fall back to earth again shattered; for these
> vague ecstasies of imaginary love, would exhaust her more than
> the wildest orgies.
>
> Elle accusait Léon de ses espoirs déçus, comme s'il l'avait tra-
> hie . . .
> Elle n'en continuait pas moins à lui écrire des lettres amou-
> reuses, en vertu de cette idée, qu'une femme doit toujours écrire
> à son amant.
> Mais, en écrivant, elle percevait un autre homme, un fantôme
> fait de ses plus ardents souvenirs, de ses lectures les plus belles,
> de ses convoitises les plus fortes; et il devenait à la fin si vérita-
> ble, et accessible, qu'elle en palpitait émerveillée, sans pouvoir

le nettement imaginer, tant il se perdait, comme un dieu, sous l'abondance de ses attributs . . . Elle le sentait près d'elle, il allait venir et l'enlèverait tout entière dans un baiser. Ensuite elle retombait à plat, brisée; car ces élans d'amour vague la fatiguaient plus que de grandes débauches. (pp. 211–212/312)

The "but" signals the passage from one stage to another, the final subordination of love to writing, the metamorphosis of writing dictated by conventions into writing that flows from the heart. The latter writing is diametrically opposed to conversation-communication in that it presupposes the absence of a receiver, compensates for a lack, thereby embracing emptiness. As Freud demonstrates in *The Poet and Daydreaming*, the fictive character, like this composite being who is sketched by Emma's pen, is the product of all the unsatisfied desires of its creator. Transcoded into psychoanalytic terminology, the "phantom" that Emma perceives is a phantasm. Moreover, writing, such as Emma practices it (such as Flaubert practiced it), is a solitary pleasure: the phantasmic scene is one of seduction. The pleasure that Emma experiences in rewriting Léon, in giving herself a lover three times hyperbolic, is intensely erotic.

To write is to leave the prey for the shadow, and, in the end, writing is to become the shadow itself: the author-phantom must succeed the character-phantom. Thus, just before swallowing the arsenic, Emma appears to Justin "majestic as a phantom" ("majestueuse comme un fantôme" [p. 229/334]). The apprenticeship of the heroine-artist can lead only to death, but to an exemplary death, because suicide generates language. In the novel to die a natural death *(belle mort)* is to commit suicide, because suicide is the very act that links the coming to writing with the renunciation of life. Like Madame de Tourvel, like Julie, Emma does not die without having written a last letter: "She sat down at her writing-table and wrote a letter, which she sealed slowly, adding the date and the hour" ("Elle s'assit à son secrétaire, et écrivit une lettre qu'elle cacheta lentement, ajoutant la date du jour et l'heure" [p.230/335]). Of this letter we know only the first words; " 'Let no one be blamed . . .' " (" 'Qu'on n'accuse personne . . .' " [p. 231/336]). The fragmentary state of this letter is highly significant, because the gap created by the ellipsis leaves forever unanswered the essential question: in this ultimate letter, *ultima verba,* does Emma complete the final stages of her apprenticeship, does she succeed in inventing for herself a writing that goes beyond clichés, beyond the romantic lies that they carry with them? The first words are

19

only a (negative) repetition of Rodolphe's words, tending to invalidate any hypothesis of last-minute literary conversion. This letter immediately evokes the imitative circuit. If, in the letter that Charles composes right after Emma's death, we find both thematic (novelistic ideas) and stylistic (use of the imperative: " 'Let no one try to overrule me' ") echoes of Emma's previous letters, we are struck, too, by the firmness of expression resulting from a very bold use of asyndeton. In fact, one could cite this passage as an example of Flaubertian enunciation which, according to Barthes' formula, is seized by "a generalized asyndeton":[26]

> "I wish her to be buried in her wedding dress, with white shoes, and a wreath. Her hair is to be spread out over her shoulders. Three coffins, one oak, one mahogany, one of lead. Let no one try to overrule me; I shall have the strength to resist him. She is to be covered with a large piece of green velvet. This is my wish; see that it is done."
>
> *Je veux qu'on l'enterre dans sa robe de noces, avec des souliers blancs, une couronne. On lui étalera ses cheveux sur les épaules; trois cercueils, un de chêne, un d'acajou, un de plomb. Qu'on ne me dise rien, j'aurai de la force. On lui mettra par-dessus toute une grande pièce de velours vert. Je le veux. Faites-le.* (p. 239/346)

Is this writing a personal find of Charles', whose writing up to this point vied in ineptitude with his speech (note the fifteen drafts that he writes to have Dr. Larivière come *before* Emma's death), or can one see in it the pale reflection, traces, of Emma's last letter?

In the Flaubertian novelistic universe, in which substitution chains organize the narrative, nothing is less evident than the principles of closure that govern this neurotic serialization. Since in Emma's mind the Viscount = Léon = Rodolphe (p. 106), what prevents her from continuing indefinitely this substitution of one lover for another? In theory the series is open-ended; the resources of a substitutive rhetoric and logic are inexhaustible.[27] In effect, Emma's death is not synchronic with the exhaustion of the narrative because, after her death, she is replaced by other characters: formerly the *subject* of substitution, she becomes its *object*. Thus Félicité, her maid, wears her dresses: "[she] was about her former mistress's height and often, on seeing her from behind, Charles thought she had come back . . ." ("elle était à peu près de sa taille, souvent Charles, en l'apercevant par derrière, était saisi d'une illusion . . ." [p. 249/359]); and Charles begins to imitate her:

20

To please her, as if she were still living, he adopted her taste, her ideas; he bought patent leather boots and took to wearing white cravats. He waxed his mustache and, just like her, signed promissory notes.

Pour lui plaire, comme si elle vivait encore, il adopta ses prédilections, ses idées; il acheta des bottes vernies, il prit l'usage des cravates blanches. Il mettait du cosmétique à ses moustaches, il souscrivit comme elle des billets à ordre. (p. 250/360)

But, on the actantial plane, on the plane of the novel's structuring opposition, Emma/Homais, Emma is succeeded by the blind man, a Beckettian character whose *symbolic* value has for a long time preoccupied the critics,[28] and whose function still remains to be pinpointed. According to our reading, his function is above all heuristic: whereas the opposition between Emma and Homais is implicit, concealed by anagrams, that between the blind man and Homais is explicit, manifest on the plane of events.

The blind man's doubling of Emma is prepared a long time in advance: from his first appearance the blind man finds in Emma a listener; his melancholic song evokes an echo in Emma's mind (p. 193/291); later she gives him her last five-franc coin (see in this scene the opposition: Emma's excessive generosity vs. Homais's excessive greed; by her *gift,* Emma is united with the blind man against Homais [p. 219]). Finally, on her deathbed, Emma hears the blind man, believes she sees him, and pronounces her last words: " 'The blind man!' " (" ' L'aveugle!' " [p. 238/344]). The seme common to Emma and the blind man is monstrosity, physical in the one, moral in the other. It is precisely the blind man's monstrosity that brings upon him Homais' hostility: Homais would like to cure the blind man, that is, reduce his difference, "normalize" him. The blind man/Homais sequence only repeats the clubfoot/Homais sequence; in both cases the science preached by the pharmacist is never anything but the means of replacing heterogeneity with homogeneity, thereby earning the gratitude and esteem of his clients. Nevertheless, unlike the crippled clubfoot, the blind-man-ever-blind flouts Homais, publicly exhibiting the wounds that the pharmacist's recommendations and pomades could not cure. Homais, unable to silence this embarrassing witness to the inefficacy of his speech, begins to pursue him through writing; a fierce fight ensues between the garrulous blind man and the prolix pharmacist:

He managed so well that the fellow was locked up. But he was released. He began again, and so did Homais. It was a struggle. Homais won out, for his foe was condemned to life-long confinement in an asylum.

Il fit si bien qu'on l'incarcéra. Mais on le relâcha. Il recommença et Homais aussi recommença. C'était une lutte. Il eut la victoire; car son ennemi fut condamné à une réclusion perpétuelle dans un hospice. (p. 251/362)

The superimposition of the Emma/Homais//blind man/Homais rivalries reveal within writing the same opposition that we detected above at the center of speech: efficacy vs. inefficacy. While Emma's writing remains, so to speak, a dead letter, transforming nothing, producing no impact on the external world, Homais' writing is able to exile, if not kill, and becomes a means of social advancement.

Moreover, this superimposition permits the disengagement of an attribute, an invariant qualification of the *victim:* the victim, woman or blind man, is a being who lacks an essential organ, in fact, as Freud repeats at several points, the same organ, since according to his theory blindness = castration. The victim's final failure is inscribed in his/her body; Emma's monstrosity is physical as much as it is moral. The blind man's doubling of Emma punctuates the text, assures its readability: woman, this "defective" monster *("monstre à la manque"),* is the privileged figure of the writer, and especially of the writer Flaubert, a "failed girl" *("fille manquée")* according to Sartre's thesis. It would, moreover, be easy to demonstrate that Emma's writing apprenticeship is consistent with an attempt to change sex, to reverse castration. The refusal of femininity, the temptation of virility, are not given once and for all from the beginning; before going that route, Emma will try to follow the path of integration, to accept the feminine destiny that Freud charts for the "normal" woman: marriage and maternity. But, just as marriage ends in failure, Charles being unable to succeed *in Emma's place,* motherhood ends in disappointment: George, the phantasmic phallic-son, turns out to be only Berthe, a child worthy of Charles. Thus, much before Freud, Flaubert well understood that in order for maternity to fully satisfy penis envy, the child must be male (which would condemn at least half of all women to inevitable neurosis):

> She hoped for a son; he would be strong and dark; she would call him George; and this idea of having a male child was like

an expected revenge for all her impotence in the past. A man, at least, is free; he can explore all passions and all countries, overcome obstacles, taste of the most distant pleasures. But a woman is always hampered. Being inert as well as pliable, she has against her the weakness of the flesh and the inequity of the law. . . .

She gave birth on a Sunday at about six o'clock, as the sun was rising.

"It's a girl!" said Charles.

She turned her head away and fainted.

Elle souhaitait un fils; il serait fort et brun; elle l'appellerait Georges, et cette idée d'avoir pour enfant un mâle était comme la revanche en espoir de toutes ses impuissances passées. Un homme, au moins, est libre; il peut parcourir les passions et les pays, traverser les obstacles, mordre aux bonheurs les plus lointains. Mais une femme est empêchée continuellement. Inerte et flexible à la fois, elle a contre elle les mollesses de la chair avec les dépendances de la loi . . .

Elle accoucha un dimanche, vers six heures, au soleil levant.

—C'est une fille! dit Charles.

Elle tourna la tête et s'évanouit. (p. 63/122–123)

Unable to obtain a phallus by "phallic proxy,"[29] Emma seeks to satisfy her desire to change sex through transvestism. Partial at the beginning of the novel, the disguise is completed just before Emma's death:

Like a man, she wore a tortoise-shell eyeglass thrust between two buttons of her blouse.

Elle portait, comme un homme, passé entre deux boutons de son corsage, un lorgnon d'écaille. (pp. 11–12/50)

. . . she parted it [her hair] on one side and rolled it under, like a man's.

. . . elle se fit une raie sur le côté de la tête et roula ses cheveux en-dessous, comme un homme. (p. 89/157)

"Could I go riding without proper clothes?"

"You must order a riding outfit," he answered.

The riding-habit decided her.

—Eh! comment veux-tu que je monte à cheval puisque je n'ai pas d'amazone?

—Il faut t'en commander une! répondit-il.

L'amazone la décida. (p. 113/186)

On that day of Mid-Lent she did not return to Yonville; that evening she went to a masked ball. She wore velvet breeches, red stockings, a peruke, and a three-cornered hat cocked over one ear.

Le jour de la mi-carême, elle ne rentra pas à Yonville; elle alla le soir au bal masqué. Elle mit un pantalon de velours et des bas rouges, avec une perruque à catogan et un lampion sur l'oreille. (p. 212/312)

But, as Sartre demonstrates, for Flaubert sexuality belongs to the realm of the imagination; disguise is, then, only an *analogon* of Emma's imaginary sex. In the last analysis, it is only on the imaginary plane, i.e., on the plane of the role *played* in the couple, that Emma's growing virility asserts itself. The order of her affairs, Rodolphe before Léon, thus assumes its meaning: whereas in her relationship with Rodolphe Emma plays the female role, traditionally passive, in her relationship with Léon the roles are reversed: "he was becoming her mistress rather than she his" ("il devenait sa maîtresse plutôt qu'elle n'était la sienne" [p. 201/300]).

It is not by chance that the writing apprenticeship and the "virility apprenticeship," if I may call it that, follow paths which ultimately converge at the time of Emma's affair with Léon, for their affair marks the triumph of the imaginary over the real, this being the precondition of all writing. If, insofar as the effect *on* the real is concerned, Homais' writing surpasses Emma's; considered in terms of the "reality effect," it is without any doubt Emma's (Flaubert's) writing that surpasses Homais' for the "reality effect" can only be achieved through a total renunciation of any real satisfaction, can only be the just reward of sublimation, i.e., castration. For Flaubert writing thus has a sex, the sex of an assumed lack, the feminine sex.

It would seem, however, that all these oppositions are outweighed by Flaubert's radical distrust of language in general, a distrust evident in Emma's most bitter discovery, namely that ". . . everything was a lie" ("Tout mentait!" [p. 206/306]). For the Flaubert of *Madame Bovary* language is constantly undermined by its potential for lying, lying in the largest sense of the term, including hyperbole as well as the willful distortion of facts, and mystified idealization as well as cynical reductionism. The generalization of lying erases both the differences between forms of writing and the differences between writing and speech. Emma's letters and Homais' published pieces thus participate in the same "a-mimesis":

24

both he and she depart from reality, embellishing facts, adjusting them to their needs. They "invent"—"Then Homais invented incidents" ("Puis Homais inventait des anecdotes" [p. 251/362]). On the other hand, Emma's idealization,—"irrealization," Sartre would say—of Léon on paper is only the resumption, the materialization of the oral self-idealization of the two lovers that occurs on the occasion of their reunion in Rouen:

> this was how they would have wished to be, *each setting up an ideal* to which they were now trying to adapt their past life. Besides, *speech is like a rolling machine that always stretches the sentiment it expresses.*
>
> c'est ainsi qu'ils auraient voulu avoir été, *l'un et l'autre se faisant un idéal* sur lequel ils ajustaient à présent leur vie passée. D'ailleurs, *la parole est un laminoir qui allonge toujours les sentiments.* (p. 169/260; emphasis mine)

Things would be too simple if there were not at least one exception to the rule; hence old Rouault appears to escape the treason of language. His annual letter enjoys a harmony both metaphoric (letter = writer) and metonymic (letter = reality contiguous to the writer). The hiatus between writer, words, and things is here reduced to a minimum. In fact, in the Flaubertian system the opposite of lying is not telling the truth, but immediacy, because the least distance between the sender and the receiver, the writing subject and the Other, as well as that between man and Things, opens a gap through which lies penetrate:

> She held the coarse paper in her fingers for some minutes. A continuous stream of spelling mistakes ran through the letter and Emma followed the kindly thought that cackled right through it like a hen half hidden in a hedge of thorns. The writing had been dried with ashes from the hearth, for a little grey powder slipped from the letter on her dress, and she almost thought she saw her father bending over the hearth to take up the tongs.
>
> Elle resta quelques minutes à tenir entre ses doigts ce gros papier. Les fautes d'orthographe s'y enlaçaient les unes aux autres, et Emma poursuivait la pensée douce qui caquetait tout au travers comme une poule à demi cachée dans une haie d'épines. On avait séché l'écriture avec les cendres du foyer, car un peu de poussière grise glissa de la lettre sur sa robe, et elle crut presque apercevoir son père se courbant vers l'âtre pour saisir les pincettes. (p. 124/200)

Examined more closely, this model of paternal writing is in fact threatened from all sides. In spite of the spelling mistakes and the intradiegetic metaphor which guarantee the writer's adherence to words and things,[30] the gap is there, manifest in the form of a lack: thought is compared to a "half hidden" hen. Adherence is thus partial, and, if this letter conveys writing matter (letter + ashes), it is the matter itself that represents "the price to be paid": the symbolic Father is, as Lacan writes, the dead Father.

Two consequences follow from this. First, for the characters who, unlike old Rouault, maintain relations with the world that are strongly mediated by written as well as spoken language, such as Emma, there is only one way in which to enjoy immediacy, and that is to step outside language. The two great erotic scenes of the novel link jouissance,[31] plenitude, with the suspension of all linguistic communication. The initiation by Rodolphe culminates in one of the great Flaubertian silences, to borrow another expression from Genette:[32]

> Silence was everywhere. . . . Then far away, beyond the wood, on the other hills, she heard a vague prolonged cry, a voice which lingered, and in silence she heard it mingling like music with the last pulsations of her throbbing nerves.
>
> Le silence était partout . . . Alors, elle entendit tout au loin, au-delà du bois, sur les autres collines, un cri vague et prolongé, une voix se traînait, et elle l'écoutait silencieusement, se mêlant comme une musique aux dernières vibrations de ses nerfs émus. (p. 116/189–190)

If in this scene the spoken word is supplanted by a nonarticulated, asemantic cry, in the coach scene the written word is torn to shreds, reduced to insignificance:

> One time, around noon, in the open country . . . a bare hand appeared under the yellow canvass curtain, and threw out *some scraps of paper that scattered* in the wind, alighting further off like white butterflies on a field of red clover all in bloom.
>
> Une fois, au milieu du jour, en pleine campagne [. . .] une main nue passa sous les petits rideaux de toile jaune et jeta *des déchirures de papier, qui se dispersèrent* au vent et s'abattirent plus loin, comme des papillons blancs, sur un champ de trèfles rouges tout en fleur. (p. 177/270; emphasis mine)

26

The euphoric form of the letter is thus the sperm-letter: in *Madame Bovary,* as in *The Temptation of Saint Anthony,* happiness is "being matter."
But if fictional characters, these "paper beings," find their happiness beyond or without language, what of the writer who is condemned to work in an articulate and signifying language? The writer cannot be for Flaubert but a pursuer of lies, making do for want of something better, with available means, i.e., language, language which is always both judge and plaintiff, source of lies and condemner of lies, poison and antidote, *pharmakon.* There is in *Madame Bovary* a character who appears to fulfill this prophylactic function. It is, as if by chance, a doctor, Doctor Larivière, a character with quasi-divine attributes: "The apparition of a god would not have caused more commotion" ("L'apparition d'un dieu n'eût pas causé plus d'émoi" [p. 233/339]).[33] Note in what terms Flaubert describes his diagnostic gifts:

> His glance, more penetrating than his scalpels, looked straight into your soul, and would *detect any lie,* regardless how well hidden.
>
> Son regard, plus tranchant que ses bistouris, vous descendait droit dans l'âme et *désarticulait tout mensonge* à travers les allégations et les pudeurs. (p. 234/339; emphasis mine)

These are exactly the same terms that Flaubert uses to define his stylistic ideal when, in a letter to Louise Colet contemporary with the writing of *Madame Bovary,* he criticizes Lamartine for not having "this medical view of life, this view of Truth."[34] Truth, it must be remembered, is for Flaubert a matter of style. To be true, the writer need only substitute for the doctor's look the equivalent instrument in his art, i.e., his style: "a style . . . precise like scientific language . . . a style that would penetrate into ideas like the probe of a stylet" (*Extraits,* p. 71). The structural homology of the two sentences in question, with, on the one hand, the scalpel glance which "looked straight into your soul," and on the other the "stylet-style" which "penetrates into ideas," underscores the identity of scriptural approach and surgical procedure. There is nothing less passive, less feminine, than the relationship with language known as "les affres du style" (pains of style): the reader of the correspondence concerning *Madame Bovary* cannot but be impressed with the aggressive and even sadistic relationship of Flaubert with the sentences and paragraphs of his novel that

27

he sets about dissecting, unscrewing, undoing, unwriting, to use expressions found throughout his letters.[35] To convey the inarticulate, one must disarticulate. As Sartre observes, "style is the silence of discourse, the silence in discourse, the imaginary and secret end of the written word."[36]

Flaubert's stylistic ideal completes his writing ideal; if Flaubert's writing refers to what one might call, playing a bit on Kristeva's terms, a "gyno-text," then his style aspires to a "phallo-text," a masculine "phenotext":

> I love above all else nervous, substantial, clear sentences with flexed muscles and a rugged complexion: I like male, not female, sentences.
>
> J'aime par-dessus tout la phrase nerveuse, substantielle, claire, au muscle saillant, à la peau bistrée: j'aime les phrases mâles et non les phrases femelles.[37]

In the last analysis the "bizarre androgyn" is neither Flaubert (Sartre) nor Emma (Baudelaire), but the book, locus of the confrontation, as well as the interpenetration of *animus* and *anima,* of the masculine and the feminine.

By definition a *restricted* thematic study cannot claim to be all-encompassing. We are thus able to take note of a final demarcation separating the new thematic criticism from the old: concerned with thematic structure or, better still, structuring themes, new thematic criticism must not go beyond the framework of the individual novel (poem, drama). (This does not, of course, exclude intertextual allusions and references.) Defining the corpus in this manner, restricted thematics reintroduces a diachronic dimension into the always synchronic or a-chronic apprehension of traditional thematic criticism, thereby substituting "a new hermeneutic, one that is syntagmatic, or metonymic" for "the classical hermeneutic that was paradigmatic (or metaphoric)."[38] As we have observed, the writing/speech paradigm overdetermines not only the actantial distribution of characters but also the consecutive progression of the narrative sequences. I mean *overdetermine* because a thematic approach cannot by itself account for the multiple functioning of a text, but, given its "intent," one cannot really do without it.

Translated by Harriet Stone

2

Smiles of the Sphinx:
Zola and the Riddle of Femininity

Tout récit ne ramène-t-il pas à Oedipe?
Roland Barthes, *Le plaisir du texte*

There has been a great deal of talk about Zola's women. Indeed, Zola's discourse on woman has in recent years become an intrinsic part of the critical discourse on Zola. It would appear as though whatever the critic's starting point, whatever the place "from which he speaks," Zola's "gyno-mythology" is an obligatory stopping place. This is hardly surprising. Woman, that mobile unit, that empty square par excellence, wanders about the entire critical landscape (political, erotic, and, more recently, thermodynamic): woman can be equated with the people, the body, or money, with all that circulates and/or is repressed. Woman is poly- or pluri-serial, poly- or pluri-valent. From all these recent "serializations" *(mises en série)* three profiles of Zola emerge: Zola as Oedipus, Zola as feminist (?), Zola "living in the feminine."[1] Now what is amazing is that despite the ideological and metalinguistic differences that separate such critics as Jean Borie, Chantal Jennings, Anna Krakowski, and Michel Serres, all concur in dealing with woman in Zola as though for him femininity were a given. Nothing could be further from the truth. For Zola, just as for Freud, woman is a "dark continent" far more disturbing than the African continent blithely colonized in *Fécondité*. In order to bring to light the problematics of femininity which haunts Zola's works, we will have to read Zola *with* Freud,

29

his contemporary: not the Freud of the Oedipus, but of the preoedipus, the author of the essays on the "riddle of femininity."[2] Moreover, it is important to recall that before grappling with the Woman as Mother that is Jocasta, Oedipus on the road to Thebes encounters that figure of Woman as Riddle that is the Sphinx.[3]

For Zola, the life of woman is marked by mysteries, and those mysteries go back to the very moment of conception. The mystery of femininity inevitably leads one back to the mystery, indeed the myth of origins. In a rarely quoted preface he wrote to the *Roman d'un inverti (The Novel of a Homosexual)*, Zola raised the following question: "In the mystery of conception has one ever thought of this. A child is born: why a boy? why a girl? No one knows."[4] The impossibility of articulating the laws that govern sexual differentiation at the moment of conception goes hand in hand with the anguished observation that subsequently there exist cases of indifferentiation:

> What an increase in obscurity and misery if nature hesitates for a moment, if a boy is born part-girl, if a girl is born part-boy! The facts are there, it happens every day. The indecision may begin with the very physical aspect, the main character traits: the man effeminate, delicate, cowardly; the woman masculine, violent, hard. (12:702)

Thus, from the outset, the riddle of femininity is intimately linked with the enigma of sexual difference; given his well-known interest in contemporary science and particularly in all matters pertaining to heredity, there is nothing surprising about these "scientific" concerns on the part of Zola. In effect he asks: what laws determine what Prosper Lucas calls the "sex of the product"? And, if nature does in some cases hesitate, indeed err, what criteria would allow us to distinguish (effeminate) men from (masculine) women? Insufficient attention has been paid to the pervasive sexual indifferentiation in Zola's fiction. Zola is the heir to an entire century of questioning of sexual roles. Indeed the nineteenth-century novel— whether it be that of Balzac, Stendhal, Gautier, or Flaubert—rehearses an interminable "crisis of distinctions,"[5] which is made manifest by the proliferation of effeminate male characters and viriloid female characters, not to mention the multiplication of borderline cases: androgyns and castrati.[6]

But when I speak of sexual indifferentiation in Zola's fiction, I do not wish to evoke his decandentist, "belle époque" side, rather I would draw attention to the cases of indifferentiation which are ascribable to fantasies, to an "infantile" theory of sexuality: I have in mind couples of adolescent lovers such as Miette and Silvère *(La Fortune des Rougon)*, or Serge and Albine *(La Faute de l'abbé Mouret)*, couples which Angus Wilson long ago qualified as "intersexual."[7] One need only scrutinize the most consummate elaboration of this type of idyll, *La Joie de vivre*, to be led to modify Wilson's formula. For the couple made up by Pauline Quenu and her cousin Lazare Chanteau is a pseudo-fraternal, a *unisexual* couple: for Zola, just as for Freud, "a little girl is a little man": "Lazare, from the very first day, had accepted her as though she were a boy, a small brother" ("Lazare, dès le premier jour l'avait acceptée comme un garçon, un frère cadet").[8] Only a brutal event can disrupt this idyll, relegating the men to one side, the women to another: and that event is the young girl's menstruation. This irruption of difference, this bloody reminder of castration destroys forever what Luce Irigaray calls "an old dream of symmetry."[9] Here Zola parts ways with Freud and rejoins Michelet for whom menstruation is also the obsessional symptom of femininity. Zola cannot conceive of puberty, that is female puberty, as anything but an (unpleasant) surprise:

> The girl was sitting up in bed, with her covers thrown back, white with terror, and screaming continuously for her aunt; her bare, parted legs were stained with blood, and she was staring at what had come out of her, all her habitual courage driven away by the shock.
>
> Assise au milieu du lit, les couvertures rejetées, la jeune fille appelait sa tante d'un cri continu, blanche de terreur; et elle écartait sa nudité ensanglantée, elle regardait ce qui était sorti d'elle, frappée d'une surprise dont la secousse avait emporté toute sa bravoure habituelle. (p. 49/ 3:853)

The scene of menstruation is, as it were, doubled by the childbirth scene, the "bloody motherhood" ("maternité ensanglantée") of Louise, Lazare's wife, reproducing the "bloody nudity" ("nudité ensanglantée") of Pauline. If puberty is an unpleasant surprise, maternity is a form of rape, the exhibition of woman's mutilated genitalia:

31

Thus brutally exposed to the light, all the disturbing mystery had gone from that delicate skin with its secret places . . . nothing remained but suffering humanity, childbirth amidst blood and ordure, the mother's womb strained to bursting-point, the red slit stretched agonisingly, like the wound made by an axe in the trunk of some great tree, spilling its lifeblood.

A la grande clarté brutale, le mystère troublant s'en était allé de la peau si délicate aux endroits secrets . . . et il ne restait que l'humanité douloureuse, l'enfantement dans le sang et dans l'ordure, faisant craquer le ventre des mères, élargissant jusqu'à l'horreur la fente rouge, pareille au coup de hache qui ouvre le tronc et laisse couler la vie des grands arbres. (p. 264/ 3:1096)

It is only late in life, very precisely as of the last of the *Rougon-Macquart, Le Docteur Pascal,* that Zola will consecrate woman mother and promote the ideology of family-ism—an "especially sticky" ideology in Barthes' words.[10] Unlike Louise, Clotilde, the female protagonist of *Docteur Pascal,* will give birth easily, the consecration of motherhood entailing the easing of childbirth. By locking woman into motherhood, Zola rejoins Freud, for whom the only so-called normal femininity is the one defined by marriage and motherhood. When Krakowski asserts that "Zola's heroines are first and foremost physically and psychically mothers" (p. 148), one should see in this identification (not to say reduction) of femininity with (or to) motherhood, a makeshift, a desperate attempt to institute difference there where it is lacking. It would appear that at first, woman in Zola wants to be a man (suffers from what Freud calls a "masculinity complex"), or rather, that not wanting to recognize sexual difference, castration, Zola remains mired in the denial of Otherness that is male narcissism. Thus, in his preparatory notes for the *Rougon-Macquart,* the young Zola writes in a text bearing the revealing title, *Différences Between me and Balzac:* "Balzac says he wants to depict men, women, and things. I, on the other hand, treat men and women as indistinguishable, nevertheless recognizing the natural differences" ("Balzac dit qu'il veut peindre les hommes, les femmes et les choses. Moi, des hommes et des femmes, je ne fais qu'un, en admettant cependant les différences de nature" [5:1737]).

Even in those cases where Zola seems to recognize the natural differences, the riddle of femininity remains central, subsisting in the form of a structuring novelistic principle. In Zola a character's femininity institutes from the moment she is named an enigma whose solution will not necessarily be synchronous with the closure of the text; it would then constitute a structural variant of the "hermeneutic code" elaborated by Barthes: "Narratively, an enigma leads from a question to an answer, *through a certain number of delays.* Of these delays, the main one is unquestionably the feint, the misleading answer, the lie, what we call a *snare.*"[11]

In order to test out this hypothesis, let us consider, however briefly, the exemplary case of Nana; indeed, from the very first pages of the novel an insistent question is posed by all of the characters: who is Nana?

> The man standing in front of the playbills spelt it out loud; others uttered it in a questioning tone as they passed; while the women, at once uneasy and smiling, repeated it softly with an air of surprise. Nobody knew Nana.[12]
>
> Les hommes qui se plantaient devant les affiches, l'épelaient à voix haute; d'autres le jetaient en passant sur un ton d'interrogation; tandis que les femmes, inquiètes et souriantes, le répétaient doucement, d'un air de surprise. Personne ne connaissait Nana. (2:1100)

The entire first chapter consists in the deferral of Nana's appearance, in the exploitation of the enigma constituted by her name: "Was it Nana at last? The girl was certainly keeping them waiting" ("Etait-ce Nana enfin? Cette Nana se faisait bien attendre" [p. 31/ 2:1106]. The reader, like the audience, is kept in suspense and even becomes frustrated by this suspense: "Such a long wait had ended up by annoying the audience" ("Une attente si prolongée avait fini par irriter le public" [p. 32/ 2:1107]). But Nana's appearance on stage does not solve the mystery, only gives it fresh impetus; as soon as they see her all the men in the audience try to place her, as they all experience the same impression of *déjà vu:*

> "But I know the girl," cried Steiner, as soon as he caught sight of Fauchery. "I'm certain I've seen her somewhere [. . .] At the Casino, I think . . .
> "As for me," said the journalist, "I don't know where it was; like you, I've certainly met her before . . ."
>
> —Mais je la connais! cria Steiner, dès qu'il aperçut Fauchery. Pour sûr, je l'ai vue quelque part . . . Au Casino, je crois . . .

33

—Moi, je ne sais plus au juste, dit le journaliste; je suis comme vous, je l'ai certainement rencontrée . . . (p. 34/ 2:1109)

If Nana's past is a relatively easy riddle to which the narrative will in time provide some answers, the riddle of her femininity is far more complex:

> All of a sudden, in the good-natured child the woman stood revealed, a disturbing woman with all the impulsive madness of her sex, opening the gates of the unknown world of desire.
>
> Tout d'un coup, dans la bonne enfant, la femme se dressait, inquiétante, apportant le coup de folie de son sexe, ouvrant l'inconnu du désir. (pp. 44–45/ 2:1118)

It is around this unknown, which manifests itself as a gaping void, a trap, that is, a snare that the novel is woven and it ends as it began by a series of question marks; thus Nana's last appearance on stage is marked by a silence worthy of a sphinx:

> She didn't say a word: the authors had even cut the line or two they had given her, because they were superfluous. No, not a single word: it was more impressive that way, and she took the audience's breath away by simply showing herself.
>
> Elle ne disait pas un mot, même les auteurs lui avaient coupé une réplique, parce que ça gênait; non, rien du tout, c'était plus grand, et elle vous retournait son public, rien qu'à se montrer. (p. 459/ 2:1476)

This final enigmatic appearance is followed by a no less enigmatic disappearance, translated on the plane of the diegesis by an explicit ellipsis:

> Months went by, and she began to be forgotten. When her name was mentioned in her old haunts, the strangest stories were told, and everybody gave the most contradictory and far-fetched information.
>
> Des mois se passèrent. On l'oubliait. Lorsque son nom revenait, parmi ces messieurs et ces dames, les plus étranges histoires circulaient, chacun donnait des renseignements opposés et prodigieux. (p. 454/ 2:1471)

At the end of the novel, just as in the beginning, Nana is elusive, that obscure object of desire; her name evokes curiosity, elicits commentaries; the gap her absence-presence opens in the text is the matrix of fictions: "A legend was in the making" ("Une légende se formait" [ibid.]). In a word, Nana is the enigmatic, which is to say hermeneutic object par excellence.

Hélène Grandjean, the heroine of *Une Page d'amour*—a novel which despite obvious differences is linked to *Nana* not only by contiguity (they follow each other in the series) but also by homology (their structures are identical: the opposition known/unknown)—is another matter altogether. Eclipsed on the one hand by *Nana,* on the other by *L'Assommoir,* the central panel of the feminine trypitch embedded in the *Rougon-Macquart* is a little-known novel. This critical neglect seems to me unfortunate because it is precisely in this half-toned novel that Zola yields up both his myth and his demythification of femininity. Between the stories of the mother (Gervaise) and the daughter (Nana) we have the story of the relationship of a widowed mother and her only daughter. Following the sudden illness and death of her husband, on the morning after their arrival in Paris, Hélène (née Mouret) finds herself alone with her daughter Jeanne, an intellectually precocious but sickly child. It is at the bedside of her sick daughter that Hélène meets her neighbor, the young and seductive Dr. Henri Deberle. The (very brief) affair that will result from this meeting will be the direct cause of Jeanne's death—Jeanne dies literally consumed by jealousy. Finally, Hélène accepts the marriage proposal of Mr. Rambaud, devoted family friend, and leaves Paris for Marseille, closing the geographic as well as erotic circle.

It is no accident that in a novel which bears the title *Une Page d'amour,* the posing of the riddle is linked to a literary activity and Nana, the actress, is replaced by Hélène, the reader: woman's status goes from mere hermeneutic object to a more complex combination of hermeneutic object and subject. In one respect Hélène's reading of fiction *(Ivanhoe)* is peculiar; it is a reading characterized by voluntary deferral, a reading whose discontinuous rhythm mimes and scans the enigmas already encoded in the original text:

> She derived enjoyment from not satisfying her curiosity all at once. The story swelled her with an emotion that was stifling

her. . . . There was a great charm in being ignorant, half divining, giving herself up to a slow initiation, with the dim idea that she was beginning her youth over again.[13]

Elle prenait une jouissance à ne point satisfaire tout de suite sa curiosité. Le récit la gonflait d'une émotion qui l'étouffait . . . Il y avait là un grand charme: ignorer, deviner à demi, s'abandonner à une lente initiation, avec le sentiment obscur qu'elle recommençait sa jeunesse. (2:847)

As opposed to the typical protagonist of a naturalist novel who, according to Philippe Hamon, suffers from an "Asmodeus complex,"[14] bringing what we might call a "heuristic" code into play, Hélène institutes a "hermetic" code as a way of life: a calm if not merry widow living in seclusion, she withdraws into her apartment in Passy and wants to know nothing of what she sees from her window, for the corollary of the devalorization of curiosity is the denaturing of glass objects, in this instance a window with a magnificent view of Paris. If we consider enigma as the invariant of the text, an element of the novel which has often disturbed and baffled the critics (with the sole exception of Mallarmé, see 2:1621)— namely the five lengthy descriptions of Paris threaded through the text— takes on its full meaning: Paris, that unknown city is the double of Henri (let us note in passing the homophony of the second syllable: *ris/ri*), that unknown man with whom Hélène will live out her novel, or rather her page of love:

> They knew nothing of Paris . . . Then they continued to look at Paris, without further seeking to recognize it. It was very pleasant to have it there and yet be unfamiliar with it.
>
> Elles ne savaient rien de Paris [. . .] Alors, elles continuèrent à regarder Paris, sans chercher davantage à le connaître. Cela était très doux, de l'avoir là et de l'ignorer. (1:126, 127/ 2:854)

> Why need she know Henri? It seemed to her sweeter to ignore him . . .
>
> Qu'avait-elle besoin de connaître Henri? Il lui semblait plus doux de l'ignorer. (1:253/ 2:911)

The network of ignorance is not limited to Hélène, it extends to all of the female characters in the novel (whereas the male characters all possess forms of prestigious knowledge: Henri Deberle, the doctor; l'abbé Ram-

36

baud, the priest; Mr. Rambaud, the do-it-yourself man, and Malignon, the seductor and lifeguard): thus Juliette, Dr. Deberle's wife, makes a point of preserving the ignorance, of protecting the innocence of her younger sister Pauline, sending her out to play in the garden when the conversation comes too close to revelations about taboo subjects; on the other hand, Jeanne, Hélène's sickly daughter, is tortured by her "childish ignorance" ("ignorance d'enfant" [2:214/ 2:1030]). The anxiety she experiences when looking out over Paris—"if she could have raised the roofs" ("si elle avait pu soulever les toitures!" [ibid./2:1029])—is something like the dysphoric side of the Asmodeus complex. For her, death signifies access to the unknown, to the knowledge forbidden her in her lifetime:

> At last, then, she was going to know, she would place herself on the domes and on the spires, a few strokes of her wings, and she would see the forbidden things that were hidden from children.
>
> Enfin, elle allait donc savoir, elle se poserait sur les dômes et sur les flèches, elle verrait, en sept ou huit coups d'ailes, les choses défendues que l'on cache aux enfants. (2:309/ 2:1070)

Whether the enigma is soothing or fatal, chosen or imposed from the outside, it pertains to only one form of knowledge, the erotic knowledge possessed by Malignon. All of these female lacks of curiosity converge on one place, Malignon's pied-à-terre. Only the desire to taste of an unknown pleasure, only "curiosity" (2:181/ 2:1015) drive Juliette to set up a rendez-vous there with Malignon. Like Jeanne she is after an unnamed form of knowledge; in this novel the verb to know is (at least in French) intransitive: [15] "She had only to shut her eyes, she would know all" ("Elle n'avait qu'à fermer les yeux, elle saurait" [2:184/ 2:1017]). Finally, however, Juliette leaves the apartment as ignorant as when she arrived, first because at the last minute she recoils from Malignon's clumsy advances, second because her rendezvous is interrupted by the unexpected arrival of Hélène, who has forewarned Henri of his wife's betrayal by means of an anonymous letter. After these comings and goings worthy of a boulevard comedy, couple number one, Juliette/Malignon, make room for couple number two, Hélène/Henri, and the act of love interrupted or delayed by Hélène's *snare* is consummated. [16] But the chain of substitutions does not end there, for in a second substitution that is as tragic as the

first is comic, it is the daughter who is the reluctant victim of the knowledge her mother had set out to acquire unbeknownst to her. In a scene
only Zola could have imagined, Jeanne looses her virginity by proxy, while
her mother remains so to speak intact:

> When they teased her, when they tickled her in spite of her
> laughter, she had sometimes felt that exasperated shiver. All rigid,
> she waited, her innocent and pure limbs in revolt. From her in-
> nermost being, from her awakened woman's nature, a keen pang
> started, as if she had received a blow from afar.

> Lorsqu'on la taquinait, qu'on la chatouillait malgré ses rires, elle
> avait eu parfois ce frisson exaspéré. Toute raidie, elle attendait
> dans une révolte de ses membres innocents et vierges. Et, du
> fond de son être, de son sexe de femme éveillé, une vive douleur
> jaillit comme un coup reçu de loin. (2:217/ 2:1031)

> She trembled at the thought of the passionate joys that she had
> not known. Reminiscences occurred to her, and she felt all too
> late that her senses were awakening, accompanied by an intense
> unsatisfied desire.

> Elle frissonnait de la volupté qu'elle n'avait point éprouvée. Des
> souvenirs lui revenaient, ses sens s'éveillaient trop tard, avec un
> immense désir inassouvi. (2:253–254/ 2:1046)

Hélène will not advance beyond this stage in her erotic education: she
will go from her initial lack of curiosity to her final serenity, with a brief
frustration at the critical moment. Desire can only be fully experienced as
an after-effect. At the end of the novel it is as though Hélène's passion
for Henri had never existed; the page of love is subjected to a sort of
retrospective censorship, a delayed bracketing: "Had she, then, been mad
for a year?" ("Elle avait donc été folle pendant un an?" [2:352/ 2:1089]).
After her daughter's death, after her remarriage of convenience with Mr.
Rambaud, Hélène returns to her earlier state of willed ignorance, what
was referred to in the age of classicism as her "repos": "she again grew
calm, without a desire, without curiosity, and continued her measured
march on her direct road" ("elle redevenait très calme, sans un désir, sans
une curiosité, continuant sa marche lente sur la route toute droite"
[2:353/ibid.]). Henri, like Paris, will remain forever unknown to her:

> Then Hélène said within herself that she did not know Henri
> . . . On the last as on the first day, to her he was a stranger.

Smiles of the Sphinx: Zola

Et Hélène se disait qu'elle ne connaissait pas Henri . . . Au dernier comme au premier jour, il lui restait étranger. (2:354–355/ 2:1090)

~~Then Hélène's glance wandered for the last time over the impassive city; it, too, remained unknown to her.~~

Alors, Hélène, une dernière fois, embrassa d'un regard la ville impassible, qui, elle aussi, lui restait inconnue. (2:358/ 2:1091–1092)

The time has perhaps come to attempt to solve the mystery, to name if not to answer the riddle: that stranger, that unknown (Henri-Paris) are they not quite simply the concretization, the projection of the part of Hélène that remains forever alien to her: her libido (cf. "the unknown world of desire" in *Nana*). Female sexual desire is, to borrow Malebranche's celebrated characterization of the imagination: "the madwoman in the house" ("la folle du logis"). When Hélène desires Henri, she no longer recognizes herself, she is as though dispossessed by another: "It seemed to her that she heard the voice of an unknown wicked and sensual woman . . ." ("C'était comme une femme méchante et sensuelle qu'elle ne connaissait point" [2:143/ 2:999]); "Her being had ceased to belong to her, another was controlling her" ("Son être avait cessé de lui appartenir, l'autre personne agissait en elle" [2:352–353/ 2:1089]). In the grip of sexual attraction, Hélène thinks she is the victim of a demonic possession; female sexuality is a form of estrangement, of "unheimlich," which invades the body: the riddle of femininity is then in the end on the order of the uncanny.

The hypothetical connection between these two Freudian concerns stands in need of clarification as it is apt to shed light on the novel's underlying logic. We are, indeed, far from having exhausted the questions raised by *Une Page d'amour*. There remains at least one major riddle: why does Zola choose to inflect one of the most hackneyed clichés of the nineteenth-century novel, the conflict between passion and maternal love, the "bad mothers" punished for their illicit love affairs by the sickness/death of their child? The examples are both too numerous and too well known to be cited here; we will retain the most convincing case from our point of view: that of Mme Arnoux in *L'Education sentimentale*. Though she has two children, a boy and a girl, it is the boy's and not the girl's illness that prevents her from keeping her rendez-vous with Frédéric Moreau. Zola's brilliant modulation of this theme consists in opposing the mother/lover relationship not to the canonic mother/son relationship, but rather to the all-important mother/daughter relationship. If this new twist to an old stereotype strikes me as significant it is because according to Freud the riddle of femininity is grounded precisely in the most archaic phase of the little girl's development, the one where she takes her mother for her unique love object, technically speaking, the preoedipal phase. According to Freud there is no more inexorable censorship than that affecting this phase, this "pre-history" which, in an often quoted comparison, Freud likens to the Minoan-Mycenean civilization whose traces are buried beneath the superior layers of Greek civilization (*S.E.* 21:226). On the level of the logic of the unconscious, there would then be a necessary link between Hélène's "cold life" ("froideur" [1:242/ 2:906]) and the sickness and death of Jeanne.

Aside from the fact that Zola transposes the preoedipal to the age of puberty, Hélène and Jeanne's relationship is characterized by the same features as the mother/daughter relationship in the preoedipal phase, as reconstructed by Freud. First, both Zola and Freud consider that this phase is a critical, indeed decisive phase for the health of the future woman:

> She is at the period of life when a woman's health is decided.
> Elle est à l'époque où la santé d'une femme se décide. (1:24/ 2:809)

> . . . the suspicion that this phase of attachment to the mother is especially intimately related to the aetiology of hysteria [. . .] that in this dependence on the mother we have the germ of later paranoia in women. (Freud, *S.E.* 21:227).

This phase is indeed marked by an exclusive attachment to the mother and Jeanne loves her mother with a "controlling adoration" ("adoration tyrannique" [1:41/ 2:816]) which admits of no sharing. The exclusiveness of this dual relationship is readily apparent in a characteristic symptom:

> Nothing now existed for her but her large doll . . . She thus took refuge in the love of her big doll . . . She drew her doll to her still closer, her last love.
> Plus rien existait pour elle que sa grande poupée . . . Elle se réfugiait ainsi dans l'amour de sa grande poupée . . . Elle serra davantage sa poupée, son dernier amour. (2:1068, 1069, 1071)

. . . we must not overlook the fact . . . that the little girl's preference for dolls is probably evidence of the exclusiveness of her attachment to her mother, with complete neglect of her father-object. (Freud, *S.E.* 21:237)

Although, or rather, because it is exclusive, this love is ambivalent; thus Jeanne displays a characteristic fear, when she accuses her mother of wishing to kill her by forcing her to swallow a potion:

No, it is poisoning me.

Non, ça m'empoisonne. (2:19/ 2:945) [17]

. . . we discover the fear of being murdered or poisoned . . . already present in this pre-Oedipus period, in relation to the mother. (Freud, *S.E.* 22:120)

Finally Jeanne dies of having "seen" the primal scene, of not having been able to possess her mother exclusively; she dies at the decisive moment when she must give up the mother-object and come under the sway of the Oedipus complex. Jeanne pushes the "foreclosure"—to borrow a Lacanian term—of the male signifier to its logical extreme: rather than acknowledge its existence, she dies. Now it seems to me that the daughter's failure—her inability to integrate the mediating phallus and cross the threshold of the Oedipus—is not unrelated to the mother's frigidity—her inability to experience jouissance other than in such eminently solitary activities as reading, sewing, and, above all, riding on a swing:

When she was a young girl she swung for hours, and the memory of those distant parties filled her with a dull desire.

Lorsqu'elle était jeune fille, elle se balançait pendant des heures, et le souvenir de ces lointaines parties l'emplissaient d'un sourd désir. (1:97/ 2:841)

It was her enjoyment, those ascents and those descents that made her giddy.

C'était sa jouissance, ces montées et ces descentes, qui lui donnaient un vertige. (1:100/ 2:843)

The swing episode, which is presented as the height of innocence, is highly significant: for one thing, it is the one time Hélène appears perfectly natural, her ingenuousness shining through "the cold perfection of

41

her great beauty" ("la correction froide de sa grande beauté" [2:841]). For another, Jeanne, who also enjoys swinging, far prefers to be the spectator of maternal jouissance:

> She was most anxious to see her mother fly, as she called it, taking still more delight in looking at her than in swinging herself.
>
> Elle avait la passion de voir sa mère s'envoler, comme elle le disait, prenant plus de joie encore à la regarder qu'à se balancer elle-même. (1:96/ 2:841)

We have here the nexus of the complex mother-daughter relationship: both privilege masturbatory pleasure as a sexual activity, the daughter in order to keep her mother to herself, the mother, to keep herself from men: Henri's sudden arrival on the scene brings their game to an abrupt halt, for, rather than exhibiting her jouissance in front of Henri, Hélène jumps off the swing, spraining her ankle in the fall.

The intimate complicity that exists between Hélène and Jeanne exceeds the bounds of a more or less neurotic dependence; one would have to invoke not a dual relationship, but a splitting. Jeanne is then Hélène's Other, the "bad woman," and, in fact, Zola does describe Jeanne in almost precisely these terms: "she had the air of a jealous and desperate woman" ("elle avait sa figure de femme jalouse et méchante" [1:54/ 2:961]). Jeanne, she who wants to know while refusing knowledge, *is* her mother's repressed. As the logic of the narrative obeys the laws of the unconscious, Jeanne's death is inevitable. The fact that the final scene in the novel is situated in the snow-covered cemetery of Passy is surely not coincidental: the grave buried beneath the snow is in some sense the projection in time and in space of Hélène's frigidity. Burial, tearing out of the page (à propos of Jeanne's death, Zola attributes this thought to Hélène: "it seemed to her that a page from the book of her life had been torn away" ["il lui semblait qu'une page de sa vie était arrachée," 2:337/ 2:1083]), covering over with snow, all reinscribe the inexorable repression of the preoedipal phase. In light of this analysis, the curious tonality of the novel's closure takes on its full significance. Hélène's rêverie is interrupted by her husband, Mr. Rambaud, who says:

> "I am certain that you have forgotten the fishing rods!"
> "Oh! quite!" she exclaimed, surprised, and vexed at her forgetfulness . . .

—Je suis sûr que tu as oublié les cannes à pêche!

—Oh! absolument! cria-t-elle, surprise et fâchée de son manque de mémoire . . . (2:359/ 2:1092)

If we now compare Hélène, the bourgeois lady from the provinces, and Nana, the Parisian courtesan, we find that their sexualities are curiously similar, if only on the plane of the signifier; thus both of Hélène's husbands treat her like a beautiful statue:

Charles still kissed her marble-like feet . . .

Charles baisait toujours ses pieds de marbre . . . (1:114/ 2:848)

On the wedding night, he also [Mr. Rambaud] had kissed her bare feet as beautiful as those of a marble statue which were once again turning to stone.

Le soir des noces, lui aussi avait baisé ses pieds nus, ses beaux pieds de statue qui redevenaient de marbre. (2:352/ 2:1089; translation modified)

Even if we were unaware of the metonymic link between the foot and the female genitalia which the fetishist turns to account, the simple superimposition of the marble imagery in *Une Page d'amour* and *Nana* would apprise of us of the fact:

And Nana, in front of this fascinated audience . . . remained victorious by virtue of her marble flesh, and that sex of hers which was powerful enough to destroy this whole assembly and remain unaffected in return.

Et Nana, en face de ce public pâmé . . . restait victorieuse avec sa chair de marbre, son sexe assez fort pour détruire tout ce monde et n'en être pas entamé. (p. 46/ 2:1120)

Woman in Zola is thus an idol; instead of woman as petrifying, or at the same time as, we have petrified woman; for Zola, as I believe for Freud, feminine jouissance remains a dead letter. In a fictional universe where desire is almost always foregrounded, woman exists beyond or beneath the pleasure principle, in the margins of the page of love.

This observation fully confirms our initial hypothesis: namely that a sub-code of the hermeneutic code specially adapted to feminocentric texts must be set into place. The model of narrative intelligibility Barthes derived from the Oedipus myth is not, as he implicitly posits, universally valid: it bears the stamp of its patriarchal origins and cannot account for texts whose organizing principles are grounded in the pre-Oedipus.[18] I would propose to call this new code, the "hieratic code," in both senses of the word: depending on whether the adjective applies to a pose or a form of writing, it means either "majestic stiffness" or "cursive hieroglyphic." This double meaning is actualized in *Salammbô*, a novel whose "hieraticism" is particularly conspicuous.[19] The word is used to qualify both an object of value Salammbô sends to her fiancé Narr'Havas—"a crown of rock salt, ornamented with hieratic designs" ("une couronne de sel gemme, ornée de dessins hiératiques")[20]—and Salammbô herself: "she sat perfectly upright in a hieratic attitude" ("elle restait toute droite, dans une attitude hiératique" [p. 363/306]).

The advantage the hieratic code presents is that it takes over a semantic network which includes woman, writing, and stone. In order to test out the benefits to be derived from this code, let us take as a case in point a novel by Balzac which does not seem in any way related to *Une Page d'amour* and *Nana: La Peau de chagrin*. *La Peau de chagrin*, one of Balzac's "philosophical fictions," is the story of a suicide deferred. Part One recounts how on the verge of committing suicide Raphael de Valentin, the novel's protagonist, receives from the hands of a mysterious antique dealer a talisman which figures the economy of desire: the price of wish fulfillment is a diminution of life, represented by the shrinkage of the skin. The acceptance by Raphael of the magic ass's skin seals the Faustian compact which temporarily extends his life. Part Two consists in an extended flashback centered on Raphael's tale of his vain love for the courtesan Foedora, the so-called "woman without a heart" ("la femme sans coeur"). In Part III, after having gone to great lengths to stretch the shrinking skin, Raphael expires in the arms of his loving fiancée, Pauline. Read in the light of the hieratic code, the underlying logic of the narrative is revealed: there exists a close and necessary connection between Parts One and Two, because Foedora is no more than the feminine face or aspect of the central Enigma whose scriptural form or side is the Talisman. The splitting or, to be more exact, the doubling of the scriptural enigma by the sexual is determined by a strict symmetry, for if the skin is feminine by virtue of its ductility and pliability, woman is textual by virtue of her mystery: "she was more than a woman: she was a romantic novel" ("c'était plus qu'une femme, c'était un roman").[21] What is more, however, the hardness of woman is contrasted with the suppleness of leather, for Foedora has, of course, "splendid shoulders, worthy of the Venus de Milo" ("belles épaules dignes de la Vénus de Milo") and the "hateful smile of a marble statue" ("le détestable sourire d'une statue de marbre" [p. 135/168]), when it is not the "laugh of the Medusa" of which Hélène Cixous speaks.[22]

The fact that woman is petrified *(médusée)* at least as much as (if not more than) petrifying *(médusante)* emerges clearly in a curious fantasy Raphael has concerning Pauline: "she was the child of my creation, a statue I had fashioned. Like a second Pygmalion, I tried to turn back into marble this living, warmly coloured, speaking and feeling virgin" ("c'était mon enfant, ma statue. Pygmalion nouveau, je voulais faire d'une vierge vivante et colorée, sensible et parlante, un marbre" [p. 115/150]). In the end, the hieratic code is another name for an inverted, perverted, or perhaps simply a restored Pygmalion myth, for, before the statue could be transformed into woman, woman had to be turned to stone. When Freud undertook his analysis of Jensen's *Gradiva,* he was guided by a sure instinct, for the "dreams" and "delerium" of Norbert Hanold, the young German archeologist in love with a woman of stone, are but extreme manifestations of a mytho-pathology which was particularly rampant in nineteenth-century literature. At that moment of literary history, woman's literariness seems to be bound up with her being turned into marble, her enigmatization.

If the hieratic code governs *Une Page d'amour* as well as *La Peau de chagrin, Nana* as well as *Salammbô,* in what does the vaunted difference between Zola and Balzac (see above), Zola and his predecessors consist? The difference operates on two planes: first, the social: in Zola the riddle of femininity has gone from an aristocratic model to a bourgeois and even popular one; second, the intersection in Zola of the hermeneutic and the heuristic has repercussions on the hieratic. As a result, instead of total (death), petrification becomes partial: if Jeanne is buried under a marble gravestone, "a simple column" ("une simple colonne" [2:1084]), Hélène survives, though partially petrified. Do the degradation of the enigma and the survival of the petrified woman signify progress or rather the persistence of the myth?

In order to answer this question let us return to *La Peau de chagrin* which can be read as a veritable allegory of the persistence of the enigma:

> The old man presented his stiletto to the stranger, who took it and attempted to cut into the skin at the place where the words

were inscribed; but when he had removed a thin layer of leather the letters still showed so clear and so identical with those which were printed on the surface that, for a moment, he had the impression that he had removed nothing.

Le vieillard présenta son stylet à l'inconnu, qui le prit et tenta d'entamer la Peau à l'endroit où les paroles se trouvaient écrites; mais, quand il eut enlevé une légère couche de cuir, les lettres y reparurent si nettes et tellement conformes à celles qui étaient imprimées sur la surface, que, pendant un moment, il crut n'en avoir rien ôté. (p. 50/87)

Similarly—and this follows from the equivalence posited above between Foedora and the Talisman—when Raphael spies on Foedora in the hope of penetrating her mystery, he finds only "one more mystery in this preeminently mysterious woman" ("un mystère de plus dans cette femme déjà si mystérieuse" [p. 161/193]), and this mystery within a mystery is nothing other than her singing, yet another example of solitary pleasure: "she appeared to be listening to herself, to be feeling a sensual delight which was all her own; it was as if she were enjoying all the thrills of love" ("elle paraissait s'écouter elle-même et ressentir une volupté qui lui fût particulière; elle éprouvait comme une jouissance d'amour" [ibid.]). The attempt to penetrate the talisman and to violate the woman without a heart are bound to fail: "The enigma concealed beneath this fair semblance of woman was born anew: so many explanations of Foedora were possible that nothing was finally explained" ("L'énigme cachée dans ce beau semblant de femme renaissait, Foedora pouvait être expliquée de tant de manières, qu'elle devenait inexplicable" [p. 164/196]). The hieratic code is then a limit-case of the hermeneutic code. Beneath the smile of the sphinx, there is always already another enigma.[23]

Approached from the angle of the riddle of femininity, Zola appears "denatured," if not "denaturalized." The familiar image of Zola, the novelist of transparency, is replaced by the image of another, less reassuring Zola: the novelist of opacity. And all the available evidence suggests that, though paradigmatic, woman is not exceptional, does not constitute an aberration.[24] The reading proposed here is then a reading against the grain, one that would emphasize "the mysteries of Zola."[25] For whatever the (forms of) knowledge conveyed by Zola's texts, he always took into account the unknown and unknowable. There is in Zola a residue which escapes all grids; the fact that this residue should for a long time appear in a feminine guise should come as no surprise to the readers of the *Rougon-Macquart,* a novelistic cycle whose "origins" are bound up with the intimate secrets of Tante Dide, the ancestor figure who stands first in a long line of Sphinx-Women. Let us recall briefly the main elements of this clinical case: mute, rigid, living the life of a mummy (1:134–135), ever since the birth of her first child, Tante Dide has suffered from a nervous condition, she is subject to periodic crises of hysteria during which what is mimed is, of course, what is forbidden:

> She remained rigid on her bed with her eyes open; then she was seized by a fit of gasping and she began to flail about; she had the terrifying strength of those hysterical women who must be tied down to keep them from breaking their heads against the wall. This return to her old flames, these sudden attacks shook her sore frame in a pitiful way. It was as though the fullness of her burning youthful desire had shamefully burst through the chill of her sixties.

> Elle demeurait sur son lit, rigide, les yeux ouverts; puis des hoquets la prenaient, et elle se débattait; elle avait la force effrayante de ces folles hystériques, qu'on est obligé d'attacher, pour qu'elles ne se brisent pas la tête contre les murs. Ce retour à ses anciennes ardeurs, ces brusques attaques, secouaient d'une façon navrante son pauvre corps endolori. C'était comme toute sa jeunesse de passion chaude qui éclatait honteusement dans ses froideurs de sexagénaire. (1:135)

In *Zola et les mythes,* Borie writes: "In Zola's works mothers are strictly forbidden to go out" (p. 147). I would go further and risk this conclusion: in Zola's works mothers are forbidden to experience sexual bliss. The unknowable (the riddle) is in the end nothing but the unthinkable: the Mother's jouissance.

3

Une Vie or the
Name of the Mother

The Extra-Text

Not all syllables in a literary text are equal; a hierarchy governed by a complex of still to be determined factors endows certain particles of signifying matter with a special resonance. Such a "master-syllable" is, as Jacques Derrida has shown in a celebrated footnote to his chapter on Mallarmé in *La Dissémination*—what follows may be considered as a footnote to that footnote[1]—the French *or*. The peculiar fascination exerted by this syllable over certain French writers of the *fin de siècle* period cannot I believe be ascribed solely to *or*'s reference to the precious metal gold. Consider the case of one of Mallarmé's most illustrious and prolific contemporaries, Maupassant. *Or* insists in his texts. To the examples already cited (and commented upon but in a different perspective) by Jean Paris,[2] others can be added and drawn either from

—the paradigm of novel titles: *Mont-Oriol, Fort comme la Mort* (and, of course, *Notre Cœur*, for as we shall see, below *cœur* there is always *cor*);
—the paradigm of short story titles: *Le Horla;*
  or from
—the paradigm of place names: *Normandy, Corsica,* etc.

Let us retain from this open-ended list what is from our perspective the most revealing example, *Mont-Oriol,* because the encoding of this toponym is the object of a novelistic scene. I am alluding to the scene during which the financier Andermatt informs the investors in the Society—

48

the novel tells of the creation of a spa—of the name he has found for the new watering place:

> "And notice, gentlemen, that this name is very well adapted for its purpose. People will say Mont-Oriol just as they say Mont-Dore. It impresses the eye and lingers in the ear. One reads it at a glance, catches the sound easily, and it stays in one's memory. Mont-Oriol! Mont-Oriol! The baths of Mont-Oriol!"
>
> And Andermatt made the word ring, hurling it out like a cannon-ball, and listening to the echo.
>
> "Et notez, messieurs, que ce vocable est excellent. On dira le Mont-Oriol, comme on dit le Mont-Dore.
>
> Il reste dans l'œil et dans l'oreille, on le voit bien, on l'entend bien, il demeure en nous: Mont-Oriol!—Mont Oriol!—Les bains du Mont-Oriol."
>
> Et Andermatt le faisait sonner, ce mot, le lançait comme une balle, en écoutant l'écho.[3]

Now even if Mont-Oriol is explicitly patterned on Mont-Dore and, moreover, as a note in the French edition informs us, "The made-up name of Mont-Oriol was not invented by Maupassant,"[4] nevertheless the form and the choice of this word are significant. Whether copy or borrowing, borrowing or copy, neither the common sense explanation (Mont-Oriol/Mont-Dore), nor the learned one (Maupassant's Mont-Oriol—Léon Cladel's) exhaust the genesis of this incantatory expression. Upon closer inspection, it would appear as though a suffix which can be declined, as it were— -Dore, -Oriol—had been appended to an invariable prefix: Mont. Without dwelling just yet on the persistance of the syllable *or*, our starting point, let us stop to consider the features which distinguish *Oriol* from *Dore*. What is striking is the fact that the declension of the suffix takes the form of the suppression of the initial *D* and the addition, in the opposite and symmetrical position, of the final *l*,[5] for if one admits that all work on the signifier is motivated, and further that the proper name is the privileged support of the author's drives and fantasies, could we not see in the adding of *l* to the stem *or* the anagram of *Laure*, the first name of Maupassant's mother. This oneiric etymology would seem to explain the jouissance Andermatt derives from the repetition of the word Oriol (note the triple anaphora), as well as his belief in the indelibility of his find.

Everything leads me to believe that this scene of nomination is emblematic, that what is at stake here exceeds the particular case of the mother-son relationship of Guy de Maupassant the man. What we have here is a scenario which is played out on other scenes, in other texts of fiction; hence Jean-Pierre Richard locates such a scenario in Céline's *Casse-pipe:*

> What clearer demonstration of the fact that to write here is to pronounce the forbidden word (name, first name), to appropriate it to oneself, to steal it from the father to whom it belongs . . . To write would be . . . to scatter this burning name throughout the substance of the text, thus rendering it voluptuous, because secretly bound, tensile, electrified. An always happy text then in its fleshly viability even if it appears desperate.[6]

The attention lavished in recent years on what Lacan calls the Name of the Father *(Ecrits)* seems to have somewhat obscured a fact whose significance is only beginning to be measured: the writer is someone who plays not only with the mother's body, as Barthes has written *(The Pleasure of the Text),* but also with her name. The first and maiden names of the mother also play an important part in the elaboration of the fictive text.[7] Make no mistake: this observation does not in any way signify the evacuation of the paternal metaphor, which even if one wished it is not feasible. Let us return one last time to the nomination scene in *Mont-Oriol.* There is a "generator" of the name Oriol which I have purposely held in reserve, in the wings as it were, waiting for the moment when its appearance was likely to produce the greatest effect; I am referring quite simply to "father" Oriol, the old peasant from whom Andermatt purchased the land on which he built his spa:

> For this reason, isn't it natural to call our baths the baths of Mont-Oriol? Thus we will associate with the resort, which is destined to become one of the most important in the whole world, *the name of its original owner.*
>
> N'est-il pas naturel, dès lors, d'appeler nos bains: les Bains du Mont-Oriol, et d'attacher à cette station qui deviendra une des plus importantes du monde entier, *le nom du premier propriétaire.* (8:144/ p. 134; emphasis added)

Oriol then represents far more than the anagram of the Name of the Mother; in it are inextricably bound up both the *appropriation* of the father's field (reinforced by *Mont*) and the *reparation* of this act of aggression on the plane of the symbolic; in it are condensed both the Name of the Father (fictitious) and the Name of the Mother (real). Oriol is then in some sense the master signifier, the *cipher* of Maupassant, hence its transtextual significance. What better introduction to our reading of *Une Vie*—a reading as lacunary, as riddled with blanks as the text whose form it mimes—than to place it under the sign in which the oedipal drama is joined with the inaugural gesture of all novelistic enterprises, the attribution of a title or: entitlement.

ENTITLEMENT

Everything has already been said about this title and yet everything remains to be said. The degree zero of the realist title which, as we have just seen, relies heavily on onomastic paradigms to insure mimesis,[8] *Une Vie* proclaims itself a limit-title, a wager-title. It is as though the subtitle (the title beneath the title) of all purportedly biographical novels (e.g., *Madame Bovary, Bel-Ami*) had usurped the place reserved for the title and by so doing revealed the banality disguised by the individualizing fiction of the proper name. *Une Vie* or the loss of the proper. That this loss should be the sad fate of a female protagonist is hardly surprising. On the one hand, according to a tradition extending at least as far back as the eighteenth century (and as far forward as the present: see the title of Claude Etcherelli's novel, *Elise ou la vraie vie*) has it that the archetypal literary life is lived in the feminine;[9] on the other hand, for some time now feminist theoreticians have asserted that the loss of the proper is proper to women.[10] *Une Vie* is then a title with two entries: referring to a long literary tradition, while exposing, by means of a form which is finally parodic, the truth about this fictional femininity. The heroine is no longer (never was?) the titular of her life; Jeanne's life does not belong to her. Thus this title and the novel whose matrix it is takes to its logical conclusion Flaubert's program in *Madame Bovary*, for, as Claude Duchet has pointed out: "Nothing in this title belongs to Emma and the novel will be precisely the novel of this title," that is the novel of "dispossession."[11] This formula could equally well be applied to *Une Vie*, whose plot comes down to the repetition of a minimal narrative sequence, *loss*, the naturalist novel being characterized by the overwhelming predominance of *degradation* over *amelioration*, to borrow Claude Bremond's still useful terms.

The loss of the proper name inscribed in the title will engender a whole series of losses: loss of dear ones, loss of birthplace. Let us note that these losses are prefigured not only by the anonymity of the title, but also by the female protagonist's patronym: Le *Perthuis des Vauds.*[12] *Une Vie* recounts the passage from having to non-being, from fullness to emptiness, which implies that in the case of Jeanne—and her case is in this respect typical—it is not a question of an initial "lack," but of the progressive appropriation of all she is and has by the men in her life.

DISPOSSESSIONS

In a novel where what is at stake is the loss of the proper, possession cannot in any way be taken for granted. We must therefore pay special attention to the use Maupassant makes in it of possessive pronouns, syntactical elements surcharged by the bringing into play of various forms of metalinguistic commentary, such as anaphora, italics, and quotation marks.

At the outset, Jeanne, the aristocratic young heiress who is the novel's main protagonist, lacks for nothing; on the contrary, she is defined by a generalized overabundance: very young, very rich, very pretty, this pampered only child is endowed with all the semantic features of a fairy tale princess. (Indeed it is precisely by violating the immutable scenario of the fairy tale—"Once upon a time"/"they lived happily ever after and had many children"—that Maupassant writes the denatured fairy tale that is *Une Vie*). Thus, in this sentence drawn from the first chapter of the novel, one can perceive no limit to Jeanne's virtual property; the use of free indirect discourse eliminates any doubt as to the subject of this veritable delirium of possession, and anaphora punctuates this excess:

> It was *her* sun, *her* dawn, the start of *her* life, the dawn of *her* hopes.
>
> C'était *son* soleil; *son* aurore; le commencement de *sa* vie; le lever de *ses* espérances.[13]

But anaphora—one of the privileged rhetorical figures of the discourse of excess—also serves as a warning: Jeanne's disappointments will be directly proportionate to her illusions. The proleptic value of the metacommentary seems to be confirmed by another sentence in the first chapter. The subject of the sentence is Jeanne's father:

> He wanted to show her the renovation of the mansion, of *her* mansion.
>
> Il voulait lui montrer l'embellissement du château, de *son* château. (p. 18/ 23; emphasis Maupassant's)

The convergence of the *repetition* of the word "mansion" and the underscored *difference* of the possessive adjective "her" emphasizes the irony of the syntagm, "her mansion," a useless clarification, because the magnificent Château des Peuples will never belong entirely to its charming lady. The landed analogon of Jeanne (just as the skiff *Jeanne* is her nautical double), the mansion will pass from the hands of her father to those of her husband, and from her husband's hands to those of her son, and each of these men will so seriously mismanage this property that by the end of the novel Jeanne will be quite literally dispossessed of *her* mansion, "The house, with which her whole *life* had been bound up" ("cette maison où toute sa *vie* était attachée" [p. 174/ 273]).

Whether it is a question of the father's generosity, the husband's meanness, or the son's wastefulness, the economic meddling of the men in her life will produce the same result: Jeanne's spoliation. The loss of the *proper* inevitably entails a loss of *property*. This formulation calls for two somewhat disparate remarks: 1) It is no accident that the novel which takes for its title the name, indeed the meliorative nickname of its protagonist, *Bel-Ami,* is opposed in every particular to *Une Vie:* Jeanne's slow spoliation corresponds to Bel-Ami's accelerated accumulation, while the role of *traitors* played by the men in *Une Vie* is a caricature of the role of *helpers* assigned the women in *Bel-Ami.* And, undeniable proof of the link between proper name and property, at each stage of his ascent, Bel-Ami's success—like that of that other "paysan parvenu," Julien Sorel—is crowned by a transformation, an ennobling expansion of his name: Georges Duroy→Georges Du Roy de Cantel→Baron Georges Du Roy. If the absence or presence of the proper name in the title, that is the coincidence or noncoincidence: title/proper name, entails two diametrically opposed narrative programs in Maupassant's works, what then of *Pierre et Jean,* what does this unique variant in the realist-naturalist onomastic paradigm signify (cf. *Les Sœurs Rondoli, Les Sœurs Vatard, Les Frères Zem-*

gano)? Does the doubling of the first names presage a doubling of the assets, or the opposite? Neither. *Pierre et Jean* appears as a compromise solution between *Une Vie* and *Bel-Ami:* the doubling of the first names initiates a conflictual relationship which will be resolved by the spoliation of one of the rival brothers (Pierre) and the enrichment of the other (Jean). The title is a snare: like all symbolic multiplications, the doubling of the first names compensates a lack, in this instance the elision of the family name, for therein lies the drama of *Pierre et Jean:* though they bear the same family name, the two brothers have different "names of the father." In other words, if the novel were entitled *Les Frères Roland,* there would be no drama, the family assets would be equally divided. 2) In Maupassant's fictional universe, Jeanne's fate is exemplary, because in Maupassant woman cannot manipulate the possessive without inclining toward the grotesque, when it is not the tragic. Her taking possession is illusory, her objects, ridiculous. In order to focus on the specificity of female possession, let us superimpose two texts bearing on the use of the possessive, texts which are rigorously parallel except in one respect: in the first, the possessor is a female character (Jeanne's mother), whereas in the second, the possessor is male (Andermatt, the financier):

> . . . she talked of *her* hypertrophy on every possible occasion, so often that it seemed that this condition was something peculiar to her and belonged to her as a private possession, to which no one else had any right.
> . . . elle parlait de "son" hypertrophie à tout propos et si souvent qu'il semblait que cette affection lui fût spéciale, lui appartînt comme une chose unique sur laquelle les autres n'avaient aucun droit. (p. 22/31)

> And he said "my doctor," "my experience" with the authority of a man who has in reserve unique powers. The possessive pronouns rang in his mouth with the sonorous sound of metal. And when he said, "my wife" one felt it was quite clear that the Marquis no longer had any right over his daughter since Andermatt had married her, marrying and buying having the same meaning in his mind.
> Et il disait: "Mon médecin," "mon expérience" avec une autorité d'homme qui détient des choses uniques. Les pronoms possessifs prenaient dans sa bouche des sonorités de métal. Et quand il prononçait: "Ma femme," on sentait d'une façon bien

évidente que le marquis n'avait plus aucun droit sur sa fille, puisque Andermatt l'avait épousée, épouser et acheter ayant le même sens dans son esprit. (8:118/ 114–115)[14]

Undeniably, on the metaphysical plane, the baroness and Andermatt are of a kind: it is just as absurd to claim exclusive rights over an ailment as over a doctor. But on an entirely different plane, which we might term *economic*, there is a fundamental difference between woman's and man's lot. On the one hand, a negative asset (the diseased body), on the other, positive possessions: a physician (a highly valued member of society), experience (a male prerogative in the nineteenth century), woman (the desirable body). In each case the possessions flaunted by Andermatt are either male attributes or over-valorized objects: the physician is in nineteenth-, as well as twentieth-century society, the privileged possessor of knowledge; similarly Christine, Andermatt's wife, is an object of exchange whose value is increased by her title. Indeed, Christine circulates among the men who possess her in turn without ever having any right over herself; even the child she has by her lover is easily recuperated by her sterile husband who exclaims: "Will you give me back *my* baby?" ("Veux-tu bien me rendre *ma* fille?" [8:305/ 263]). In the end, woman's part of woman is the remainder of the exchange system, that is, all that is not listed on the stock market of erotic values.

The Education of a Sentimental Woman

That the baroness' hypertrophied organ should be the heart is not an insignificant medical fact, because the ailment the baroness suffers from is both of a physical and an affective order: the baroness is a sentimental woman, a stereotypical female character in Maupassant. Her illness results not from her earthly nourishment (cf. the obesity of her male double, l'abbé Picot), rather from her spiritual fare, in other words her readings:

> In her young days she had been very pretty, as slim as a reed. After waltzing in the arms of all the officers of the Empire, she had read *Corinne*, which had made her weep; the novel had left a lasting impression on her mind.

Elle avait été fort jolie dans sa jeunesse et plus mince qu'un roseau. Après avoir valsé dans les bras de tous les uniformes de l'Empire, elle avait lu *Corinne* qui l'avait fait pleurer; et elle était demeurée depuis comme marquée de ce roman. (p. 22/31)

Going her prototype Emma Bovary one better—Emma contents herself with trying to make her life coincide with her readings—the sentimental woman somatizes her readings: the baroness suffers from a hysterical ailment; her hypertrophy is a symptom whose symbolism is easily deciphered. For having read *Cor-inne* too well, the baroness' body has become the eloquent image of her *cor* (*cor, cordis:* heart). Considering the intimate and immediate link which exists between the flesh and the letter, one being the transcription of the other, it is hardly surprising to see the baroness apply the possessive to the scriptural complement of *her* hypertrophy, her "relics":

They were all her old letters, letters from her father and mother, the Baron's letters during their engagement, and many others.

C'était toutes ses anciennes lettres, les lettres de son père et de sa mère, les lettres du baron quand elle était sa fiancée, et d'autres encore. (p. 23/32)

We will return to these relics; let us note for now that Jeanne too will have "her" relics, sentimentality being considered by Maupassant as a sort of hereditary disorder, taint or fissure—to speak like Zola—which is transmitted from mother to daughter:

. . . Jeanne preserved her letters and kept a box of "relics," though she was an entirely different person from her mother, in obedience to an inherited instinct of romantic dreaming.

. . . Jeanne aussi gardait sa correspondance, préparait sa "boîte aux reliques," obéissant, bien qu'elle différât en tout de sa mère, à une sorte d'instinct héréditaire de sentimentalité rêveuse. (p. 124/192)

The equation established in *Une Vie* between the reading of sentimental literature and obesity is operative in other texts by Maupassant, as though the obesity of the sentimental woman were, strictly speaking, a gynecological disorder. Thus the story of Mme Roland (the mother in *Pierre et Jean*) is the degraded (bourgeois) version of the baroness':

Une Vie *or the Name of the Mother*

She loved to read romances and poetry, not for their value as works of art, but for the tender and melancholy dreaminess they awoke in her. A verse, often commonplace, often bad, set the little string in vibration, as she would say . . .

Since her arrival at Havre she had become visibly stouter, and this made her once slender and supple figure rather heavy.

Elle aimait les lectures, les romans et les poésies, non pour leur valeur d'art, mais pour la songerie mélancolique et tendre qu'ils éveillaient en elle. Un vers, souvent banal, souvent mauvais, faisait vibrer la petite corde, comme elle disait . . .

Elle prenait depuis son arrivée au Havre, un embonpoint assez visible qui alourdissait sa taille autrefois très souple et mince.[15]

Let us note in passing that Mme Roland's idiolectal expression, "la petite corde," echoes COR*inne* and brings into play the matrix not to say maternal syllable *or,* whose powers of dissemination are thus confirmed.

ANATOMY AND ITS DESTINIES

What the baroness' deformed body makes manifest in the flesh *(en chair)*, in plain language *(en clair)* is the fact that the female body is, to borrow Roger Kempf's expression, "the literary body" par excellence, a palimpsest body on which the passing years cruelly inscribe their traces: such is precisely the major theme of *Fort comme la mort*. To tell the life of a woman and, through her, of Woman is tantamount to recounting the adventures of her body, a culturally coded body: the paradigm of vicissitudes is quickly exhausted. Thus, bringing into play a minimum of means, hypostatizing Woman in an ultimately limited number of female characters, Maupassant succeeds in *Une Vie* in dramatizing the poverty of this corporeal adventure.

The overt singularity of the title *Une Vie* represents in fact the sum of several lives, dissimulates a plural existence. The underlying plural of the title (*Une Vie* is made up of the lives of all its female characters) in some sense justifies the absence of the proper noun noted above; whereas in *Madame Bovary*, Emma is Woman, in *Une Vie*, Woman is hypostatized in the form of some of the main feminine stereotypes in force at the time: the Sentimental Woman, the Old Maid, the Sensualist. If there are grounds for comparing *Une Vie* to a work by Flaubert (Maupassant's master),

Reading (for) the Feminine

L'Education sentimentale rather than *Madame Bovary* would be that work,[16] for, let us recall, in *L'Education,* the feminine is incarnated in turn in the guise of Mme Arnoux, Rosanette, Mme Dambreuse, and Mlle Roque. A comparison of the major semantic axes which determine the distribution of the female characters in the two novels may help us tease out the specificity of Maupassant's problematic of sexual difference.

In Flaubert's novel these semantic axes are entirely subordinated to Frédéric Moreau's point of view: they are first what we might call the axis of profitability—will Frédéric's relationship with this woman advance his interests—second: the axis of consummation—will Frédéric consummate his desire for this woman. Thus, Mme Arnoux might be said to combine features of nonprofitability and nonconsummation. Because *Une Vie* is, unlike *L'Education,* a feminocentric novel, the vector of (male) desire that connects Frédéric to the female characters no longer functions as its central axis: its female characters have been promoted from the status of mere object to that of subject and this promotion entails a different distribution of the female actors. The great question posed by Maupassant in *Une Vie* (as well as in other texts) is: *how does reproduction (read maternity) compromise with jouissance?* A question which often (though not always) arises in the boulevard comedy form: do the lover and the husband get on well together? Thus the two major axes which organize the distribution of female roles in *Une Vie* are on the one hand the axis of reproduction (fertility vs. sterility) and the axis of eroticism (jouissance vs. nonjouissance). Because what are involved here are combinations of mutually exclusive sexual relationships, the semiotic square elaborated by A. J. Greimas some years ago, provides an apt mode of schematization

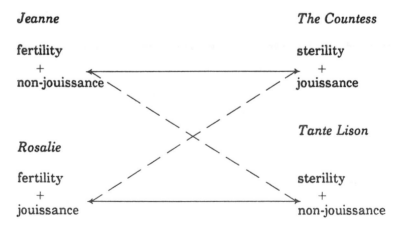

(figure 1). This schema stands in need of immediate qualification on at least two points:

1) One might legitimately wonder at the absence of the other major female protagonist, about whom much has already been said: the baroness. Strange though it may seem, upon reflection, the baroness actualizes the same combinatory as Rosalie, and it is no accident if in both cases success goes hand in hand with the splitting of the male object: the maid, like the baroness, has both a lover and a husband. That the woman should be impregnated either by the husband (the baroness), or by the lover (Rosalie) seems in keeping with the great law that rules all sexual relationships in Maupassant: *the necessary separation of the pleasant and the useful*.[17] The corollary of this law might help explain a certain number of narrative scenarios that recur with striking and seemingly arbitrary fixity and involve a woman, her husband, her lover, and one or more children: on the basis of such short stories as *Histoire d'une fille de ferme, Le Million, L'Héritage, Le Petit*, and *Monsieur Parent*, it is possible to state that if a woman has a child by her lover, she will not have one by her husband, and vice versa. The converse, however, is statistically far less frequent; in fact, it seems to be the privilege of the aristocracy: the baroness and the Countess of Guilleroy *(Fort comme la mort)*. In the bourgeoisie and the lower classes, even when there is a marriage between an aristocrat and a parvenu, things work out differently: invariably it is the lover who wins out. Thus, if there is any uncertainty as to the father, the lover is automatically designated: "She was pregnant. By her lover or her husband? How could she tell? By the lover, no doubt" ("Elle fut grosse. De son amant ou de son mari? Le pouvait-elle savoir? Mais de l'amant, sans doute," *Monsieur Jocaste*, 1:873). Thus, in the rare cases where the taboo is violated (because it is obviously a question of an interdiction), such as in *Pierre et Jean* or *Le Testament*, the lover's son is favored by the mother at the expense of the legitimate son or sons. In short: in promoting the separation of the pleasant and the useful, Maupassant does little more than place an eighteenth-century aristocratic morality in the service of an oedipal fantasy, which consists of flouting the husband (the legitimate father) by making him sterile and delegating the procreative function to the lover. We will soon see that the child gains nothing in the exchange, but let us note for now Maupassant's characteristic gesture: what he takes away with one hand, he gives back with the other. Thus the deficiencies of legitimate paternity are compensated by the quasi miraculous ease of illegitimate paternity. If we have returned here to the well-known theme

of the vicissitudes of paternity in Maupassant, it is to attempt to see how maternity is reconciled with eroticism. It emerges that Jeanne's great mistake will be to believe that one can or must find combined in one man the functions of husband, lover, and father, a romantic and bourgeois ideal which does not in any way correspond to the realities of life, of a woman's life.

2) It will be argued that Jeanne's case is far more complex than this schema allows, and, of course, that is true: as the main protagonist, Jeanne is cramped by a model which reduces her to the same level as the other characters. Any "reduction" is also an interpretation. The question then arises: what elements of the text led me to propose this interpretation?

The facts are as follows: during her honeymoon in Corsica Jeanne experiences jouissance, "that mysterious outburst of sensual emotion" ("cette étrange et véhémente secousse des sens" [p. 62/96]), that is the female orgasm (as viewed by men). But this jouissance is so fleeting, so tenuous, so limited both in time (honeymoon) and in space (Corsica), that one cannot, it seems to me, include Jeanne among those who are destined for pleasure and succeed in reconciling maternity and jouissance. The stereotypical opposition of Jeanne and Rosalie—in the nineteenth century, Hélène Cixous reminds us, "the maid is the mistress' repressed,"[18]—as well as Jeanne's refusal to identify with her mother, in particular her adulterous mother, lend further weight to our argument. What is more, Jeanne will carry her disillusionment to the point of prudishness, condemning all women who, like Rosalie, the baroness, and Gilberte—her husband's mistress—succumb to their erotic desires:

> Jeanne's sensual impulses were dead and no longer worried her; her broken heart and romantic soul were only soothed by the warm fertilizing breath of spring and she lived in a world of fancy, excited but without passion, day-dreaming, dead to all the lusts of the flesh. With a feeling of revulsion, which amounted almost to hatred, she could not understand the foul bestiality of the world.
>
> The nature of human beings now revolted her as something unnatural, and, if she bore a grudge against Gilberte, it was not because she had stolen her husband, but merely because she had fallen into the world-wide mire.
>
> Et Jeanne, dont les sens éteints ne s'agitaient plus, dont le cœur meurtri, l'âme sentimentale semblaient seuls remués par les souf-

fles tièdes et féconds, qui rêvait, exaltée sans désirs, passionnée pour des songes et morte aux besoins charnels, s'étonnait, pleine d'une répugnance qui devenait haineuse, de cette sale bestialité. L'accouplement des êtres l'indignait à présent comme une chose contre nature; et, si elle en voulait à Gilberte, ce n'était point de lui avoir pris son mari, mais du fait même d'être tombée aussi dans cette fange universelle. (p. 121/189)

If one absolutely had to categorize Jeanne, one would have to view her as a typically Victorian female type (cf. Irene, Soames' wife in Galsworthy's *The Forsyte Saga*) by whom the loss of virginity is experienced as a rape which leaves indelible traumatic traces:

> Inevitably they concluded that a young girl raised with the ideal of future tenderness and in the expectation of a disturbing mystery, which she dimly divines to be indecent and mildly impure, but distinguished, must remain deeply troubled when the duties of marriage are revealed to her by a boor.
>
> Ils arrivaient infailliblement à cette conclusion qu'une jeune fille élevée dans le rêve des tendresses futures et dans l'attente d'un mystère inquiétant, deviné indécent et gentiment impur, mais distingué, devait demeurer bouleversée quand la révélation des exigences du mariage lui était faite par un rustre.[19]

DRINKING MOTHER

> Pourquoi que tu ne bé point la mé, pé Toine? (*Toine, Contes et Nouvelles*, 1:177)

If on the plane, let us say, of events Jeanne's "frigidity" implicates both the education given her by her parents and the initiation inflicted on her by her husband, on another plane or level, the analytic, her problem is long-standing, going back to her earliest dual relationship, her relationship to her mother *(mère),* which is always—and nowhere more so than in Maupassant—a relationship to the sea *(la mer):*

> What was so painfully lacking was the sea, her mighty neighbor for twenty-five years, the sea with its salty air, its storms, the thunder of its waves, the sea which she had looked at every morning from her window at the Poplars, whose air she had

breathed day and night, which she had felt close to her and which unconsciously she had come to love like a human being.

Ce qui lui manquait si fort, c'était la mer, sa grande voisine depuis vingt-cinq ans . . . la mer que chaque matin elle voyait de sa fenêtre des Peuples, qu'elle respirait jour et nuit, qu'elle sentait près d'elle, qu'elle s'était mise à aimer comme une personne sans s'en douter. (pp. 182–183/286)

In Maupassant the love of the mother-sea takes the form not only of a thematic overinvestment in the sea and water in general, but above all of a recurrent scenario linking jouissance to the quenching of thirst.[20] Hence it is possible to range a fair number of characters in Maupassant under two headings: on the one hand, the *thirsty*, such as Bel-Ami (ch. 1 of *Bel-Ami*), or the unfortunate protagonist of *Garçon, un bock!*, or the Horla which subsists solely on milk and water; on the other hand, the *purveyors of beverages*, such as the pharmacist Marowsko, the inventor of a liqueur called "la groseillette" *(Pierre et Jean*, pp. 73–74), such as the barmaids whose erotic prestige is due only to their occupation *(Pierre et Jean, Notre Cœur*, and *L'Ermite)*, such as, finally, the giver of water at the Enval spa, endowed with the idealizing name of Marie, and who is described as follows:

This placid woman of Auvergne, wearing a little cap always snowy white and nearly covered by a large apron always very clean, that hid her working dress, slowly rose when she saw a bather coming towards her. As soon as she recognized him, she picked out his glass from a little movable, glazed cupboard, and calmly filled it with a zinc dipper.

The gloomy bather smiled, drank and returned the glass with "Thanks, Marie!" then turned away. And Marie seated herself again on her chair to wait on the next comer.

Cette calme Auvergnate, coiffée d'un petit bonnet toujours bien blanc, et presque entièrement couverte par un large tablier toujours bien propre, qui cachait sa robe de service, se levait avec lenteur dès qu'elle apercevait dans le chemin un baigneur s'en venant vers elle. L'ayant reconnu, elle choisissait son verre dans une petite armoire mobile et vitrée, puis elle l'emplissait doucement au moyen d'une écuelle de zinc emmanchée au bout d'un bâton.

Le baigneur, triste, souriait, buvait, rendait le verre en disant: "Merci, Marie!" puis se retournait et s'en allait. Et Marie se rasseyait sur sa chaise de paille pour attendre le suivant (8:2/p. 22; cf. *Mes 25 Jours*)

Everything in this scene tends to invest the act of giving water with mythical significance; the ritualized gestures and sacred character of the "guardian of the healing waters" (*Mes 25 Jours*, p. 708) represent the syncretism of pagan and Christian forms of worship and images of *alma mater*.

Thus, at first jouissance is drinking mother. But the most fully realized elaboration of this recurrent scenario cautions us against a univocal interpretation of the fantasy. I am alluding to the short story which bears the revealing title (whose apparent irony fools no one): *Idyll*. Brought together by chance in the compartment of a train, a wet-nurse gorged with milk breast-feeds a starving worker:

> He kneeled in front of her, and she leaned over him, carrying her breast to his mouth with a maternal motion. In the movement which she made when taking it in her two hands to hold it out to this man, a drop of milk appeared on the end. He drank it eagerly; then he began to nurse greedily and regularly.
>
> Il se mit à genoux devant elle; et elle se pencha vers lui, portant vers sa bouche, dans un geste de nourrice, le bout foncé de son sein. Dans le mouvement qu'elle fit en le prenant de ses deux mains pour le tendre vers cet homme, une goutte de lait apparut au sommet. Il la but vivement, saisissant comme un fruit cette lourde mamelle entre ses lèvres. Et il se mit à téter d'une façon goulue et régulière. (p. 198/ 2:1288)

What must be noted in this short story is what Paris calls the "complementarity" of the two characters: each of them *gives*, both the one who gives to drink and the one who drinks; in this act of love, both partners are satisfied:

> As she was closing up her dress, stretched by her enormous development, she said: "You have certainly done me a great favor. I thank you, Monsieur."
>
> He answered, in a grateful tone: "None at all, Madame, it is I who thank you—I hadn't had anything to eat for three days!"
>
> Elle lui dit, en faisant rentrer dans sa robe les deux gourdes vivantes qui gonflaient sa poitrine:

"Vous m'avez rendu un fameux service. Je vous remercie bien, Monsieur."
Et il répondit d'un ton reconnaissant:
"C'est moi qui vous remercie, Madame, voilà deux jours que je n'avais rien mangé!" (p. 198/2:1288–89)

Just as in a dream where the dreamer is split in two, the author is *both* the thirsty man and the wet-nurse; Maupassant's dream would then be one of self-sufficiency: to be both mother and child.

If (at best) there is no difference between giver and receiver, it follows that the giver can be either a man or a woman. Nevertheless, and in our perspective this is highly significant, there are differences between donator and donatrix. That is what emerges from the superimposition of two variants of this phantasmic scene, where only the sex of the "sender" varies:

The young people . . . suddenly caught sight of a spring of clear water spurting from a little hole in the cliff, by the side of a wooden bench which formed a resting place about the middle of the slope . . .
"Oh, how thirsty I am!" cried Madame Rosémilly.
But how could they drink? She tried to scoop up some water in her hands, but it escaped between her fingers. Jean had a bright idea; he placed a stone in the road, and she knelt on it to drink from the spring itself, which was now on a level with her mouth.

Les jeunes gens . . . aperçurent à côté d'un banc de bois qui marquait un repos vers le milieu de la valeuse, un filet d'eau claire jaillissant d'un petit trou de la falaise . . .
"Oh! que j'ai soif!" s'écria Mme Rosémilly.
Mais comment boire? Elle essayait de recueillir dans le fond de sa main l'eau qui fuyait à travers les doigts. Jean eut une idée, mit une pierre dans le chemin; et elle s'agenouilla dessus afin de puiser à la source même avec ses lèvres qui se trouvaient ainsi à la même hauteur. (4:128/169–170)

Feeling thirsty, they followed a trail of dampness over a waste of stones, which led them to a tiny spring channelled into a trough for the use of goatherds. A carpet of moss covered the ground around. Jeanne knelt down to drink and Julien followed her example. Suddenly Jeanne had a lover's inspiration. She filled her mouth with the liquid and distending her cheeks like a waterskin she conveyed to Julien that she wanted to quench his thirst lip to lip. He bent forward with his head back and his arms extended and drained at one gulp this spring of living flesh, which kindled the fire of desire in his heart.

Ils avaient soif, une trace humide les guida, à travers un chaos de pierres, jusqu'à une source toute petite, canalisée dans un bâton creux pour l'usage des chevriers. Un tapis de mousse couvrait le sol alentour. Jeanne s'agenouilla pour boire; et Julien en fit autant . . .

Soudain Jeanne eut une inspiration d'amour. Elle emplit sa bouche du clair liquide, et, les joues gonflées comme des outres, fit comprendre à Julien que, lèvre à lèvre, elle voulait le désaltérer.

Il tendit sa gorge, souriant, la tête en arrière, les bras ouverts; et il but d'un trait à cette source de chair vive qui lui versa dans les entrailles un désir enflammé. (pp. 60–61/93–94)

When Jean, the giver, searches for a means to quench Mme Rosémilly's thirst, he has an "idea" worthy of an engineer; piper of the spring, he imposes culture, masculine knowledge on (feminine) nature. In other words, Jean can only give a drink by means of a stone; he needs a helper, an instrument. The same rule does not apply to his female homonym, Jeanne: faced with the same problem, how to quench the thirst of a love object, she has not a "bright idea" but a "lover's inspiration" worthy of a mother; no appeal to technological expertise enters into play, the simple knowledge of the body is sufficient. Thus the donatrix, unlike the donator, pays in kind by transforming herself into a woman-breast.

In the end, for Jeanne, to experience jouissance is not so much *having* the mother to drink from (one risks drowning; at the very moment when Jeanne is about to leap into the sea, she moans, "Maman!" p. 140), rather *being* her, being the breast (a fantasy which would be the feminine equivalent of the masculine fantasy: being the phallus). The transformation of the man/woman relationship into a mother/child relationship is for Jeanne the royal way to jouissance. In turn devoted daughter, maternal wife, possessive mother, and, finally, fulfilled grandmother, Jeanne will never succeed in existing outside the field of motherhood.

THE SECRET (IN THE) DRAWER

The baroness' hypertrophy is then polyvalent, for not only does it make manifest the significance of the heart-body (cœur-corps), but it also concretizes the disproportionate place the Mother occupies in this fictional

universe. It is as though the mother's massive body cluttered up, indeed
invaded, the pages of the novel, in the manner of this portrait of a (seductive) mother: "She seemed so much alone, and so much at home, that
she made the whole large apartment seem absolutely empty. She lived
alone in it, filled it, gave it life" ("Elle était tellement seule, et chez elle,
qu'elle faisait le vide en tout ce grand appartement, le vide absolu. Elle
l'habitait, l'emplissait, l'animait seule" [*Un Portrait*, 6:297/1:629]). The
mother is everywhere, relayed either by the sea or by a whole series of
characters; thus, after the successive deaths which carry off the baroness
and Julien, when the family circle tightens around Paul (Jeanne's son),
even the least maternal characters—the baron and tante Lison—are called
upon to play a maternal role (whereas there is never any question of replacing the dead father):

> As he was growing fast, one of the absorbing occupations of
> his three guardians, whom the Baron called his three mothers,
> was to measure his height.
>
> Comme il grandissait vite, une des passionnantes occupations
> des trois parents que le baron appelait "ses trois mères" était de
> mesurer sa taille. (p. 155/243)

Thus, tante Lison barely in the grave, Rosalie appears to take over, taking care of her mistress as though she were "a sick child" ("un enfant
malade" [*Une Vie*, p. 271]).[21]

But these substitutive series only serve to make more manifest a profound distress, for the baroness' death creates a gap which no one can
fill. Indeed, in losing her mother, Jeanne is the victim of a double disas-
ter: at first, she mourns her mother's death, her physical death, but, in a
second stage, she gives up as lost an idealized image of her mother, she
mourns a moral death. A little (a lot) like Charles Bovary who suffers the
pangs of jealousy after the fact, Jeanne discovers her mother's adultery
the very evening she spends watching over her mother's corpse with filial
piety. In opening the famous "chest of relics," Jeanne learns the "dreadful
secret" it had always concealed. Let us stop over this piece of furniture,
for it occupies a privileged place in Maupassant's "philosophy of furniture," and governs by the frequency of its appearances and the extension
of its semantic field a "mini-corpus" which includes: *Pierre et Jean, Fort
comme la mort, Notre Cœur*, as well as *La Veillée, Comment on cause, Nos*

Lettres, Suicides, and *Souvenirs.* The number of "chests of relics" one finds in Maupassant's work, the monotony of their content, the serious consequences which always follow upon their violation, all lead me to believe that we have here one of those nodal points in which writing takes charge of neurosis, transforming a banal oedipal triangle into an individual myth. Maupassant's family romance is quite literally what is known in French as a "roman à tiroirs" (episodic novel). This is no jest:

1) The chest of relics is part of the paraphernalia of lovers; it is a common piece of furniture, as indicated by the use of the definite article in the following quotation:

> He remembered now a little miniature which he had seen in Paris on the parlor chimneypiece, once upon a time, but which had disappeared. Where was it? Lost, or hidden? . . . His mother, perhaps, kept it in *the* secret drawer where relics are hidden.
>
> Il se rappelait maintenant un petit portrait miniature vu autrefois à Paris, sur la cheminée de leur salon, et disparu à présent. Où était-il? Perdu ou caché! . . . Sa mère l'avait gardé peut-être dans *le* tiroir inconnu où l'on serre les reliques d'amour. (*Pierre et Jean*, 4:93/125)

2) It follows that this piece of furniture is in no way a female attribute:

> The painter who was making pencil-sketches . . . reread the Countess' note, then, opening a secretary-drawer, deposited it on top of the other letters which had piled up there since the beginning of their affair.
>
> Le peintre qui crayonnait des esquisses . . . relut le billet de la comtesse, puis ouvrant le tiroir d'un secrétaire, il l'y déposa sur un amas d'autres lettres entassées là depuis le début de leur liaison. (*Fort comme la mort*, p. 63)

3) A banalized piece of furniture, the relics chest is doubly linked to death, first because of its coffin-like form and content, second because of its deadliness:

> "Oh! if you cherish life, never disturb the burying-ground of old letters!"

Oh, ne touchez jamais à ce meuble, à ce cimetière des corre-
spondances d'autrefois, si vous tenez à la vie! (1:117/826)

4) Whatever the example chosen, the violation of the chest sooner or
later leads to the disappearance, indeed the destruction of its entire contents, fire constituting an integral part, as it were, of the semantic field of
the relics drawer: "Above all burn this letter" ("Surtout brûle cette lettre"
[p. 31/204]); similarly, in *Fort comme la mort,* on his deathbed, Olivier
will ask of his lover the supreme sacrifice; to burn the love letters she
herself wrote.

What then is the dangerous message these letters bear? These letters,
these relics all testify (with a single exception and we shall see in a moment that this exception only confirms the rule) to the mother's "fall into
carnality," which is to say to her jouissance, and for the child (daughter
as well as son, Jeanne as well as Pierre), there is no more shameful and
above all no more painful family secret. For, while easily putting up with
a puppet father (Mr. Roland in *Pierre et Jean*), the child does not tolerate
at all well the retroactive revelation of the existence of the formidable rival that is the mother's lover. When they are given, the names of the lovers bear eloquent testimony to the mixed feelings of fear and hatred they
inspire: Paul d'Ennemare (*Une Vie;* en a marre = fed up with) on the one
hand, Mr. Maréchal (*Pierre et Jean*) on the other. The substitution of the
lover for the father is labor lost: not only does the father's hold emerge
strengthened, but in the process of attempting to secure exclusive rights
over the mother, the author of this scenario finds nothing better to do
than to "blacken" and degrade her.

But, as we mentioned earlier, there exists one variant which at first sight
seems out of place in this homogeneous corpus: I am alluding to the drama
of the protagonist of *Suicides* who, unlike the other children, finds in his
secretary evidence not of his mother's infidelity, rather of the faithful love,
not to say gratitude, he feels for his mother. Here is the relic whose re-
discovery causes his death:

" 'My Dear Little Mamma:
" 'I am to-day seven years old. It is the age of reason. I take
advantage of it to thank you for having brought me into this
world.
" 'Your little son, who loves you.
" 'Robert' "

Une Vie *or the Name of the Mother*

"Ma petite maman chérie,
  "J'ai aujourd'hui sept ans. C'est l'âge de raison, j'en profite pour
te remercier de m'avoir donné le jour.
                    "Ton petit garçon qui t'adore,
                    "Robert." (1:119/2:828)[22]

All one has to do is to read Freud's essay, "A Special Type of Object-Choice Made by Men," to remove the apparent contradiction between the son's letter and the letters to or from the lover: for, according to Freud, the feelings of gratitude toward the mother are bound up with the desire to save the loved one, to redeem the "whore." The burning of the letters to/from the mother is the form that the child's "reparation" takes in Maupassant. By representing the ritual purification by fire of the fallen mother, the author discharges his "debt" with exemplary honor. And yet this propitiatory gesture of the good little boy goes hand in hand with a form of appropriation unlike those considered above: for what is sacrificed is none other than *the mother's text*. We might say, in somewhat schematic terms, that what authorizes the son's text is the pulverization, the dispersion of a maternal *Ur-text*. And it is Maupassant himself who stresses the fact that the letters to/from the mother constitute not only her very being, but her greatest claim to fame:

> She looked at it, these square things which contained all she had known how to say of her love, everything she had been able to tear of it from herself to give to him, with a little ink, on white paper . . . It was the soul of her soul, the heart of her heart.

> Elle regardait cela, ces petites choses carrées qui contenaient tout ce qu'elle avait su dire de son amour, tout ce qu'elle avait pu en arracher d'elle pour le lui donner, avec un peu d'encre, sur du papier blanc . . . C'était l'âme de son âme, le cœur de son cœur. (*Fort comme la mort*, p. 245)

> Think that never, do you understand, never, does a woman burn, tear, or destroy the letters in which it is told her that she is loved. That is our whole life, our whole hope, expectation, and dream. These little papers which bear our name in caressing terms are relics which we adore; they are chapels in which we are the saints. Our love letters are our titles to beauty, grace, seduction, the intimate vanity of our womanhood; they are the treasures of our heart. No, a woman never destroys these secret and precious archives of her life.

69

Songez donc que jamais, vous entendez bien, jamais une femme ne brûle, ne déchire, ne détruit les lettres où on lui dit qu'elle est aimée. Toute notre vie est là, tout notre espoir, toute notre attente, tout notre rêve. Ces petits papiers qui portent notre nom et nous caressent avec de douces choses, sont des reliques, et nous adorons les chapelles, nous autres, surtout les chapelles dont nous sommes les saintes. Nos lettres d'amour, ce sont nos titres de beauté, nos titres de grâce et de séduction, notre orgueil intime de femmes, ce sont les trésors de notre cœur. Non, non, jamais une femme ne détruit ces archives secrètes et délicieuses de sa vie. (6:314–315/ 1:1107)

Let us note that if the destruction of the mother's letters takes place in an aggressive and dysphoric register, in *Bel-Ami* Maupasant represents the euphoric mode of the relationship between the mother and the son's texts. I am referring to the very unusual type of relationship Mme Forrestier maintains with the men in her life. Like a modern muse, while preserving her complete autonomy, she takes pleasure in forming young journalists by having them write what she dictates to them, she nurtures their articles with her own substance; the ideal bountiful mother for a writer, she gives them her voice. Writing *à deux,* man and woman, mother and son, would seem to be the supreme form of happiness (*Bel-Ami,* p. 265).[23]

BLANKS

Up until now we have been concerned with only one aspect of the drawer: its contents. It is time to speak of the form of the container. What then is a drawer? An enclosed space which mediates between emptiness and fullness: "When the chimney was full and the drawer empty" ("Quand la cheminée fut pleine et le tiroir vide" [*Fort comme la mort,* p. 245]). Now, as Eugénie Lemoine-Luccioni notes: "The play of emptiness and fullness is . . . central to the female imaginary. Woman has an easy means by which to fill the emptiness: to get fat or pregnant."[24] The drawer, metaphor for Jeanne's life: indeed, all that which at first simulates fullness—wealth, marriage, motherhood—turns out to be but a snare, a false plenitude which hides a hole, a chasm:

But as they lived simply, what they had would have been enough, if there had not been in the house *a bottomless* and ever-open *outlet*, the Baron's generosity; this was always drying up the money in their hands as the sun dries up the water in the marshes.

Comme ils vivaient simplement, ce revenu aurait suffi s'il n'y avait eu dans la maison *un trou sans fond* toujours ouvert, la bonté. Elle tarissait l'argent dans leurs mains comme le soleil tarit l'eau des marécages. (p. 11/12)

Why should one fall into marriage so quickly, as into *an abyss* suddenly yawning before one's feet?

Pourquoi tomber si vite dans le mariage comme dans *un trou* sous vos pas? (p. 49/73)

Then her womb seemed to *discharge*.

Il lui sembla soudain que tout son ventre se *vidait* brusquement. (p. 105/163)

By the end of the novel, struggling against the pull of the void into which money and family members are sucked will become Jeanne's only reason for living. Lacking plentitude in the present, she will attempt to banish emptiness from her past, by filling in the blanks in her memory, transforming the tattered tissue of her life into a smooth, seamless texture:

> Suddenly an idea came into her mind, which soon developed into a terrible, permanent, haunting obsession. She wanted to recall almost day by day everything she had done . . . She had underlined the important days in her life, and sometimes she managed to recover a whole month, putting together day by day, by grouping and connecting one day with another, all the little incidents that had preceded or followed the important date.

> Et une idée la saisit qui fut bientôt une obsession terrible, incessante, acharnée. Elle voulait retrouver presque jour par jour ce qu'elle avait fait . . .
> Elle avait marqué de traits les dates mémorables de son histoire, et elle parvenait parfois à retrouver un mois entier, reconstituant un à un, groupant, rattachant l'un à l'autre tous les petits faits qui avaient précédé ou suivi un événement important. (p. 195/307)

The relics and other material traces (old calendars, gold pin, Poulet's ladder) then take on their full significance: they are part of a mnemonic machine destined not only to supplement failures of memory, but to make up for a failed life. In keeping with her faith in the redemptive powers of memory, Jeanne saves her memories the way others place stock market shares in a vault. Having been unable to live her life forward, as a project, woman, that is sentimental woman, lives retrospectively. Having attained old age, she retains only the desire to tell her story or to be told another's:

> Jeanne sometimes replaced Rosalie and took Mama out for her walk, when she recalled memories of her childhood.
> Jeanne parfois remplaçait Rosalie et promenait petite mère qui lui racontait des souvenirs d'enfance. (p. 23/33)

> Jeanne, sitting up in bed, wanted to know the whole story and said: "Come now, *tell me everything*, my dear girl, *all about your life*. It will do me good after all I have suffered."
> Alors Jeanne, s'asseyant sur son lit, envahie d'un besoin de savoir: "Voyons, *raconte-moi tout*, ma fille, *toute ta vie*. Cela me fera du bien aujourd'hui." (pp. 172–73/269)

Telling one's life, one's whole life, down to the smallest detail is an activity traditionally assigned to women.[25] Rosalie and Jeanne only pick up again the never-interrupted narrative thread of Ronsard's old woman chatting with her servant by the fireside. It would appear that the autobiographical, not to say novelistic project is the revenge of the weak. One might then well ask why Jeanne does not seek to counter the horrors of the void by the anguish of the blank page, in short: Why doesn't Jeanne attempt to write her life story? The answer to this question is given somewhat obliquely in the following:

> She kept whispering: "Pullet, darling little Pullet!" as if she were talking to him. His name sometimes put an end to her dreams, and she would spend hours trying to *write* the letters of his name *in the air* with an outstretched finger. She traced the letters slowly in front of the fire, imagining that she could see them; then, thinking that she had made a mistake, she began again with the P, her arm trembling with fatigue, forcing herself to complete the name; when she had finished it, she began all over again.

Et, tout bas, ses lèvres murmuraient: "Poulet, mon petit Poulet," comme si elle lui eût parlé; et, sa rêverie s'arrêtant sur ce mot, elle essayait parfois pendant des heures d'*écrire dans le vide,* de son doigt tendu, les lettres qui le composaient. Elle les traçait lentement, devant le feu, s'imaginant les voir, puis, croyant s'être trompée, elle recommençait le P d'un bras tremblant de fatigue, s'efforçant de dessiner le nom jusqu'au bout; puis, quand elle avait fini, elle recommençait. (pp. 193–194/304)

Writing for Jeanne is not signing her own name, rather incessantly inscribing the name of her son; if Emma desires a son and is disconsolate at having a daughter, Jeanne's life testifies to the failure to which any attempt to live and especially to write one's life by phallic proxy inevitably leads.

As far as emptiness goes, however, there is worse: consider the case of a female character about whom I have said little thus far (about whom little is said in the novel), a character who represents what we might term the degree zero of femininity, not to say of character itself.[26] I refer to tante Lison:

> She had made no place for herself; she was one of those people who remain strangers even to their relations, like unexplored country, whose death leaves no gap, no void in a house . . .

> Elle ne tenait point de place; c'était un de ces êtres qui demeurent inconnus même à leurs proches, comme inexplorés, et dont la mort ne fait ni trou ni vide dans une maison . . . (p. 41/61)

If tante Lison's death goes unnoticed, it is simply because in life she was the embodiment of emptiness: one could call her a phantom character. Now the seemingly banal first name of this "under-qualified" (Hamon, p. 123) character is the object of one of those metalinguistic commentaries that are always indicative of an added meaning:

> Her name was Lise, a name which seemed to embarrass her by its suggestion of sprightly youth. When it became obvious that she was not the marrying type and probably would never marry, they took to calling her Lison instead of Lise.

73

Elle s'appelait Lise et semblait gênée par ce nom pimpant et jeune.
Quand on avait vu qu'elle ne se mariait pas, qu'elle ne se mari-
erait sans doute point, de Lise on avait fait Lison. (p. 40/60; cf.
Par un soir de printemps, 2:307)

Marriage would, of course, have entailed a change of civil status bearing on the family name, celibacy will then provoke a transformation of
the suffix of the first name: Lison is the name of a failed woman, a bi-
sexual name, one might say, since it is the name of the locomotive in
Zola's *La Bête humaine*, which is, as Jean Borie has shown, a herma-
phroditic monster.[27] What is more, if one reads this passage literally, it
posits the equation: Lison = Lise + on. Lison thus represents the conjunction of the proper name of the individual and what one critic has called
"the current family name" of the *doxa:* the indefinite pronoun *on.*[28] And,
finally, Lison can also be understood as an imperative addressed to the
reader (Lison = lisons, let us read), which suggests that the empty square
temporarily occupied by tante Lison is the one which the future reader
will occupy, also on a temporary basis.

ENCORE

It follows that the thematics of emptiness are bound up with onomas-
tics. This is the logical consequence of Hamon's remark to the effect that:
"the classical (readerly) narrative . . . abhors a semantic vacuum (and the
proper name is, by definition, a meaningless term, a 'blank' word, an 'asé-
mantème' in Guillaume's terminology)."[29] In Maupassant this abhorr-
ence turns to vertigo, which explains the extraordinary inflation of motivation, the thirst for nominal "transparency" one finds in his works which
goes beyond anything one finds in Flaubert or even Zola. Thus in Maupassant's fiction the proper name is often replaced by the "hyperseman-
ticized" name that is the surname: *Bel-Ami* is only the most striking example of this type of substitution. Among the very numerous surnames
one finds in Maupassant, we might distinguish four large classes:
1) synecdochic surnames: in the majority of examples noted, the motivation involves a link between the physical appearance of the character
and his/her surname:

74

Une Vie *or the Name of the Mother*

Among her friends she was called the Goddess, because of her proud bearing, her big black eyes, the nobility of her figure.

On l'appelait, parmi ses amis, la Déesse, à cause de son allure fière, de ses grands yeux noirs, de toute la noblesse de sa personne. (1:824)

. . . an *embonpoint* unusual for her age, which had earned for her the sobriquet of Boule de Suif ("Tallow-Ball").

Son embonpoint précoce . . . lui avait valu le surnom de Boule de suif. (4:13/ 2:122)

2) quotation surnames: in a rather limited number of cases, the surname takes up a characteristic expression of the character:

Mica! mica! mica! in reply to everything. I shall call you Mademoiselle *Mica*, I think.

Mica! mica! mica! pour tout. Je ne vous appellerai plus que mademoiselle Mica. (3:306/ 1:1273)

3) portrait surnames: a complex and, to the best of my knowledge, unique instance where the surname is determined both by the character's physique and idiolect:

Ever since his arrival in France, his friends had called him Mlle Fifi. This surname derived from his smart figure, narrow waist, which seemed to be held by a corset, and pale face with its barely visible nascent mustache, as well as from the habit he had acquired to signify his sovereign contempt for men and things of using at every turn the French locution—*fi, fi, then*—which he pronounced with a slight hiss.

Depuis son entrée en France, ses camarades ne l'appelaient plus que Mlle Fifi. Ce surnom lui venait de sa tournure coquette, de sa taille fine qu'on aurait dit tenue en un corset, de sa figure pâle où sa naissante moustache apparaissait à peine, et aussi de l'habitude qu'il avait prise, pour exprimer son souverain mépris des êtres et des choses, d'employer à tout moment la locution française—*fi, fi, donc*, qu'il prononçait avec un léger sifflement. (2:155–156)

4) enigma surnames: these are borderline cases, rare but significant, where motivation wavers or is entirely lacking:

75

Reading (for) the Feminine

In Argenteuil she was called Queen Hortense. No one knew why. Perhaps it was because she had a commanding voice; perhaps because she was tall, bony, imperious; perhaps because she governed a kingdom of servants, chickens, dogs, cats, canaries, parrots, and all the animals so dear to an old maid's heart.

On l'appelait, dans Argenteuil, la reine Hortense. Personne ne sut jamais pourquoi. Peut-être parce qu'elle parlait ferme comme un officier qui commande? Peut-être parce qu'elle était grande, osseuse, impérieuse? Peut-être parce qu'elle gouvernait un peuple de bêtes domestiques, poules, chiens, chats, serins et perruches, de ces bêtes chères aux vieilles filles? (5:1/ 2:829)

But, and this is perhaps the key point, whatever the degree of nominal transparency, Maupassant never relies on the reader's cultural competence to decode the surname; the surname is always—as was the case for tante Lison—accompanied by an explanation; the surname is a "meta-name." Maupassant's quasi-pedagogical concern has to do, at least in part, with the fact that with few exceptions (La reine Hortense or Monsieur Jocaste), the surnames he favors rely on a purely local system of references. The surname is then the hyperbolical guarantor of mimesis, out-classing the mere name as producer of a "reality effect."

But if the surname occupies a privileged position in Maupassant's on-omastics, it is above all because he suffers from a generalized anxiety of nomination. Whether the semantic void manifests itself where the Name of the Father is lacking, or where the unnamable appears, the anxiety of nomination responds to only one remedy: the inscription of the name there where it is lacking. The steps taken by little Simon in his desperate search for a figurehead (*prête-nom*: literally name-lender) father in *Le Papa de Simon* are not all that different from those taken by the narrator of the *Horla* who listens with rapt attention to the sounds of the invisible (2:1093 and 1118). And yet even this anxiety-producing lack admits of an exception, and it is to be found precisely at the end of *Une Vie*. Let us recall briefly the final scene in the novel: beside herself with joy, Jeanne comes home with her infant granddaughter, whom Paul entrusted to Rosalie after the child's mother died in labor. Now this child who arrives in the nick of time to save Jeanne, this infant savior, has no first name and only barely a family name, since Paul married the infant's mother on her deathbed solely for the sake of legitimacy. The exhaustion of the fiction coincides with a moment of respite, between two downbeats, two rites

76

of passage, birth and baptism, the time of limbo where the signifier is suspended, but where this lack is the source not of anxiety but of joy. Though the infant's anonymity echoes that of the title, it resonates otherwise: evoking not loss but promise. The place assigned the reader by Maupassant is precise and it is indeed that of tante Lison; the ideal reader figured in Maupassant's work is a godmother.

4

L'Ensorcelée:
The Scandalized Woman

One evening, at vespers in the Church of Blanchelande, a small community in Normandy, Jeanne le Hardouey, who is the wife of a well-to-do peasant but who was born de Feuardent, is struck by the sight of an unknown priest with a somber and imposing bearing. He is the abbé de la Croix-Jugan, a former monk of equally aristocratic ancestry, who has come to "expiate by an exemplary life" ("racheter par une vie exemplaire")[1] his double crime: his activities as a leader of the Chouannerie and his attempted suicide. On the way home Jeanne encounters a shepherd known as "le pâtre" whom her husband had refused to employ; he curses her in the following terms: "You will remember the vespers you have just left for many a day, Mistress le Hardouey" ("Vous vous souviendrez longtemps des vêpres d'où vous sortez, maîtresse le Hardouey" [p. 96/ 111]). Fascinated by the abbé, cursed by the shepherd, Jeanne also comes under the (bad) influence of la Clotte, a paralyzed old spinner who was in her youth a companion in debauchery of both the abbé and Jeanne's father. As her confidant (not to say analyst), she shares and feeds the aristocratic fire of Jeanne, who is known as "the misallied." It is then at la Clotte's that Jeanne meets the abbé with whom she has fallen madly in love, but who counters her passion with a maddening indifference. When Jeanne ends up drowning herself, as though to appease the fire that marks her forehead with a red stigma, la Clotte attends her funeral. This act provokes an unleashing of violence: la Clotte is stoned by the crowd and dies of her injuries. This lapidation does not, however, restore peace and harmony to the community of Blanchelande; this sacrifice does not found a ritual. On the contrary: on the very Easter day when the abbé is at last entitled to preach mass once again, he is struck down on the altar by Thomas le Hardouey, who is bent on avenging his wife's death. Thomas van-

78

ishes without leaving a trace and it is then and only then that the ritual the narrative undertakes to explain is established: the mass of the abbé de la Croix-Jugan.

Summarized in this fashion, Barbey d'Aurevilly's *L'Ensorcelée* appears to be a text which lends itself to a Girardian reading while at the same time eluding its grasp. In this fictional universe where violence and the sacred mesh and merge, we do, of course, find the major narrative sequences whose quasi-mechanical succession characterizes the narrative of victimage: 1) the crisis of distinctions; 2) reciprocal violence; 3) collective violence; 4) the restoration of peace and the institution of interdictions and rituals.[2] But the laws of what one might call the *sacrificial syntax* are violated: thus collective violence (the lapidation of la Clotte) is *followed* by reciprocal violence (the murder of the abbé) which founds a ritual. The question arises: what relationship if any is there between this syntagmatic slippage and the sexual derangement constituted by the title? In other words: what does it mean to be bewitched in the perspective of Girard's "anthropology of victimage" (p. 171) and further, in what way does the story of the bewitched woman involve a perversion of the normal course of the "persecution-text"?[3] For the "sextual" (to borrow Hélène Cixous' celebrated neologism)[4] aberration we have just noted does not constitute the sole peculiarity of the text: not only is it a borderline case *(cas-limite)* of the persecution-text, it also features a borderline frame *(cadre-limite)* in both the literal and the figurative meanings of the word. I am referring to the de Lessay heath. I am not about to go over the ground already covered by Michel Serres in the remarkable pages he devotes to what he terms the "labyrinth-heath" in *Hermès IV,*[5] rather I would like to go on from there to interrogate more specifically the relationship between the heath and the victimage narrative.

Let us then remain on the heath, the liminal and limiting heath which the narrator crosses at night guided by maître Louis Tainnebouy, a local grazier. While chatting they observe in passing the distinctive features of the landscape: "There are no trees . . . but there are folds in the land, mounds" ("Il n'y a pas d'arbres . . . mais voilà des replis de terrain, des espèces de buttes" [p. 20/54]). It is only two pages later that this apparently gratuitous detail, seemingly placed there for the sake of local color, becomes "operational," as the unevenness of the terrain provokes an accident: "All of a sudden, at one of those folds of earth we spoke of, Maître Tainnebouy's mare reared, and might have fallen if she had not been held by so tight a rein. But when she went on, she limped" ("Tout à coup, à un de ces replis de terrain que nous nous étions signalés, la jument de maître Louis Tainnebouy trébucha, et peut-être serait-elle tombée s'il ne l'eût pas soutenue de sa main vigoureuse et d'une bride épaisse. Mais quand elle se releva elle boitai�" [p. 24/57]).

This accident draws and holds our attention because it introduces an enigma into the text, an enigma Tainnebouy formulates as follows: "How could she have hurt herself on this smooth soil, without a pebble?" ("A quoi a-t-elle pu se blesser sur ce sol uni sans cailloux?" [ibid.]). To this problem Tainnebouy proposes a hypothetical solution: someone must have cast an evil spell on the mare. Upon which Tainnebouy recalls an unpleasant encounter he had had the night before when he had refused to answer for a shepherd who was looking for work: "Well, now I remember that the shepherd sent the devil of a look at me, from under the mantle of the fireplace, and I found him wandering about the side of the stable when I went to get Blanche and go" ("Eh bien! à présent, je me rappelle que le berger m'a jeté, de dessous le manteau de la cheminée, un diable de regard, noir comme le péché, et que je l'ai trouvé qui rôdait du côté de l'écurie quand j'ai été pour prendre la *Blanche* et partir" [p. 30/62]).

Everything leads me to believe that what we have here is the matrix scene of *L'Ensorcelée*. First, as our summary indicates and as the narrator does not fail to emphasize, this scene or scenario will be repeated almost to the detail in Tainnebouy's narrative: "The shepherds of whom Maître Tainnebouy had spoken, and to whom he attributed his horse's accident, played their role in the story" ("Les bergers dont maître Tainnebouy m'avait parlé, et auxquels il imputait l'accident arrivé à son cheval, jouaient aussi leur rôle dans son histoire" [p. 40/70]). The repetition of this scene seems meant to bring out the imbrication of the frame and the diegesis on the one hand, and of the origins of the fiction and the original violence on the other. This leads us to register the other generative aspect of this scene: it gives us direct access to the crisis of distinctions which goes hand in hand with the unleashing of reciprocal violence.

Like the heath, to which they are bound both metaphorically and metonymically, the shepherds incarnate the lack of differentiation. By virtue of their wanderings, which cut them off from their origins and all human community, they are the disseminators par excellence of "bad contagion": they are, as it were, the local Jews. Now what is altogether remarkable is that despite their impeccable qualifications as scapegoat victims, the shepherds are not sacrificed. Neither victims, nor executioners, the shepherds are the spokesmen for reciprocal violence, the bearers of the truth or, at the very least, a self-evident truth of violence. Their function is essentially heuristic: witness the extraordinary scene where the shepherd shows master le Hardouey his destiny in "a small mirror, about as big as a village barber's" ("un petit miroir, grand comme la *mirette* d'un barbier de village" [p. 181/177]): le Hardouey sees there his wife and the abbé roasting his heart on a spit. What is noteworthy about this typically Aurevillian scene—there is a high consumption of hearts in Barbey's fictional universe—is that in it violence and the mirror are explicitly linked: what the shepherds make visible is not so much the violence *in* the mirror as the violence *of* the mirror.[6] In Barbey the mirror stage corresponds quite literally to the crisis of distinctions, the sequence of the sacrificial syntax during which the cycle of reciprocal violence rages out of control, while, at the same time, its truth is revealed.

Indeed, if we now return to our starting point, Tainnebouy's unfortunate encounter, we are in a position to note that the *supernatural interpretation* put forward by the grazier is countered by the *rationalist interpretation* provided by the narrator: "Nothing, indeed, could have been more natural than this tale of Maître Tainnebouy. To explain the accident to his horse there was no reason to look about for a malefactor. The shepherd, moved by *resentment,* had put something into the horse's shoe to wound her and take *revenge* upon her master" ("Rien au fond n'était plus admissible que ce récit de maître Tainnebouy. Pour expliquer l'accident arrivé à son cheval, il n'était pas besoin de creuser jusqu'à l'idée d'un maléfice. Le berger, poussé par le *ressentiment,* avait pu introduire quelque corps blessant dans le sabot du cheval pour se *venger* de son maître" [p. 30/62; emphasis added]).

We must therefore reformulate our initial assertion: maître Tainnebouy's tale *and* the narrator's interpretation taken as a unit constitute the generative cell of the novel: that is, the paradigm dissimulation/revelation.[7] In this community consumed by a bloody civil war and its no less violent aftereffects, all the characters make the same mistake, refusing to recognize the true nature of the victimage mechanism which transforms the bitterest enemies into doubles; and, each time, the narrator persists in rectifying this misapprehension. One example among many: when la Croix-Jugan discovers la Clotte's body, the narrator mingles misprision and recognition: "He, who did not know the reason for this terrible death there before his eyes, thought of the Blues, his obsession, and he said to himself that any partisan crime might relight the extinguished war" ("Lui, qui ne savait pas la raison de cette mort terrible qu'il avait là devant les yeux, pensait aux Bleus, sa fixe pensée, et il se disait que tout crime de parti pouvait rallumer la guerre éteinte" [p. 229/215–216]). In a first stage, by separating himself from the abbé, the deluded *he* implicitly opposed to he who knows, the narrator exposes the error of the purely political interpretation of the lapidation. But, in a second stage, he shows that the abbé has a perfect grasp of the dialectics of reciprocal violence. Besides, the abbé's error is only partial, for the person who stirred up the mob against la Clotte, Augé the butcher, is indeed a political enemy. And yet, as la Clotte herself so well puts it, in a sentence which sheds light on the overdetermination of the violence whose victim she is, that is not the point; what la Clotte's lapidation demonstrates is the manner in which reciprocal violence results in unanimous violence: " 'The Blues!' she said, bewildered, 'The Blues! Augé is a Blue; the son of his father. *But* they all did it—they all fell upon me—Blanchelande—all of them' " ("Les Bleus! fit-elle comme égarée, les Bleus! Augé, c'est un Bleu; c'est le fils de son père. *Mais* tous y étaient . . . tous m'ont accablée . . . Blanchelande . . . tout entier" [p. 229/215]).

Let us return to the heath, the heath which we have never really left. If we superimpose the description of the de Lessay heath on other descriptions of heaths in Barbey's writings, we find that the heath is one of those literary places, one of those romantic and novelistic landscapes particularly suited to sacrifices. In reading *Un Prêtre marié*, we find that the fold in the ground which trips up Tainnebouy's mare has a history, indeed an origin:

> Since childhood Néel had heard said by all and sundry that a hideous crime had been committed on this spot and that the man who had committed it, after having been drawn and quartered according to the laws of those times, had been exposed at the scene of his crime as a terrible lesson to all those who might pass that way.
>
> Out of pity or terror each passerby, while averting his glance, had thrown a handful of clay on this corpse which lay shattered and unburied and in time something like the head of a tombstone had arisen there. The condemned man's body seemed to

have molded this pile of dust which caused the passerby to trip in the night. Horses stumbled or fell.

Néel, dès son enfance, avait entendu dire au tiers et quart qu'un horrible crime avait été commis à cette place et que l'homme qui l'avait commis, après avoir été rompu, selon la loi du temps, avait été exposé à l'endroit même de son meurtre, comme un enseignement terrible pour ceux qui prendraient par ce chemin.

La pitié de chaque passant ou son épouvante avait jeté, en détournant les yeux, sa poignée de terre sur ce cadavre fracassé et sans sépulture et y avait formé, à la longue, comme le chevet d'une tombe. Le corps du condamné semblait avoir moulé cet amas de poussière qui, dans la nuit, faisait trébucher le passant. Les chevaux y bronchaient ou s'y abattaient.[8]

The obstacle against which Maître Tainnebouy's horse stumbles is then nothing other than the tomb of the scapegoat-victim—who is always in Barbey an unburied corpse. Now, what then is this mound, this trap, but a *skandalon,* a polysemous word whose traditional meaning Girard begins by recalling: "*Skandalon* is generally translated as scandal, obstacle, stumbling-block, road-trap. The word and its derivative *skandalidzo,* to cause a scandal, comes from the stem *skadzo,* which means 'I limp' " (p. 469). Before giving an account of the Girardian meaning of the word, let us look more closely at the restricted field of its literal and etymological meaning. Our hypothesis according to which the mare stumbles on a *skandalon* is strengthened by relating this accident to another, the discovery by the abbé of la Clotte's bloody body: "All of a sudden his fiery steed, its head high in the air, gave a start and reared back, neighing. That drew him from his revery . . . He looked at the obstacle which made the mane stand up on the neck of his black filly and saw in front of the lifted feet of the animal Clotte bleeding" ("Tout à coup son ardente monture, qui portait au vent, fit un écart et se cabra en hennissant . . . Cela le tira de sa rêverie . . . Il regarda alors l'obstacle qui faisait dresser le crin sur le cou de sa noire pouliche, et il vit, devant les pieds levés de l'animal, la Clotte sanglante" [p. 228/214]).

It is as if one cannot take a step in this novel without stumbling on a corpse. The *skandalon* insists, endlessly returning us to the violent origins of this fiction, and leading us to make mention of the purely semantic function of the obstacle, the *literariness of the skandalon* (of which Girard takes no account), that is to reflect upon our own critical progress: "stylistic effect" (Riffaterre), "isotopy-shifter" (Coquet via Greimas), or "nodal point" (Freud), the *skandalon is the detail* whose contour breaks the smooth surface of the text, bringing one's reading to a halt, and provoking the "click" (Spitzer) of interpretation.[9]

The reader has then no choice but to fall into step with the characters and experience in turn the shock of the *skandalon*. Now the characters' step is uneven: not only does Tainnebouy's mare limp, but also la Clotte (her very name evokes the verb *claudiquer:* to limp). If there were any need to adduce further proof of the link between the stumbling block and the scapegoat victim, we would cite la Clotte's "mythical infirmity" (p. 152), the diacritical mark of the *pharmakos:* "Old, poor, paralyzed from her waist to her feet" ("Vieille, pauvre, frappée de paralysie depuis la ceinture jusqu'aux pieds" [p. 114/125]). There is but a step between being the one who limps and the one who trips others up and that step is lapidation.

And yet, as noted above, la Clotte is a flawed scapegoat-victim in the sense that her lapidation lacks any power of reconciliation. In order to solve the riddle of the double victimage in *L'Ensorcelée,* we will have to bring into play another meaning of the word *skandalon* (whose semantic instability is not the least of scandals), a more specifically Girardian meaning: "The *skandalon* is the obstacle of mimetic rivalry, the model to the extent that he opposes his disciple's enterprises and becomes for him an endless source of morbid fascination" (p. 439).

The *skandalon* in *L'Ensorcelée* is then also and above all the relationship between Jeanne le Hardouey and Jehoël de la Croix-Jugan, and that from the outset: "Jeanne did not know what was the matter, but she succumbed to a *fascination* full of anguish" ("Jeanne ne savait pas ce qu'elle avait, mais elle succombait à une *fascination* pleine d'angoisse" [p. 71/93; emphasis added]). Read in the light of the *skandalon,* the relationship of fascination which links the bewitched woman to her bewitcher turns out to be irreducible to passionate love. The question then arises: if we allow that this relationship is of a *mimetic* rather than a conventionally *erotic* order, what then is the object designated to the disciple's desire by the model's desire, at the same time as the model frustrates that desire? Jeanne puts us on the right track when she says of l'abbé to la Clotte: "He loves vengeance" ("Il aime la vengeance" [p. 169/168]). Before the abbé's ar-

84

rival Jeanne's desire for revenge—she had been forced to marry beneath her station, a peasant, worse a Jacobin—lay smoldering. The abbé's arrival is the spark that ignites the fire. The daughter of a "phallic" mother, the so-called Louisine-à-la-hache whom Jeanne is said to resemble, Jeanne envies the violent masculinity of Jehoël, her proud patrician double. As long as Jeanne serves the "perilous schemes" ("périlleux desseins" [p. 161/162] of the leader of the Chouannerie, who entrusts her with secret missions, she is relatively comfortable with his indifference, but when the discouraged abbé gives up his partisan struggle, Jeanne, whose "virile nature" ("nature virile" [p. 153/155]) is deprived of an outlet, turns her violence against her model/obstacle.[10]

To grasp the mimeticism of the Jeanne/Jehoël relationship is to understand the very title of the novel; displacing the emphasis from the agent (the bewitcher) to the patient (the bewitched) does not signify the primacy of the bewitched, rather the indissociability of the two partners, which Girard describes as follows: "The scandal is always double and the distinction between the scandalous and the scandalized persons always tends to disappear, it is the scandalized person who spreads the scandal about" (p. 441). The fact that the abbé's double crime is considered as scandalous in the eyes of both the Church and the community is made quite explicit and on more than one occasion; now if in this novel the abbé is the scandalous person par excellence, then Jeanne is indeed the scandalized. In fact, in keeping with the principle uncovered by Girard, it is only by means of the effect produced by Jehoël on Jeanne that the scandal is made manifest: "the sinister and terrible character of the Abbé's person augmented before the very eyes of the people . . . while Jeanne's face marked the torment, the inner wasting to which she was a prey, as if the executioner became more terrible as his victim became more tortured" ("le caractère funèbre et terrible de toute la personne de l'abbé augmenta aux yeux des populations . . . à mesure que la physionomie de Jeanne marqua mieux les bouleversements et les dévorements intérieurs auxquels elle était en proie, comme si plus la victime était tourmentée, plus sinistre devenait le bourreau!" [p. 163/163]).

What we have then in *L'Ensorcelée* is a *scandal effect:* the bloody stigmata of the scandalized woman serve to reflect on the scandalizer the evil his presence installs in the heart of the community. That the dissemination of the scandal should fall to the woman in the couple, that the symptomatology of the bewitched woman should be on the order of hysteria, and, finally, that her attempt at a cure—killing the scandalizer—should result in her death, all these facts lead me to conclude that far from benefiting from the passage from witch to be-witched, the female protagonist loses in the bargain. Rather, more simply: she is reduced to her earliest textual role (at least in Western literature), since it is Eve's: she who spreads scandal. To entitle a novel *L'Ensorcelée,* is to proclaim the subversive role of femininity (and not, as one might think, the pathos of passivity).[11] The bewitched, that is the scandalized woman, is a woman every bit as fatal as the sorceress, but a fatal woman deprived of her main titles to fame, in particular a certain heroic hieraticism that is her main prerogative. Caught up on the one hand in a dialectic of scandal, on the other, in the triangulation of mediated desire, Jeanne is condemned to being nothing more than a privileged instrument of revelation.

Having begun by interrogating the nature of the relationship linking sexual aberration (bewitchment) and textual aberration (scrambled sacrificial syntax), we are now in a position to risk an answer: these two forms of deviation are the symptoms of a progressive *deconstruction* of sacrifice, which takes place in three stages: the revelation of the truth of reciprocal violence (this is the role of the shepherds as well as of Jeanne, whose corpse they appropriate),[12] the revelation of the inefficacy of unanimous violence (la Clotte's lapidation); the revelation of the innocence of the victim (the assassination of the abbé).

In other words: if, as I believe, the revelation of the innocence of the victim constitutes the novel's telos, then, everything is in order, but that order is not the same as that which governs the text of persecution, centered on the character of the *pharmakos;* what is involved is a new syntax, one that organizes the text of revelation, which is centered on the character of the *figura Christi.* According to this hypothesis, there would be no break between the three major narrative sequences listed above: thus Jeanne's death is followed by the elements of a conversion, the prayer of that other (scandalous) being, the unrepentant sinner, la Clotte: "What she would never do for herself, this woman, who had never asked quarter of God, she had done for Jeanne. She had prayed" ("Ce qu'elle n'aurait point fait pour elle, cette femme, qui n'avait jamais demandé quartier à Dieu, l'avait fait pour Jeanne. Elle avait prié" [p. 217/206]). And this private act of repentance leads up to the dénouement, the apotheosis of the abbé whose recaptured innocence is sanctioned by the Church in these highly significant terms:

86

L'Ensorcelée: *The Scandalized Woman*

In the minds of those who had the right to judge him the rumors concerning the former monk and Jeanne merited no belief. Now, when there is no real motive for scandal, the Church
is too strong and too maternal in her justice to take account of
an opinion, which, if she did listen to it, would show no more
than worldly wisdom. She pronounces with her usual majesty,
"Woe to him who finds occasion for scandal!" and resists the
fury of tongues and their confusion.

Dans l'esprit de ceux qui avaient le droit de juger, les bruits qui
avaient couru sur l'ancien moine et sur Jeanne ne méritaient aucune croyance. Or, quand il n'y a point de motif réel de scan-
dale, l'Eglise est trop forte et trop maternelle dans sa justice pour
tenir compte d'une opinion qui ne serait plus que du respect à
la manière du monde, si on l'écoutait. Elle prononce alors avec
sa majesté ordinaire: "Malheur à celui qui se scandalise!" et résiste à la furie des langues et à leur confusion. (p. 247/228–229)

As we know, the rehabilitation of the abbé by the Church does not
stem the progress of the scandal; on the contrary, by allowing the abbé
to officiate, the Church participates, as though in spite of itself, in the
arch scandal: the abbé's murder in the midst of mass. This scene brings
into play the ultimate meaning of the *skandalon,* always according to Girard: "The scandal par excellence is the founding victim finally revealed
and the part Christ plays in this revelation" (p. 451).

This scene gives new impetus to our interrogation, for it disrupts or,
to be more precise, interrupts the work of deconstruction. Because he is
assassinated at the very moment when he is about to consecrate the host,
la Croix-Jugan will be condemned to the eternal repetition of this failed
mass: "When I tell you that he recommended this impossible mass more
than twenty times, I do not lie" ("Quand je vous dirais qu'il recommença
plus de vingt fois c'te messe impossible, j'ne vous mentirais pas" [pp. 274–
275/249]). What does this ending which resists closure signify? And, what
is more, what is the significance of the fact that the only eyewitness account of this implausible mass is that of a minor character, a certain Pierre
Cloud, a blacksmith by trade, whose narrative constitutes in some sense
the crowning event (or *clou,* literally, nail) of a story that begins with the
unshoeing of a horse? To answer these two questions is to say that the
incompletion of the work of deconstruction and the incompletion of the
work of *verification* go hand in hand. Indeed, in the two final paragraphs
of the novel, the narrator raises the problem of the reliability of the

testimony he has obtained second-hand, the problem of *Nachträg-lichkeit.*

. . . I admit for an instant I had ceased to belong to the nineteenth century and I believed everything that Tainnebouy told me, as he believed it.

Later I wished to justify my faith, by following up the habits and fancies of this sad time, and I came back to spend a few months in the neighborhood of Blanchelande. I was determined to spend the night at the hole in the portal, like Pierre Cloud, the blacksmith, and to see with my own eyes what he had seen, but as the times when the nine strokes of the Abbé de la Croix-Jugan's mass rang out were irregular and far apart, although they still heard them ring at times, as the old people in the countryside told me, and my affairs took me away from the neighborhood, I never carried out my plan.

. . . je conviens que je cessai d'être un instant du xixᵉ siècle, et que je crus à tout ce que m'avait dit Tainnebouy, comme il y croyait.

Plus tard, j'ai voulu me justifier ma croyance, par une suite des habitudes et des manies de ce triste temps, et je revins vivre quelques mois dans les environs de Blanchelande. J'étais déterminé à passer une nuit aux trous du portail, comme Pierre Cloud, le forgeron, et à voir de mes yeux ce qu'il avait vu. Mais comme les époques étaient fort irrégulières et distantes auxquelles sonnaient les neufs coups de la messe de l'abbé de la Croix-Jugan, quoiqu'on les entendît retentir parfois encore, me dirent les anciens du pays, mes affaires m'ayant obligé à quitter la contrée, je ne pus jamais réaliser mon projet. (p. 276/250)

This closure (or nonclosure) is just as "theoretical" in its own way as is the liminal description of the heath, but whereas the heath takes over the plurality of possible critical paths, what seems to me to be inscribed in this closing paragraph is a questioning of the particular path I have chosen, a critique of my reading. The opposition sketched here, between the scientific mind eager for evidence and the religious mind which takes things on faith, is in the very terms of the polemic provoked by Girard's work: he is often criticized for founding his system on a postulated, nonverifiable event, about which there exists no direct testimony.[13] The course adopted by the skeptical narrator, who would like to occupy Pierre Cloud's position, anticipates that of all skeptical readers, both the reader of *L'En-*

sorcelée and the reader of this reading of that text: what we have here is a double *mise en abîme*. What then does the narrator's evasion signify? That Truth must forever remain veiled, the founding event, forever mediated? A non-negligible detail of the narrative lends weight to this interpretation: throughout the entire novel the dreadfully disfigured face of the abbé is barred, hidden by a black cowl; it is only at the moment of this apotheosis, that is death, that he throws off his mask: "The cowl had gone and the ideal head of the Abbé could be seen without any veil" ("Le capuchon avait disparu et la tête idéale de l'abbé put être vue sans aucun voile" [p. 254/233]). But no sooner has the victim's face been unveiled than the murderer's is hidden: "After the shot the man turned around, but he had a black veil over his face" ("Quand le coup fut parti, l'homme se retourna, mais il avait . . . un crêpe noir sur la figure" [p. 262/240]).

In refusing to block the holes of the portal, the narrator brings into play what we might call the logic of the nail.[14] Taking on the role of *scapegoat-narrator* he could say with Lacan:

> The truth . . . is that which runs after truth—and that is where I am running, where I am taking you, like Actaeon's hounds, after me. When I find the goddess's hiding place, I will no doubt be changed into a stag, and you can devour me, but we still have a little way to go yet.[15]

5

Eugénie Grandet:
Mirrors and Melancholia

If, at this early stage, one can discern anything like a consensus among critics of French literature working in Lacan's wake, it would be that modern texts—the classical *Bildungsroman* as well as modern autobiographies[1]—rehearse a recurrent developmental saga: the successful or failed but, in any event, necessary passage from the Imaginary into the Symbolic, from the dangerous seductions of the mirror stage into the sobering realities of the law of the father.[2] What remains unexplored are the specificities—if any—of the feminocentric examples of these genres. What, one might ask, are the literary consequences of the anatomical differences between the sexes at the point of articulation of the Imaginary and the Symbolic? And this question implies another: what is the incidence of sexual difference on each of these psychic registers?

To raise these questions is not merely to perform the "ritual" of feminist hermeneutics: the subjection of all paradigms to the test of sexual discrimination in the name of the search for a sometimes elusive feminine specificity. What is at issue in what follows—and I am anticipating a good deal—is the ongoing recuperation of Lacan's developmental schema which attempts to suppress the Imaginary and its discourse. It is perhaps not a coincidence that it should be a female Lacanian, Shoshana Felman, who would write: "It has been understood in France and elsewhere, on the basis of Lacan's theory, that the 'specular' is to be eliminated, that the term 'imaginary' is above all a *pejorative* term, subordinated to the 'positive' that is constituted here by the antithesis of the 'real' or of the 'symbolic.' But this is not the case."[3] What follows attempts to restore the

Eugénie Grandet: *Mirrors and Melancholia*

Imaginary to its rightful pride of place, viewing it not as a stage to be outgrown, but as an ineradicable constituent of the human psyche and, more important, as the essential, indeed the only matrix of fantasy and fiction. To do so does not, however, signify an uncritical endorsement of the Imaginary: for if as the maternal register the Imaginary has been negatively valorized by certain male critics, as the empire of the specular it has, as we shall see, come under attack by one feminist psychoanalyst and not the least, Luce Irigaray.

I have chosen *Eugénie Grandet* as my text at least in part because, as is becoming increasingly evident, Balzac's fiction dwells with particular insistence on precisely the junction of the Imaginary and the Symbolic. And within the Balzac canon few works body forth as nakedly as does *Eugénie Grandet* the imbrication of the maternal and paternal spheres of influence. In a great literary tradition—the French psychological novel—characterized by the conspicuous absence of either mothers (as in *Manon Lescaut* and *Madame Bovary*) or fathers (as in *La Princesse de Clèves* and *L'Education sentimentale*), *Eugénie Grandet* stands out as a novel where the oedipal configuration is writ large, as a unique nuclear family romance.

From the outset, Eugénie's relationship with her mother is described as both unusually close and closed, confined as they both are to the womblike locus of the Grandet's living room:

> In the window nearest the door stood a straw-bottomed chair, raised on blocks of wood so that Madame Grandet as she sat could look out at passers-by in the street. A work-table of bleached cherry-wood filled the other window recess, and Eugénie Grandet's little armchair was set close by. Day after day, from April to November, for the last fifteen years, time had passed peacefully for mother and daughter here, in constant work.

> Dans la croisée la plus rapprochée de la porte, se trouvait une chaise de paille dont les pieds étaient montés sur des patins, afin d'élever madame Grandet à une hauteur qui lui permît de voir les passants. Une travailleuse en bois de merisier déteint remplissait l'embrasure, et le petit fauteuil d'Eugénie Grandet était placé tout auprès. Depuis quinze ans, toutes les journées de la mère et de la fille s'étaient paisiblement écoulées à cette place, dans un travail constant, à compter du mois d'avril jusqu'au mois de novembre.[4]

Not only the living room, but the whole of "Monsieur Grandet's house" (p. 37) images a mother-daughter relationship that is quite literally monstrous: "Indeed, the lives of the famous Hungarian sisters, attached to one another by one of nature's errors, could scarcely have been more closely joined in sympathetic feeling than those of Eugénie and her mother, living as they did always together in the recess by the window, together in church, breathing the same air even while they slept" ("la vie des célèbres sœurs hongroises, attachées l'une à l'autre par une erreur de la nature, n'avait pas été plus intime que ne l'était celle d'Eugénie et de sa mère, toujours ensemble dans cette embrasure de croisée, ensemble à l'église, et dormant ensemble dans le même air" [p. 105/ 71]). This final notation—the conclusive hyperbole—draws our attention to a bizarre and telling architectural feature of the house's second story sleeping quarters: "Madame Grandet had a bedroom beside Eugénie's with a glass door between. Her husband's room was separated from hers by a partition" ("Madame Grandet avait une chambre contiguë à celle d'Eugénie, chez qui l'on entrait par une porte vitrée. La chambre du maître était séparée de celle de sa femme par une cloison" [p. 88/58]).

Balzac has here taken the mother-daughter relationship far beyond the paradigmatic bounds set forth in Madame de La Fayette's *Princesse de Clèves,* where, however strong the filial bond, the generational differences that structure society are in no danger of collapsing. In *Eugénie Grandet,* on the other hand, the necessary distance between mother and daughter has been reduced to catastrophically narrow proportions—only the most fragile of barriers, a glass pane, prevents their total fusion—catastrophic because in the end fatal to both members of the dyad: to the mother, who dies of what we might call "terminal identification," and to the daughter, who survives but never transcends her homosexual bond with her mother.[5]

What I am suggesting is that the extreme, even pathological nature of Eugénie's love for her cousin Charles bears the unmistakable stamp of its matrix: Eugénie's intense and persistent attachment to her mother. It is "this desperate paradise of the dual relationship"[6] that Charles' sudden arrival on the scene serves both to reveal and to reinforce. This observation brings us to what is surely the most characteristic manifestation of the Imaginary in everyday life, romantic love, in this instance Eugénie's narcissistic passion for her cousin. As Freud remarks in his essay, "On Narcissism: An Introduction" (1914), "over-valuation" is a distinctive "narcissistic stigma in the case of object-choice"[7] and Eugénie's overestimation verges on idolatry; at first sight she falls in love not so much with a man, as with a graven image:

> It seemed to Eugénie, who had never in her life seen such a paragon of beauty, so wonderfully dressed, that her cousin was a seraph come from heaven . . . In fact, if such a comparison can convey the emotions of an ignorant girl who spent all her time darning stockings and patching her father's clothes, who had passed her life by that window under the dirty wainscoting, looking in the silent street outside to see scarcely one passerby in an hour, the sight of this exquisite youth gave Eugénie the sensations of aesthetic delight that a young man finds in looking at the fanciful portraits of women drawn by Westall for English *Keepsakes,* and engraved by the Findens with a burin so skillful that you hesitate to breathe on the vellum for fear the celestial vision should disappear.
>
> Eugénie, à qui le type d'une perfection semblable, soit dans la mise, soit dans la personne, était entièrement inconnu, crut voir en son cousin une créature descendue de quelque région séraphique . . . Enfin, si toutefois cette image peut résumer les impressions que le jeune élégant produisit sur une ignorante fille sans cesse occupée à rapetasser des bas, à ravauder la garderobe de son père, et dont la vie s'était écoulée sous ces crasseux lambris sans voir dans la rue silencieuse plus d'un passant par heure, la vue de son cousin fit sourdre en son cœur les émotions de fine volupté que causent à un jeune homme les fantastiques figures de femmes dessinées par Westall dans les Keepsake anglais, et gravées par les Finden d'un burin si habile, qu'on a peur, en soufflant sur le velin, de faire envoler ces apparitions célestes. (p. 73/47)

The reference to Freud is, however, problematic, for, it will be recalled, in the essay on narcissism, Freud clearly distinguishes between male and female types of narcissistic object-choice, and, according to this typology—which, Freud remarks, is "of course not universal"—the telltale overestimation is a male prerogative. As for "the purest and truest" feminine type of women: "Strictly speaking, it is only themselves that such women love with an intensity comparable to that of man's love for them. Nor does their need lie in the direction of loving, but of being loved" (*S.E.* 14:89). Eugénie—who loves according to the masculine model— would then be a "case of female narcissism running counter to the psychoanalytic theory," a theory amply corroborated by Balzac in other novels. The myth of female narcissism is, indeed, alive and well in Balzac's fictional universe: one has only to think of the "woman without a heart," the courtesan Foedora in *La Peau de chagrin,* a woman who lives in a state of autarchic splendor which drives her would be lovers to distraction. What, under these circumstances, are we to make of Eugénie's "unfeminine" object-choice? We might begin by simply rejecting Freud's distinction—a step many other critics have taken before us[8]—and seek to divorce gender from narcissism. This is, of course, precisely the strategic move Lacan effectuates in his return to and departure from Freud's writings on narcissism: the mirror stage during which the narcissistic foundation of the ego is laid is presented as unisexual, before sexual difference.

Now, inasmuch as it has been said, accurately I think, that narcissism is "the keystone of the Lacanian system"[9] (and is also to my mind the key to our understanding of *Eugénie Grandet*), the question raised by a Lacanian reading of feminocentric literature is the question raised by Juliet Mitchell, with reference to preoedipal infantile development: "Is there any [gender-bound] differentiation . . . within this level of the Imaginary relationship epitomized (though not completely) by narcissism?"[10] In other words: is the difference between the sexes operative during the formative mirror stage? Does the female infant perceive her *imago* differently from the male infant, does she perceive herself as different (inferior to) the ideal (male) model? Is there a specifically female entry point into the Imaginary? Mitchell hedges her answer: "Everything Freud writes confirms that there is no important psychological differentiation in this pre-Oedipal situation. But this situation is not a stage, not an amount of time, but a level. At another level, the culturally determined implication of the sexual difference is always in waiting."[11] According to this Lacano-Derridean formulation of the question, sexual difference is inscribed from the outset, but its revelation is deferred: Mitchell seems to subscribe to the notion of something we might call sexual differ*a*nce.

Had Mitchell had the benefit of reading Luce Irigaray's feminist post-Lacanian deconstruction of Freud's two essays on femininity, as well as of Lacan's *Encore,* her answer would have been, I am quite certain, less contorted and more audacious. One cannot come away from a reading of either *Speculum* or *Ce Sexe qui n'en est pas un* still believing in the myth of a sort of prelapsarian pre-Oedipus, indeed in the innocence of the very notion of the mirror stage. Lacan's mirror, as Irigaray shows, is but the

94

most recent avatar of a philosophical topos, the plane mirror which has been, at least since Plato, in the service of a philosophical tradition dedicated to valorizing sameness, symmetry, and most important of all, visibility: the phallus as unique sexual standard. According to Irigaray, the mirror stage is not in any sense of the word, neutral; the figure in the mirror is implicitly male:

> And, *as far as the organism is concerned, what happens when the mirror reveals nothing?* No sex, for example. As is the case for the little girl. To say that "the sex (of the congener) matters little" in the constituent effects of the mirror image, and further that "the specular image seems to be the threshold of the visible world," does not that amount to stressing that the female sex will be excluded from it? And that it is a male or an asexual body that will determine the features of the *Gestalt*, that irreducible matrix of the introduction of the subject into the social order. Hence its functioning according to laws so foreign to the feminine?[12]

Far from being the ecstatic experience that it is for the male infant, the mirror stage, still according to Irigaray, deals the little girl the first of her "narcissistic wounds."[13] Under the sway of the prevailing scopic economy, the female Imaginary—for that is what I have been describing here—cannot but be marked by an alienation far more radical than that affecting the male ego, a sort of secondary alienation grafted onto the primary alienation constitutive of the ego in the Lacanian scheme. Consequently, contemplating her image in the mirror, a woman in love can but experience a devastating sense of inadequacy, a dysphoria far in excess of the loss of "self-regard" which is the corollary of the idealization of the love object.[14] When, the morning after Charles' unexpected arrival from Paris, Eugénie looks at herself in the mirror, her narcissism is definitely of the negative sort: "She rose restlessly to her feet again and again, to go to her mirror and look at her face, in just the spirit of a conscientious writer reading his work through, criticizing it and saying hard things about it to himself: 'I am not good looking enough for him!'" ("Elle se leva fréquemment, se mit devant son miroir, et s'y regarda comme un auteur de bonne foi contemple son œuvre pour se critiquer, et se dire des injures à lui-même.—Je ne suis pas assez belle pour lui" [p. 94/62]). Balzac's analogy is eloquent: first, because it attests to Eugénie's status as an artifact, an object of communication and exchange, and second, because it reveals the always implicit presence of a male observer in all scenes of female auto-contemplation. As John Berger so aptly notes in his *Ways of Seeing:* "The surveyor of woman in herself is male: the surveyed female."[15]

Balzac, however, does not content himself with revealing the hidden mainspring of female narcissism—male mediation—he also exposes the prime mediator which, under patriarchy, can only be the father, "the sole possible agent of her [the little girl's] narcissization."[16] There is then a second mirror scene, which takes place after Grandet has locked Eugénie up in her room for refusing to tell him what she has done with her gold:

> Next day Grandet went to take a few turns round his little garden, as he had formed the habit of doing ever since Eugénie had been locked up. He chose for his walk a time when Eugénie was accustomed to brush her hair, by the window. When the cooper had walked to the big walnut tree and beyond it, he used to stand there hidden by its trunk for several minutes, watching his daughter brushing out her long chestnut locks . . .
>
> He often sat for some time on the crumbling wooden seat where Charles and Eugénie had sworn that they would love each other for ever, while Eugénie in her turn stole stealthy glances at her father or watched him in her mirror.
>
> Le lendemain, suivant une habitude prise par Grandet depuis la réclusion d'Eugénie, il vint faire un certain nombre de tours dans son petit jardin. Il avait pris pour cette promenade le moment où Eugénie se peignait. Quand le bonhomme arrivait au gros noyer, il se cachait derrière le tronc de l'arbre, restait pendant quelques instants à contempler les longs cheveux de sa fille . . . Souvent il demeurait assis sur le petit banc de bois pourri où Charles et Eugénie s'étaient juré un éternel amour, pendant qu'elle regardait aussi son père à la dérobée ou dans son miroir. (p. 204/146)

What is remarkable about this scene is less its frankly erotic overtones—in this otherwise chaste novel no man shall ever desire Eugénie with the perverse intensity of her fetishistic father—than its exemplary allegorization of the interpenetration of the Imaginary and the Symbolic, for, it should be emphasized, the separation of these two registers may be a useful heuristic device or a sought after therapeutic ideal, but it is hardly an existential reality. If, on the one hand, the capture of Grandet's image in his daughter's looking glass attests to the persistent pull of the imaginary field, on the other, Eugénie's very imprisonment testifies to the overriding force of the father's law. The Imaginary is, as it were, contained or recontained within the Symbolic. Far from being the matrifocal romance we have made it out to be, *Eugénie Grandet* is one of Balzac's major patriarchal manifestoes. Neither pathetic (like Old Goriot, the "Christ of paternity"), nor a mad scientist (like Balthazar Claës in *La Recherche de l'absolu)*, nor a prisoner of sex (like Baron Hulot in *La Cousine Bette)*, to name a few unworthy Balzacian bearers of the phallic standard, Grandet—as his surname indicates—is a uniquely strong father figure. To reduce him to the reassuringly familiar figure of the Miser is to miss his salient function as a fount of law: "his most trivial acts had the weight of judicial decisions" ("Sa parole, son vêtement, ses gestes, le clignement de ses yeux faisaient loi dans le pays" [p. 42/23]). The "bourgeois tragedy" ("tragédie bourgeoise" [p. 185/131]) enacted in the very classical twenty-four hour time frame encompassing Charles' arrival in the provincial town of Saumur, Eugénie's enamoration, and Grandet's "sovereign decree" ("l'arrêt paternel et souverain" [p. 100/67]) forbidding their union is the tragedy of the Symbolic as it shapes a female destiny; *Eugénie Grandet* is Iphigenia transposed into an era when more "than in any previous era money is the force behind the law, politically and socially" ("plus qu'en aucun autre temps, l'argent domine les lois, la politique et les mœurs" [p. 126/87]), and, Mammon, it turns out, is as pitiless a deity as Artemis.

The particular crisis-day Balzac has chosen to focus on is, let us recall, Eugénie's twenty-third birthday and the morning after, an occasion whose inaugural significance is repeatedly underscored, first by constant references to Eugénie as a child, second by the reiteration of the formula "for the first time," as in "After dinner, when the question of Eugénie's marriage had been raised for the first time" ("Après ce dîner, où, pour la première fois, il fut question du mariage d'Eugénie" [p. 59/36]); "Nanon burst out laughing at this joke, the first she had ever heard her young mistress make" ("Nanon laissa échapper un gros rire en entendant la première plaisanterie que sa jeune maîtresse eût jamais faite" [p. 76/49]); "For the first time in her life she wished to look her best" ("souhaitant, pour la première fois de sa vie, de paraître à son avantage" [p. 92/61]). Eugénie's birthday is in fact a re-birthday, the occasion upon which, emerging from a prolonged childhood, she becomes aware in a cascading series of revelations, both of the workings of, and her place in, two of the homologous, interlocking exchange systems that constitute patriarchal culture: marriage and finance.[17] What Eugénie begins to understand is that even as she enjoyed the shelter of the symbiotic mother-daughter relationship, even then she lived under the sway of the Symbolic, the order in which she was inscribed before her birth: "For the first time in her life the sight of her father struck terror into Eugénie's heart. She realized that he was master of her fate" ("Pour la première fois, elle eut dans le cœur de la terreur à l'aspect de son père, vit en lui le maître de son sort" [p. 96/65]).

The question then becomes: how does Eugénie negotiate the passage from the Imaginary into the Symbolic, or rather, how does she reconcile their conflicting imperatives? The answer to these questions is deferred nine years, during which time first Eugénie's mother dies, then her father, leaving her an immensely wealthy heiress, free to marry the love to whom she has remained true, while he was off in India making his fortune. After nine long years of silence, he finally writes her, only to announce his engagement to someone else. Devastated by this cruel blow, Eugénie is ready to retire to a convent, but is dissuaded by her local pastor, who tells her: "If you wish to work out your salvation, there are only two courses open to you to follow, either you must leave the world or you must live in it and obey its laws, you must follow either your earthly destiny or your heavenly vocation" ("Si vous voulez faire votre salut, vous n'avez que deux voies à suivre, ou quitter le monde ou en suivre les lois. Obéir à votre destinée terrestre ou à votre destinée céleste" [p. 237/170]).

It is at this juncture in the novel that Eugénie ceases to be a type and reveals herself to be what she has in fact been all along: a case. In a remarkable display of neurotic ingenuity, Eugénie charts a third course, one inconceivable in the binary (masculine) logic of the pastor, but closely patterned on the princess of Clèves' controversial and often misunderstood choice. However, whereas the princess reconciles the imperiousness of desire with the imperatives of society by electing to live alternately "in the convent" and "in the world," Eugénie selects conjunction over disjunction, a poly-syndeton is the figure of her destiny, she shall be *both married and a virgin*: "Such is the story of this woman, who is in the world but not of the world" ("Telle est l'histoire de cette femme qui n'est pas du monde au milieu du monde" [p. 200/179]).[18] Eugénie shall marry her faithful suitor, M. de Bonfons, but on one condition, namely that the marriage remain unconsummated, for, as she informs him: "I must tell you frankly that I cherish memories which time will never efface. All I have to offer my husband is friendship" ("Je ne dois pas vous tromper, monsieur. J'ai dans le cœur un sentiment inextinguible. L'amitié sera le seul sentiment que je puisse accorder à mon mari" [p. 241/174]). In short, Eugénie submits to the laws of exchange but without relinquishing her most autistic fantasy; against all expectations grounded in masculine developmental models, she enters into the Symbolic, while remaining fixated in the Imaginary.

What, then, are we to make of this bizarre final solution, of this extraordinary blank upon which the novel closes? We might begin by naming it, borrowing again from Irigaray, "the 'melancholic' solution."[19] This borrowing must be qualified, however, for it raises questions regarding the divergences between what we might call Balzac's "theory of femininity" and Irigaray's and, ultimately, the nature of Eugénie's narcissism. Having shown the devastating analogy between Freud's description of the little girl's reaction to the discovery of castration (in "Femininity") and the symptomatology of melancholia (as analyzed in "Mourning and Melancholia"), Irigaray goes on to conclude:

> In fact it is not melancholia that the little girl shall choose as her privileged mode of retreat. Possibly she has too few narcissistic reserves . . . The economy of female narcissism, the fragility of the little girl's, of the woman's "ego" render almost impossible the constitution—at least in any prevailing and stable form—of this syndrome. Which is not to say that the sexuality of the "dark continent" does not exhibit many of its symptoms. But they will be dissociated rather than organized in any permanent and coherent fashion . . .[20]

Precisely because what is involved here is not the suffocating application of a clinical grid to a literary text, rather, to use Felman's suggestive term, a recognition of their mutual implication,[21] the lack of congruence between Balzac's theory and Irigaray's should not be taken to signify a flaw in Balzac's pre-Freudian intuitions. What it does signify is that in fiction the "melancholic solution" is made possible and plausible by the facts of literary history. *Eugénie Grandet* is a case study of that dread romantic disease, melancholy. But there is more: Eugénie's adoption of the melancholic solution points up a hitherto hidden aspect of her narcissism: its evolution. Negative at the outset, Eugénie's narcissism ripens in the course of the novel, so much so that in the end she has become in the most ordinary, positive, not to say Freudian sense of the term, a narcissist:

> This chorus of praise was something quite new to Eugénie, and embarrassed her at first, but little by little her ear attuned itself to hearing her beauty acclaimed, however gross the flattery might be, so that if some newcomer had considered her plain, the criticism would have touched her more nearly than it would have done eight years before. In the end she came to love this homage, which she secretly laid at her idol's feet. So, by degrees, she became accustomed to allowing herself to be treated as a queen, and to seeing her court full every evening.
>
> Ce concert d'éloges, nouveaux pour Eugénie, la fit d'abord rougir; mais insensiblement, et quelques grossiers que fussent les compliments, son oreille s'accoutuma si bien à entendre vanter sa beauté, que si quelque nouveau venu l'eût trouvée laide, ce reproche lui aurait été beaucoup plus sensible alors que huit ans auparavant. Puis elle finit par aimer des douceurs qu'elle mettait secrètement aux pieds de son idole. Elle s'habitua donc par degrés à se laisser traiter en souveraine et à voir sa cour pleine tous les soirs. (p. 223/160)

Eugénie's melancholy is then firmly rooted in her strong reserves of narcissism, reserves drawn from her seduction of/identification with her father.

Melancholy pervades the novel; from the first page to the last, there is a perfect, characteristically Balzacian adequation between the container (house) and the contained (Eugénie): "In some country towns there exist houses whose appearance weighs as heavily upon the spirits as the gloomiest cloister, the most dismal ruin, or the dreariest stretch of barren land" ("Il se trouve dans certaines villes de province des maisons dont la vue inspire une mélancolie égale à celle que provoquent les cloîtres les plus sombres, les landes les plus ternes ou les ruines les plus tristes" [p. 33/17]); "The house at Saumur, cold, sunless, always overshadowed by the ramparts and gloomy, is like her life" ("La maison de Saumur, maison sans soleil, sans chaleur, sans cesse ombragée, mélancolique, est l'image de sa vie" [p. 247/178–179]). This observation should not be taken to mean that Eugénie's character is in any sort of mechanical, naturalistic way determined by her environment; rather it is meant to stress the fact that melancholy serves as a unifying principle of the novel. Indeed, if Eugénie's melancholy is determined by any single factor, it is by her identification with her mother. Their complicity is sealed by what I would term a "stoical pact"; Madame Grandet's dying words—"there is happiness only in heaven" ("il n'y a de bonheur que dans le ciel" [p. 213/153])[22]—become Eugénie's guiding maxim, indeed constitute the maxim that ensures the verisimilitude of this self-styled implausible narrative.[23] Thus, when all hopes of happiness here on earth are dashed by Charles' cynical letter, Eugénie is destroyed but not surprised:

> She raised her eyes towards heaven, remembering the last words of her mother . . . then, thinking of her mother's death and the life which had preceded it, which seemed to foretell what her own would be, she looked at her destiny face to face, and read it at a glance. There was nothing left for her to do but to develop her wings, aspire towards heaven, and live a life of prayer until the day of her deliverance. "My mother was right," she said weeping. "One can only suffer and die."

> Elle jeta ses regards au ciel, en pensant aux dernières paroles de sa mère . . . puis, Eugénie, se souvenant de cette mort et de cette vie prophétique, mesura d'un regard toute sa destinée. Elle n'avait plus qu'à déployer ses ailes, tendre au ciel, et vivre en prières jusqu'au jour de sa délivrance.—Ma mère avait raison, dit-elle en pleurant. Souffrir et mourir. (p. 236/170)

The axis of sexual difference, for Balzac, runs parallel with the axis of algomania. On one level, the most explicit (not to say superficial), *Eugénie Grandet* is a novel whose central thesis is "doloristic," in keeping with a deep Romantic fascination with pain as a fundamental ontological experience. Through her identification with her mother, Eugénie assumes her femininity, for her mother's last words are in fact nothing but a brief quotation from the complete "text" of women's lives:

> In every situation women are bound to suffer more than men, and feel their troubles more acutely. Men have physical robustness, and exercise some control over their circumstances. They are active and busy, can think of other matters in the present, look forward to the future and find consolation in it. That was what Charles was doing. But women stay at home, alone with their grief, and there is nothing to distract them from it. They plumb the depths of the abyss of sorrow . . . and fill it with the sound of their prayers and tears. And that was Eugénie's

fate. She was taking the first steps along her destined path. In love and sorrow, feeling and self-sacrifice, will always lie the theme of women's lives, and Eugénie was to be in everything a woman, save in what should have been her consolation.

En toute situation, les femmes ont plus de causes de douleur que n'en a l'homme, et souffrent plus que lui. L'homme a sa force, et l'exercice de sa puissance: il agit, il va, il s'occupe, il embrasse l'avenir et y trouve des consolations. Ainsi faisait Charles. Mais la femme demeure, elle reste face à face avec le chagrin dont rien ne la distrait, elle descend jusqu'au fond de l'abîme qu'il a ouvert, le mesure et souvent le comble de ses vœux et de ses larmes. Ainsi faisait Eugénie. Elle s'initiait à sa destinée. Sentir, aimer, souffrir, se dévouer, sera toujours le texte de la vie des femmes. Eugénie devait être toute la femme, moins ce qui la console. (p. 182/129)

Eugénie Grandet (daughter of Felix!) is then the paradigmatic Romantic heroine (indeed, the paradigmatic Romantic hero is a heroine), and her suffering must be excessive. It is, however, the very hyperbolic nature of Eugenie's eroto-monomania that transforms the Romantic lie into a certain kind of fictional and even theoretical truth.

It is time now to return to the question of narcissism, which we have not in fact ever really departed from, for, according to Freud, melancholia is intimately bound up with narcissism, melancholia often taking the form of a regression from a narcissistic object-choice to narcissism. But, as Freud remarks: "The conclusion which our theory would require—namely, that the disposition to fall ill to melancholia (or some part of that disposition) lies in the predominance of the narcissistic type of object-choice—has unfortunately not yet been confirmed by observation" (*S.E.* 14:250). *Eugénie Grandet* offers us, I would argue, precious literary confirmation of Freud's hypothetical conclusion, for, viewed in this optic, Eugénie's undying passion for Charles appears to be motivated by a more insidious form of narcissism than the one we had diagnosed at the outset; if, as we have noted, Eugénie is initially bedazzled by Charles' ornithological perfections—he is compared to both a peacock and a phoenix—ultimately she falls in love with his extreme sorrow. Grief stricken by the news of his father's suicide, Charles appears to Eugénie as her *idealized melancholic double,*[24] her love is a love for a *fallen dandy:* "His grief was unaffected, sincere, and deeply felt, and the tense, drawn look of suffering gave him the pathetic charm women find so attractive. Eugénie found it so, and was more in love than ever. Perhaps, too, his misfortunes had brought him closer to her. Charles was not now the wealthy and handsome young man living in a sphere out of her reach that he had been when she first saw him; he was a relative in deep and terrible distress, and grief levels all distinctions" ("Il ne jouait pas la douleur, il souffrait véritablement, et le voile étendu sur ses traits par la peine lui donnait cet air intéressant qui plaît tant aux femmes. Eugénie l'en aima bien davantage. Peut-être aussi le malheur l'avait-il rapproché d'elle. Charles n'était plus ce riche et beau jeune homme placé dans une sphère inabordable pour elle; mais un parent plongé dans une effroyable misère. La misère enfante l'égalité" [pp. 135–136/94].

In a very real sense the narcissistic object Eugénie chooses to love—and it is of the essence that she does choose: "there and then she vowed to herself that she would love him always" ("elle se jura d'abord à elle-même de l'aimer toujours" [p. 158/111])—is melancholy itself: "theirs was a first passion with all its childish ways, all the more tender and dear to their hearts because their hearts were surrounded by shadows. The mourning crêpe in which their love had been wrapped at its birth only brought it into closer harmony with their surroundings in the tumble-down old country house" ("ce fut la passion première avec tous ses enfantillages, d'autant plus caressants pour leurs cœurs, qu'ils étaient enveloppés de mélancolie. En se débattant à sa naissance sous les crêpes du deuil, cet amour n'en était d'ailleurs que mieux en harmonie avec la simplicité provinciale de cette maison en ruines" [p. 169/119–201]). Small wonder, given the nature and depth of her identification with both her mother and her cousin—and in the kinship system depicted in nineteenth-century French novels, "a cousin is better than a brother, he can marry you" ("un cousin est mieux qu'un frère, il peut t'épouser" [p. 174/124])—small wonder that Eugénie responds to Charles' desertion by withdrawing from life and regressing into narcissism: she has always already been in mourning.

Indeed, the entire novel can be read as a variant of the folk theme analyzed by Freud in his essay "The Theme of the Three Caskets" (1913), a particularly interesting variant because in contradistinction to the several examples cited by Freud, which all center on *"a man's choice between three women"* (*S.E.* 12:292), *Eugénie Grandet* features a situation in which a female protagonist chooses from among three suitors (the number three is particularly insistent in this novel: there are the three women, Madame

Grandet, Nanon, and Eugénie, the three Cruchot and the three des Grassins). Furthermore, two of these suitors offer Eugénie caskets. There is first the silver workbox Adolphe des Grassins gives Eugénie on her birthday: "He kissed Eugénie on both cheeks and offered her a workbox with fittings of silver gilt. It was a trumpery enough piece of goods, in spite of the little shield bearing the initials E.G. carefully engraved in Gothic characters, a detail which made the whole thing appear more imposing and better finished than it in fact was"("[Il]l'embrassa sur les deux joues, et lui offrit une boîte à ouvrage dont tous les ustensiles étaient en vermeil, véritable marchandise de pacotille, malgré l'écusson sur lequel un E.G. gothique assez bien gravé pouvait faire croire à une façon très soignée" [p. 63/39]). Then there is the gold dressing-case Charles gives Eugénie in exchange for the gold purse she offers him: "He took up the box, drew it from its leather cover, opened it and sadly showed his wondering cousin a dressing-case shining with gold, in which the fine workmanship of the fittings greatly enhanced the value of the precious metal" ("Il alla prendre la boîte, la sortit du fourreau, l'ouvrit et montra tristement à sa cousine émerveillée un nécessaire où le travail donnait à l'or un prix bien supérieur à celui de son poids" [pp. 162–163/115]).

Now in a seemingly radical departure from the male model of this "ancient theme," Eugénie, the miser's daughter, chooses the solid gold casket. But this deviation does not in effect call into question the main thrust of Freud's analysis, for in *Eugénie Grandet* the gold casket stands for death, just as surely as the lead one does in *The Merchant of Venice:* the dressing-case is in fact a reliquary, containing the portraits of Charles' dead parents.

A potentially more disruptive disparity between the male and female versions of the theme would appear to be the absence of the third casket. While it is worth recalling here one of the basic principles of the structural analysis of myth, namely that all the constituent units or mythemes of a myth are not present or necessarily present in a particular version of the myth,[25] I think we need not invoke this principle here: a reading attentive to detail will show that the missing element is not missing, simply concealed and displaced. The third casket is manifested in the novel, but it does not participate in the system of exchange; it is as it were out of circulation. It takes the form of an awkward and enigmatic analogy which protrudes from the surface of the text in the course of the description of the Grandet's garden: "At the far end of the courtyard the eight dilapidated steps leading to the garden gate were half-buried under high-growing plants, and looked like the tombstone of some medieval knight, put there by his widow at the time of the Crusades, and neglected ever since" ("Enfin les huits marches qui régnaient au fond de la cour et menaient à la porte du jardin, étaient disjointes et ensevelies sous de hautes plantes comme le tombeau d'un chevalier enterré par sa veuve au temps des croisades" [p. 92/61–62]). Atropos the inexorable is, then, present in the novel, in the appropriate textual form of a figure of speech that cannot be turned away from. On one level we might "recuperate" this extended simile, this hypertrophied detail by reading it as a commentary on, or *mise en abîme* of, the main plot: when Charles goes off to the Far East like some sort of latter-day Crusader, Eugénie erects an empty crypt, a cenotaph in his memory, conflating mourning and melancholia. "The object has not perhaps actually died, but has become lost as an object of love (e.g., the deserted bride)" (*S.E.* 14:245). But this reading, while perfectly plausible, fails to take into account the most arresting feature of this mininarrative, its form, its very incongruity. To right this misappropriation would entail reading this detail not as a symbol, but rather as an allegory of the workings of the Symbolic order, which, according to Lacan, is always under the aegis of a dead man, the primal father of Freud's *Totem and Taboo*. This is surely not the place to attempt to read "The Theme of the Three Caskets" in conjunction with *Totem and Taboo* (both texts appeared in 1913), but based on what we have seen so far, it would appear that Eugénie's love of death is the wages of the subject's entry into the Symbolic.

The question then becomes: why does the daughter pay a higher price? Or rather: why does the son successfully perform the work of mourning, while the daughter remains mired in melancholia? These are the questions raised by the deliberately parallel but antithetical destinies of Eugénie and Charles Grandet. Indeed, as Charles' cynical letter to Eugénie makes clear, Eugénie's male counterpart has no trouble making a smooth and easy transition from one psychic register into the other: "The death of our parents is in the natural order of things, and we must follow them in our turn. I hope that you are consoled by this time. Time cures every pain, as I have found by experience. Yes, my dear cousin, I'm sorry to say boyhood's illusions are over for me . . . I am a man now, where I was a child when I went away" ("La mort de nos parents est dans la nature, et nous devons leur succéder. J'espère que vous êtes aujourd'hui consolée. Rien ne résiste au temps, je l'éprouve. Oui, ma chère cousine, malheureusement pour moi, le moment des illusions est passé . . . D'enfant que j'étais au départ, je suis devenu homme au retour" [p. 233/167]). I would suggest that a tentative answer to these questions might be teased out of Freud's essay on narcissism. However questionable not to say mystified Freud's remarks on female narcissism, there is one observation in that famous or infamous passage that bears rereading. Speculating on why it should be that "the purest and truest" type of female should upon reaching adolescence enter into an autarchic state of self-love, Freud writes: "Women, especially if they grow up with good looks, develop a certain self-contentment which compensates them for the social restrictions that are imposed upon them in their choice of object" (*S.E.* 14:88–89). Seen in this light, it would appear that the female protagonist's melancholic retreat into narcissism may in fact be the only form of autonomy available to her in a society where woman's assigned function in the Symbolic is to guarantee the transmission of the phallus. Eugénie's sentimental education—she receives no other—culminates, like that of the princess of Clèves' before her, in what I would call a lucid romanticism, a refusal to decide in the terms offered by the culture.[26]

Like Eugénie I find myself poised between two equally compelling contradictory impulses—the revalorization of a psychic register often connoted as feminine and associated with a-social behavior, and the denunciation of a social order which both condemns women to deviancy and defines its terms. I refuse to opt for one of two readings, Eugénie as heroine of the Imaginary, Eugénie as victim of the Symbolic. My double reading inhabits the paradoxical space allotted woman under patriarchy, a space neither inside nor outside, where what appears as lack in one order shows up as excess in another. Eugénie's half-hearted entry into the Symbolic (the unconsummated marriage) may thus be viewed as subversive at the same time as her retreat into the Imaginary (the undying love for Charles) appears as a measure of woman's limited options under patriarchy. This much can be affirmed, however. When one compares Eugénie's destiny not to Charles', but to that of Lucien de Rubempré, the protagonist of *Illusions perdues* and *Splendeurs et misères des courtisanes* and Eugénie's true melancholic double, the benefits to be derived from fetishistic undecidability are made manifest: for, whereas Lucien cannot survive the loss of his illusions, Eugénie can and does. Now the advantages of death-in-life over suicide may not be overwhelming in everyday life, but in fiction, survival is everything, particularly for a female protagonist. To the extent that, as Leo Bersani has written, "The realistic novel is the 'mirror stage' of literature,"[27] any nineteenth-century novel that imagines for its protagonist a life beyond adolescence represents something of a generic triumph. However bittersweet, Eugénie's survival into the present of the narrator's enunciation—"Such is the story of this woman, who *is* in the world, but not of the world" (p. 248; emphasis added)—suggests that as long as the Imaginary persists unbound below the baseline of the Symbolic, the classical text and with it the (female) protagonist's options will remain open.

II
BREAKING THE CHAIN

6

Salammbô Bound

La Décoration! tout est dans ce mot: et je conseillerais à une dame, hésitant à qui confier les dessins d'un Bijou désiré, de le demander, ce dessin, à l'Architecte qui lui construit un hôtel, plutôt qu'à la faiseuse illustre qui lui apporte sa robe de gala. Tel, en un mot, l'art du bijou.
Stéphane Mallarmé, *Proses diverses*

We are not done turning to account the group of texts that constitute the dossier of the so-called *Salammbô* controversy, an appendix that has come in the course of time to be an integral part of the text of the novel, just as the record of the *Madame Bovary* trial proceedings is henceforth included in any complete edition of that novel. Indeed, though many other controversies have occupied the forefront of the French literary scene since 1862, the questions raised by the critics of *Salammbô* remain current. It is then via this "after-text" that I would like to approach this novel which is in its own way as impregnable as the city of Carthage which it represents. This roundabout approach serves to pose from the outset one of the major problems raised by *Salammbô:* that of access. For, according to its critics—and by Flaubert's own admission—one of the novel's major structural flaws is its faulty perspective, faulty in the double meaning of the word: both lacking and distorted. I quote Sainte-Beuve, but I could substitute either Froehner or Dusolier, because they too score the same peculiarity:

> In many, many places one recognizes the work of the consummate craftsman; each part of the structure is executed with care,

rather too much than too little: I see doors, walls, locks, vaults, well wrought, well built, each separately; nowhere do I see the architect. The author does not stand above his work: he is too close to it, he has got his nose pressed against it. He seems not to have considered it before and after as a whole, nor at any moment to dominate it. At no time did he step far back enough from his work to put himself in the reader's place.[1]

Now, when in response to Sainte-Beuve, Flaubert does step back, does put himself in the reader's place, he in some sense concedes the merits of the criticism by acknowledging the incongruity of his work: "The pedestal is too large for the statue. Now as 'too much' is never a transgression, but 'not enough' is, one hundred pages more would have been needed, relating to Salammbô alone."[2]

Let us stop for a moment to consider Flaubert's self-criticism for, whether or not it is "sincere,"[3] it is noteworthy because of the presuppositions it ratifies, presuppositions that underlie not only the *Salammbô* controversy, but the battle of realism itself. At first Flaubert sanctions the principle of aesthetic economy which grounds a significant number of objections addressed to realist writers: namely that that which one gives to description, one takes away from character, or, on another level, that which one gives to the detail, one takes away from the whole. Thus Froehner exclaims: "If only M. Flaubert had neglected the detail to save the whole!" (CHH, p. 384). But, in a second step, Flaubert formulates a maxim which clearly sets him off from his critics, namely: there is no such thing as the guilt of excess. Or as he writes about the first *Education:* "it is always because of an *absence* that a book is weak."[4] In short, to make up for the novel's flaw, for what Jacques Neefs calls its "constitutive inadequacy,"[5] one should enlarge the statue and not shrink the pedestal. Flaubert's conclusion—"one hundred pages more would have been needed, relating to Salammbô alone"—is at the very least paradoxical, if one recalls that in creating the character of Salammbô, Flaubert was bound by no constraint of an archeological order: "My business will (I think) be entitled 'Salammbô, Carthaginian novel.' That's the name of Hamilcar's daughter invented by yours truly."[6] Why then have brought into being a character who is both supernumerary on the historical plane and inadequate on the diegetic? And, to go straight to the point, is there any relationship between the paradoxical role devolved upon Salammbô and her femininity?

Salammbô *Bound*

These questions lead us to note a constant feature of the criticism devoted to *Salammbô:* the deafening silence when it is not the final judgment that hangs over the character of Salammbô. As usual it is Sainte-Beuve who sets the tone when he writes: "That Salammbô whose person and passion were supposed to motivate the book and the action, is piquante, bizarre, artfully composed and contrived, I readily agree, but she does not animate anything and finally is not interesting."[7] Given the principle of aesthetic economy articulated above, the corollary of this execution of Salammbô is the promotion of Carthage, because Carthage is opposed to Salammbô as the pedestal is to the statue, the collective to the individual, the political to the sexual, the masculine to the feminine, to cite the principal paradigms that traverse the critical discourse on *Salammbô*. Indeed, if the part of the *Correspondance* regarding the genesis of the novel attests to the interchangeability of the woman and the city in Flaubert's mind—he always refers to his work in progress as Carthage—this equivalence masks an opposition that is soon revealed as a hierarchy. Thus Maurice Bardèche, the author of the preface that precedes the text of the novel in the magnificent Club de l'Honnête Homme edition, resolves the aporia of the Salammbô/Carthage relationship by simply evacuating Salammbô:

> Is it her destiny which is being played out or Carthage's? We come slowly, painfully to take an interest in Carthage; we do not at any moment succeed in becoming interested in Salammbô . . . In sum, there is an abyss the author does not succeed in having us bridge between the romantic and extravagant love poem upon which he has erected his plot and the historical events which interest him and which he has undertaken to recount. Let us conclude that the fragile priestess painted like a doll was but a pretext, that Flaubert did not dare dispense with her, that he was perhaps mistaken, but that finally since this point was not essential in his eyes, it is absurd to use it to prosecute him. (CHH, p. 18)

Whether one proposes to bracket the character of Salammbô, or emphasizes the homology of the love and war stories, or even goes so far as to privilege the sexual, the opposition of Salammbô and Carthage remains one of the fundamental assumptions of the critics. Now it seems to me that this assumption must be interrogated, because, as the manuscripts and the final version of *Salammbô* make readily apparent, it is not always so easy in this novel to separate the woman from the city, that is, the accessory from the essential, to borrow Flaubert's revealing vocabulary as it is taken up and elaborated upon by Bardèche. Indeed, basing himself on one of Flaubert's notations in an early draft—"The historical events are nothing but an *accessory* of the novel" (CHH, p. 36; emphasis added)— the author of the preface notes that in the course of the successive revisions of the scenarios, the relationship between the accessory and the essential is reversed: "In the final scenario it is definitely the Mercenaries who triumph. The subject is their dramatic rebellion against Carthage, it is no longer the love of Mâtho for Salammbô. That which was initially the accessory to the novel has become the entire novel" (CHH, p. 37).

Having observed that the elaboration of the final scenario goes hand in hand with the generalization of the accessory, how can one not end up questioning the opposition of the accessory and the essential, indeed the very category of the accessory? It will perhaps be obvious to certain readers that I am here following the line of inquiry opened up by Derrida, particularly in *La Vérité en peinture,* where, in the course of a discussion of the *parergon,* that is, the ornament in Kant's aesthetic, Derrida insists on the extreme difficulty of tracing a clear boundary between the clothes and the statue, the clothes that cover a statue serving as the privileged example of the *parergon:*

> This demarcation of the center and of the integrity of the representation, of its inside and its outside, may already appear strange. One wonders besides where should the clothes be made to begin. Where does a *parergon* begin, where does it end. Are all clothes *parerga?*[8]

This is precisely the question raised by the descriptions of Salammbô, for finally Salammbô is a clothed statue and it becomes literally impossible to say where the female body ends and the clothing begins, it is as though her finery were stuck to her skin:

> Mâtho did not hear; he was staring at her, and her garments, that were for him blended with her body: the sheen of the fabrics was like the splendour of her skin, something special, peculiar to her alone: her eyes and diamonds sparkled; the polish of her finger-nails were a continuation of the lustre of jewels that bedecked her fingers. (p. 231)

> Mâtho n'entendait pas; il la contemplait, et les vêtements, pour lui, se confondaient avec le corps. La moire des étoffes était, comme la splendeur de sa peau, quelque chose de spécial et n'appartenait qu'à elle. Ses yeux, ses diamants étincelaient; le poli de ses ongles continuait la finesse des pierres qui chargeaient ses doigts.[9]

If, as I believe, in *Salammbô* synecdoche takes precedence over metonymy, entailing the invasion of the body of the novel by details that evoke the leprosy that slowly eats away at the Suffet Hanno's skin, it follows that the question of the relationship of woman and city is to be posed in terms other than those of mutual exclusion. What is more: if, as I have just shown, it is vain to attempt to separate the ornament from the ornamented, it is because what we have here is what I would call an *ornamental text*. What does this signify? I am, of course, hardly the first critic to draw attention to what Victor Brombert calls the "Parnassian aesthetic"[10] which presides over the writing of *Salammbô*. If I have proposed another expression to account for the ornate quality of the novel, it is precisely to draw attention away from *Salammbô*'s place in literary history and to attempt to think through what is covered over by the gangue of historical labels. And what is true of literary history is also true of the study of genres: to say that *Salammbô* is an ornamental text is not tantamount to proposing a generic reclassification of this reputedly unclassifiable work. Thus Bardèche speaks of the ornamental quality of *Salammbô* only to bring this limit-text under the sway of the epic. That would be fine with me were it not for the fact that, as the following quotation makes clear, this taxonomic rectification leaves intact the accessory/essential opposition under interrogation:

> The ornaments are also those of the epic. The "beauties" of *Salammbô* are battles, moonlit cemeteries, passes, orgies, extraordinary or horrifying actions . . . One feels very strongly that for him these are "major productions," whose proportions and savage grandeur are meant to ensure his book the deathless dignity of the masterpiece, and which do in fact do so. These huge mosaics are purely ornamental. *Salammbô* is like a palace one visits to contemplate them. (CHH, p. 22)

To say that a text is ornamental necessarily implies a revalorization of the ornamental, an unthinkable operation as long as a modernist aesthetic totally dedicated to a bleached writing hostile to all decorative elements held sway. *Salammbô,* a "purple" text according to Flaubert's celebrated word,[11] might well be the precursor text of postmodernism and as such requires the elaboration of a hermeneutic specially adapted to its texture. For, as E. H. Gombrich points out in his great book on decorative art, the ornamental calls into play an entirely different mode of perception or reception than either painting or speech: "Painting, like speaking, implicitly demands attention whether or not it receives it. Decoration cannot make this demand. It normally depends for its effect on the fluctuating attention we can spare while we scan our surroundings."[12] And he goes on to say: "Those critics who feel overwhelmed by the assault on their senses made by the profusion of ornament and have therefore condemned it as tasteless and barbaric may have misunderstood what was expected of them" (p. 116). Indeed, according to Gombrich, the spectator, who like the visitor to the Alhambra is confronted with a bewildering profusion of ornaments, is not expected to look at everything, to pay equal attention to all the details. On the contrary, he is free to choose his sightline, to let his gaze wander, to scan the whole until a detail catches his passing glance. And, just as the analyst's "evenly poised attention" fastens onto certain details of the analysand's discourse—details which insist or stand out—the fluctuating attention of the spectator of decorative art is attracted—and we can recognize here the Gestaltist assumptions that link Gombrich's work to that of the theoreticians of *Rezeptionsaesthetik*[13]—by any gap, any break in the decorative order: "The disturbance of regularity such as a flaw in a smooth fabric can act like a magnet to the eye" (p. 110). And Gombrich goes on to give an example of just such an eye-catching irregularity, a necklace with a missing bead: "In the case of the necklace it is the missing bead, the gap between the equal units, which obtrudes on our attention" (p. 111). Now there is in *Salammbô* just such a gap, not a broken necklace, but a broken chain, and it is on this detail that my evenly poised attention, my wandering viewpoint came to settle. This detail is, to borrow Barthes' term, the *punctum* of the novel, that which in the text "pricks me," but also, Barthes adds in a meaningful parenthesis, "bruises me, is poignant to me."[14] I am referring to the gold chainlet which Salammbô wears between her ankles "to regulate her steps" ("pour régler sa marche" [p. 14/36]). We shall learn subsequently (in the chapter entitled "In the Tent," about which more later), that this chainlet, which hobbles Salammbô's walk, serves as an index both of her rank and her virginity:

Finally he slept; then, disengaging herself from his arms, she placed one foot on the ground, and she saw that her chainlet was broken.

In great families the virgins were accustomed to respect these little shackles with almost the same reverence as if they were religious symbols. Salammbô, blushing, rolled around her ankles the two ends of her dishonoured gold chainlet.

Il s'endormit. Alors, en se dégageant de son bras, elle posa un pied par terre, et elle s'aperçut que sa chaînette était brisée.

On accoutumait les vierges dans les grandes familles à respecter ces entraves comme une chose presque religieuse, et Salammbô, en rougissant, roula autour de ses jambes les deux tronçons de la chaîne d'or. (p. 238/212)

It is then a *Kosmos* (order, ornament), that is, an ornament which is very precisely not *purely* ornamental. Indeed, as the Hindu art historian Ananda Coomaraswamy reminds us, the very notion of the "purely ornamental" is but a modern degradation of the original function of ornament which is always and everywhere of a magical and metaphysical order. Thus in his article on ornament he proposes to demonstrate that "most of these words which imply for us the notion of something adventitious and luxurious, added to utilities but not essential to their efficacy, originally implied a completion or fulfillment of the artifact or other object in question; [that] to 'decorate' an object or person originally meant to endow the object or person with its or his 'necessary accidents,' with a view to 'proper' operation." [15]

It is no accident if in his reading of the novel Sainte-Beuve speaks of this chainlet with supreme contempt; thus, à propos of Salammbô's first appearance in the midst of the mercenaries' feast, he writes: "She thus descends amongst the Barbarians, walking in measured steps and even a little impeded by *heaven knows what gold chainlet* she drags about between her feet" (CHH, p. 417; emphasis added). This contempt is no surprise coming from a critic who, as we have seen, flaunts his lack of interest in the character of Salammbô. The case of the author of the preface we have cited so often is more complex: while admitting his lack of interest in Salammbô, he demonstrates his interest in the chainlet. Alluding to the scene where Hamilcar, seeing his daughter return with the Zaïmph, observes that the chainlet is broken, Bardèche writes: "there remains only for us to consider with some degree of perplexity, like Hamilcar, the broken chainlet between Salammbô's ankles, to which we are free to attribute whatever meaning we please" (CHH, p. 25). The gap in the chainlet opens up the text to the plural of interpretations; it is the breach through which the interpreter enters the text, as though breaking and entering. What a shame then that the very same critic who was the first to intuit the significance of the broken chainlet should feel obliged some pages later to fill the gap and bring to a halt the free play of interpretation: "The broken chainlet attached to Salammbô's ankles is, of course, as clear a symbol for Flaubert as the pieces of paper which are thrown from the lowered windows of the fiacre in *Madame Bovary*. These 'signs' were well understood by the reading public . . . They seem a bit pale and singularly timid to today's readers [lecteurs]" (CHH, p. 37). On the contrary it seems to me—but it is true that I am a female reader and a goldsmith's daughter to boot!—that this chainlet throws into sharp relief the central enigma of this narrative aptly described as "enigmatic" by Jean Rousset, namely: what happened under the tent?[16] What matters, of course, is not to discover what *really* happened under the tent, but rather to give full play to the uncertainty that marks the central event of the story. What needs to be emphasized is that the novel is organized—and this from the earliest drafts on—around a scene of interrupted defloration, a *hymen,* in the double sense that Derrida gives to this word:

> The hymen, the consummation of differends, the continuity and confusion of the coitus, merges with what it seems to be derived from: the hymen as protective screen, the jewel box of virginity, the vaginal partition, the fine, invisible veil which, in front of the hystera, stands *between* the inside and the outside of a woman, and consequently between desire and fulfillment. It is neither desire nor pleasure but between the two.[17]

What does this mean? What would a text subject to the "law" or the "logic" of the hymen be like? It would be—I am quoting Derrida—a *perverse* text: "Nothing is more vicious than this suspense, this distance played at; nothing is more perverse than this rending penetration that leaves a virgin womb intact."[18] In the end this perversion comes to mime, when it is not become one with the perversion par excellence which is fetishism, both for Freud and Lacan. Indeed, if one reads Freud's essay on "Fetishism" in the light of what Derrida has to say about it either in "The Double Session" or *Glas,* one begins to understand that the celebrated split of the fetishist, he who says of castration in the words of Octave

Mannoni, "I know, but all the same" ("Je sais bien, mais quand même"), is something like the paradigm of undecidability. For the fetishist, let us recall, woman is castrated and not castrated at the same time, a situation Freud describes as follows: "It is not true that, after the child has made his observation of the woman, he has preserved unaltered his belief that women have a phallus. He has retained that belief but has also given it up."[19]

The scene under the tent is to be read as a sort of primal scene of fetishism, for it shows the original and intimate relationship that links the fetish and the shiny, the undecidable and the ornamental. Let us recall that in Freud's essay, he speaks of a young man, "who had exalted a certain 'shine on the nose' into a fetishistic precondition: the surprising explanation of this was that the patient had been brought up in an English nursery but had later come to Germany, where he forgot his mother-tongue, almost completely. The fetish, which originated from his earliest childhood, had to be understood in English, not German. The 'shine on the nose' [in German '*Glanz auf der Nase*']—was in reality a '*glance* at the nose.' "[20] However seductive, Freud's explanation presents the disadvantage, as Guy Rosolato has shown, of causing the German to disappear in favor of the English, thereby obscuring the link between that which is fetishized and that which shines, a link which, again according to Rosolato, is grounded in the *Glanz* whose signifier insists in the young man's lexicon:

> We must therefore take up again the indication given earlier, along with the hidden word, to find in the *glans* itself, in the organ, the initial tegumentary brilliance, but precisely attained at the summit of erection, outside of any envelope, appearing. Let us stop at this point to emphasize how essential it is for the fetishist to find this glistening, witness to his desire.[21]

In the scene under the tent, when Mâtho contemplates Salammbô, he is fascinated—and let us note in passing that in Latin *fascinum* means male organ—by a certain gleam: "She wore for ear-rings two tiny balances of sapphires, supporting a hollow pearl filled with liquid perfume, which percolated through minute perforations, moistening her bare shoulders. Mâtho watched it slowly trickle down" ("Elle avait pour pendants d'oreilles deux petites balances de saphir supportant une perle creuse, pleine d'un parfum liquide. Par les trous de la perle, de moment en moment, une goutelette qui tombait mouillait son épaule nue. Mâtho la regardait tomber" [pp. 231–232/207]).[22]

Flaubert's fetishism is hardly news. What remains to be studied are its manifestations in their specificity, for it is in the nature of the fetish to be, like the purloined letter, both perfectly visible and totally ignored: "The meaning of the fetish is not known to other people, so the fetish is not withheld from him: it is easily accessible" (p. 154). If, then, we interrogate the specificity of the chainlet, it appears that its brilliance tends to mask its function, which is to bind Salammbô's ankles. Upon closer inspection it appears that the chainlet belongs to a very particular form of fetish mentioned by Freud at the end of his essay: the bound feet of Chinese women. "Another variant, which is also a parallel to fetishism in social psychology, might be seen in the Chinese custom of mutilating the female foot and then revering it like a fetish" (p. 157). This is perhaps the place to note that when Flaubert compares Salammbô to a statue mounted on a pedestal he should be taken quite literally. From the bound ankles of Salammbô to the bound feet of Chinese women, there is not far to go, and that would account at least in part for the veneration she elicits. When Froehner described *Salammbô* as a *"carthachinoiserie"* he was closer to the mark than he could know!

It is then surely not by chance that of all the details in *Salammbô*, it is the detail of the chainlet which caught and held my attention: what is at stake here is the fate of the female protagonist under fetishism, a regime which bears certain resemblances to the feudal regime described by Julia Kristeva in *Des Chinoises:*

> Freud saw in the custom of foot-binding the symbol of the castration of woman which Chinese civilization was unique in admitting. If by "castration" we understand the necessity for something to be excluded so that the socio-symbolic order may be built—the cutting off of one part of the whole as such may be constituted as an alliance of homogeneous parts—it is interesting to note that for Chinese feudal civilization this "superfluous" quality was found in women. Is it simply a matter of knowing that woman does not have a penis? But then the insistence of underlining what's "missing" in woman by additional symbols (crippling the foot) would tend to prove that they're not all that certain; that some doubt still persists.[23]

Salammbô *Bound*

Kristeva's text is doubly valuable to us because it stresses both the political stakes of castration and the doubt betrayed by the supplement of the fetish. Indeed, Salammbô's destiny bears eloquent witness to the threat the doubt embodied by the daughter constitutes for the socio-symbolic order incarnated by the father. For Hamilcar—as for the critic—doubt is properly speaking unbearable. Upon returning to Carthage, Hamilcar learns of the rumors regarding Mâtho's night visit to Salammbô. As a result, the reunion of father and daughter takes place under the sign of doubt, doubt that Hamilcar is not about to resolve, since he has sworn before the Council of the Hundred that he will not speak of the incident to Salammbô: "Hamilcar struggled against his inclination to break his oath. However, he kept it from pride, or *through dread of putting an end to his uncertainty*, and scanned her full in the face, trying with all his might to discover what she hid at the bottom of her heart" ("Hamilcar combattait l'envie de rompre son serment. Il le tenait par orgueil, ou *par crainte d'en finir avec son incertitude:* et il la regardait en face, de toutes ses forces, pour saisir ce qu'elle cachait au fond de son cœur" [p. 184/142; emphasis added]). Further along in the novel, just like the critic who hastens to bring the enigmatic sign back to the fold of interpretation, Hamilcar rushes to bring his errant daughter back under his sway; in the blink of an eye he will go from the recognition that the chainlet is broken to the engagement of his daughter with Narr'Havas: "His eyes alternately scanned her and the Zaïmph; and he noticed that her chainlet was broken. Then he quivered, seized by a *terrible suspicion*. But quickly resuming his impassibility, he looked at Narr'Havas askance without turning his face" ("Ses yeux se portaient alternativement sur le zaïmph et sur elle, et il remarqua que sa chaînette était rompue. Alors il frissonna, saisi par un *soupçon terrible*. Mais reprenant vite son impassibilité, il considéra Narr'Havas obliquement, sans tourner la figure" [p. 246/217, emphasis added]).

By going to Mâtho, by submitting to his caresses, by allowing the chainlet to be broken, Salammbô breaks the social contract which subordinates her to the law of the father for, as Tony Tanner has convincingly argued in *Adultery and the Novel,* for women and especially for daughters, the relationship to the city in the sense of the *polis* is entirely mediated by the father (or paternal surrogates, such as the priest Schahabarim). To speak of woman and the city, of woman in the ancient city, is always in one way or another to speak of the father-daughter relation-

121

ship. This would explain the highly significant language of the first person Salammbô meets after leaving Mâtho, old Giscon:

> —"Ah! I was there!" cried he. "I heard you panting with lust like a prostitute, and when he told you of his passion, you permitted him to kiss your hands! But if the madness of your unchastity impelled you, at least you should have done as the wild beasts, which hide themselves to couple, and not thus have displayed your shame almost before the very eyes of your father!"
>
> —"Ah! j'étais là!" s'écria-t-il. "Je t'ai entendue râler d'amour comme une prostituée; puis il te racontait son désir, et tu te laissais baiser les mains! Mais, si la fureur de ton impudicité te poussait, tu devais faire au moins comme les bêtes fauves qui se cachent dans leurs accouplements, et ne pas étaler ta honte jusque sous les yeux de ton père!" (p. 241/214)

Nonetheless, during the brief interval that separates the scenes under Mâtho's and Hamilcar's tents, Salammbô enjoys a rare freedom, a freedom which takes the form of a mobility in sharp contrast with her customary hieratic attitude:

> She *threw* the Zaïmph around her waist, gathered up her veils, mantle, and scarf—"*I go there*" she ejaculated, and disappeared.
>
> Elle *jeta* le zaïmph autour de sa taille, ramassa *vivement* ses voiles, son manteau, son écharpe. —"*J'y cours*" s'écria-t-elle; et, s'échappant, Salammbô disparut. (p. 242/214)
>
> . . . taking the hem of her robe between her teeth, in three *bounds* she attained the platform.
>
> Elle prit avec ses dents le bas de sa robe qui la gênait, et, en trois *bonds,* elle se trouva sur la plate-forme. (p. 242/215)
>
> She *quickly* dismounted.
>
> Elle *sauta* vite à bas de son cheval. (p. 245/217)

Considering the unbinding of energy produced by the rupture of the chainlet and the social contract it figures—because originally the decorative and decorum are inseparable—it is hardly surprising to note that Salammbô's reinscription in the circuit of symbolic exchange goes hand in hand with the putting back into place of her yoke, results finally in her rebinding: "their thumbs were tied together with a thong of leather" ("On attacha leurs pouces l'un contre l'autre avec une lanière de bœuf" [p. 246/218]).

As Hamilcar discovers, however, it is not so easy to check the doubt and disorder spread by his daughter. Even after the engagement, Hamilcar keeps questioning Salammbô about what really happened under the tent, but he keeps coming up against her enigmatic silence:

> But the Suffet always reverted to Mâtho, under the pretext of acquiring military information. He could not understand how she had employed the hours passed in his tent. Salammbô did not mention Gisco . . . She said that the *Schalischim* appeared furious, that he had shouted a great deal, and afterwards went to sleep. Salammbô told nothing more, perhaps from shame, or possibly from an excess of innocence, which caused her to attach no importance to the kisses of the soldier.
>
> . . . le Suffète revenait toujours à Mâtho, sous prétexte de renseignements militaires. Il ne comprenait rien à l'emploi des heures qu'elle avait passées dans la tente. En effet, Salammbô ne parlait pas de Giscon . . . Elle disait que le schalischim paraissait furieux, qu'il avait crié beaucoup, puis qu'il s'était endormi. Salammbô n'en racontait pas davantage, par honte peut-être, ou bien par un excès de candeur faisant qu'elle n'attachait guère d'importance aux baisers du soldat. (pp. 282–283/247)

It is only in the final chapter that the work of rebinding is completed and doubt held in check, if not conjured. It is as though the chainlet had multiplied, ensheathing Salammbô's entire body; the female protagonist has become ornamental from head to toe, *"a perfect phallus for perverse desire,"* to quote Jean Baudrillard:[24]

> From her ankles to her hips she was enveloped in a network of tiny links, in imitation of the scales of a fish, and lustrous as polished mother-of-pearl . . . Her headdress was made of peacocks' plumage, starred with jewels; a wide, ample mantle, white as snow, fell behind her—her elbows were close against her body; her knees pressed together; circlets of diamonds were clasped on her arms; she sat perfectly upright in a hieratic attitude.
>
> Des chevilles aux hanches, elle était prise dans un réseau de mailles étroites imitant les écailles d'un poisson et qui luisaient comme de la nacre . . . Elle avait une coiffe faite avec des plumes

de paon étoilées de pierreries; un large manteau, blanc comme de la neige, retombait derrière elle,—et les coudes au corps, les genoux serrés, avec des cercles de diamants au haut des bras, elle restait toute droite, dans une attitude hiératique. (pp. 362–363/ 306)

But this is not Salammbô's final incarnation. Shortly after this apotheosis of woman as statue, of bound woman, Salammbô crumbles as though struck by lightning. This unriveting takes place immediately after the mutilation of Mâtho's corpse by the priest Schahabarim:

> Salammbô arose, like her consort, grasping a cup in her hand, to drink also. She fell, with her head lying over the back of the throne, pallid, stiff, her lips parted—and her loosened hair hung to the ground.
>
> Salammbô se leva comme son époux, avec une coupe à la main, afin de boire aussi. Elle retomba, la tête en arrière, par-dessus le dossier du trône,—blême, raidie, les lèvres ouvertes,—et ses cheveux dénoués pendaient jusqu'à terre. (p. 369/311)

Of all the deaths in Flaubert's fiction, Salammbô's is by far the most spectacular, the most theatrical, and the one which has received the least attention from the critics. Yet the sentence that marks the closure of *Salammbô*—"Thus died Hamilcar's daughter, for having touched the Veil of Tanit" ("Ainsi mourut la fille d'Hamilcar pour avoir touché au manteau de Tanit" [ibid.])—clearly indicates the significance Flaubert attributes to the *manner* in which Salammbô dies. In their haste to discover what lies hidden *behind* Tanit's cloak, the critics have not given full play to the word "thus" ("ainsi"). In the light of the preceding analysis, it seems to me that the privileged detail in the description of this unnatural, or better yet, unnaturalized death, is the undoing of the hair. We know that the hair is a corporeal attribute highly prized by the fetishist. In addition, Coomaraswamy notes: "the putting of one's hair in order is primarily a matter of decorum."[25]

If, as I believe, we must attribute the same symbolic or rather semiotic value to the undoing of the hair as to the breaking of the chainlet, what then does the dénouement—in its double meaning of closure and unknotting—of *Salammbô* mean? In order to answer this question, we must return to the final sentence and more particularly to the syntagm which follows "thus died" ("ainsi mourut"), that is the periphrasis, "Hamilcar's daughter"("la fille d'Hamilcar"). For if we fold the last sentence over the first—"It was in Hamilcar's gardens, at Megara, on the outskirts of Carthage" ("C'était à Mégara, faubourg de Carthage, dans les jardins d'Hamilcar" [p. 28/1])—we discover that in both cases, whether it be a question of the gardens or the daughter of Hamilcar, it is a question of the father as proprietor. We are under the sway of the father—at least of the paternal function—and just as Emma is first and foremost Charles' wife, Salammbô is above all Hamilcar's daughter. Her death only confirms the hegemony of the father's law: because if Salammbô dies "for having touched the Veil of Tanit"—I say "if" because no narrative voice assumes this explanation—that is tantamount to saying that she dies for having violated a taboo, and taboo, Freud repeatedly asserts, comes under the jurisdiction of the father's will. But—and it is here that the detail of the undone hair comes into play—by her extravagant death, Salammbô also subverts the patriarchal order: not only does she die making a mockery of the proprieties, she also refuses to play the role of object of value and exchange assigned by her father and the phallo-theocracy he represents.

Viewed either as a sacrifice which restores order to the city or as a deus ex machina which links the daughter of Hamilcar to the daughter of Agamemnon—Iphigenia may well be the paradigmatic daughter in Western literature—Salammbô's death interests us above all because its implausibility exposes the workings of the ornamental, that is the fetishistic text. No nineteenth-century French novelist has gone further than Flaubert in laying bare the function of the female protagonist: since Salammbô did not exist, she had to be invented, for the ornamental text is the product of the close play of binding and unbinding female energy. Salammbô's famous immobility is but a surface effect which covers over a movement which is of the order of female desire; the binding of Salammbô is the price paid for the work's polished surface and that binding is not stable. Once the novel has been written, the source of the energy tapped by the ornamental text can be sacrificed.

Let us return then in closing to our starting point: the question of perspective. It might seem that by privileging the detail of the chainlet we have done little more than follow the perceptual path traced by Flaubert in his *Correspondance* when he writes: "The detail grabs you and lays hold of you and the more it engages you the less you grasp the whole; then, gradually, things harmonize and place themselves according to all the requirements of perspective."[26] Nothing could be further from the truth: in what precedes, it is not a question of bringing *Salammbô* back under the regime of perspective which has ordered observation since the Renaissance. On the contrary, it is a question of valorizing positively that which Sainte-Beuve, Froehner, and even Flaubert considered the principal flaw of the novel: the lack of a privileged vantage point. To the multiplication of perspectives *in Salammbô*—well studied by Rousset—corresponds heretofore the multiplication of perspectives *on Salammbô*, that is Carthage. For in modern philosophical discourse, "perspectivism" is linked to the city, as this quotation from Nietzsche shows: "it is another town that corresponds to each point of view, and each point of view is another town."[27] Today it is no longer a question of destroying but rather of deconstructing Carthage, which may be the only way to save it.

7

Naturalizing Woman:
Germinie Lacerteux

Read or reread in a feminist perspective, Barthes' *S/Z* yields some rather surprising finds; for example, the suggestion, tucked away in the commentary on lexie No. 439, that the moment at which the writerly breaks through the readerly is precisely the moment at which the doxal discourse on femininity is heard in its full disoriginated force:

> (439) *This was woman herself, with her sudden fears, her irrational whims, her instinctive worries, her impetuous boldness, her fussings, and her delicious sensibility.* *SEM. Femininity. The source of this phrase cannot be discerned. Who is speaking? Is it Sarrasine? the narrator? the author? Balzac-the-author? Balzac-the-man? romanticism? bourgeoisie? universal wisdom? The intersection of all these origins creates the writing.[1]

Since, according to Barthes and others, disorigination and the uncertainty it provokes in the reader are the hallmarks of modernity, it is possible to infer from this passage that, paradoxically, far from constituting the dated residue of discarded modes of representation, the realist's discourse on femininity constitutes a privileged locus of *écriture*.

Now disorigination is in Barthes' poetics inseparable from what he calls naturalization, the process whereby bourgeois ideology converts the cultural into the natural: the use of uncertainty in the discourse on femininity is then to make a purely conventional and historically determined representation of femininity appear to be eternal, always already and forever after true. By making it impossible to ascribe this discourse to a single authorizing source, the Balzacian text accredits it as a universal truth. My concern in what follows is what happens when naturalization in Barthes' sense becomes coextensive with naturalization in the more restricted sense my title expressly plays on: that is, the process whereby realist modes of representation are converted into those of naturalism. And, to be more specific and to account for the second term in my title, my question is: how does naturalism naturalize woman?

There is perhaps no better place to seek answers to these questions than in what is commonly acknowledged to be *a* if not *the* founding text of naturalism, the Goncourts' *Germinie Lacerteux*. It is, I will argue, no accident that the inaugural text of naturalism concerns the relationship of a maid and her mistress, for one way of defining naturalism—there are, of course, others—is as the moment in the history of representation of women when the axis of class difference comes to lean on the axis of sexual difference, thereby creating a new type: *la femme du peuple*. It is then this *anaclitic* relationship between gender and class which I would like to de-naturalize here.

The dyadic relationship between Germinie and her mistress, Mlle de Varandeuil, might at the outset be viewed as a projection of the Goncourts' own, which according to their *Journal* was coded as a lesbian relationship, involving two men with *imaginary* female sexes:

> We are now like women living together, whose healths are intermingled, whose periods are simultaneous: we get our migraines on the same day.
>
> Nous sommes maintenant commes des femmes qui vivent ensemble, dont les santés se mêlent, dont les règles viennent en même temps: nos migraines viennent le même jour.[2]

This is not to suggest that the relationship between mistress and servant is in any sense erotic, but that it is suffused with an affective intensity that emphasizes their complicity rather than their differences, particularly those pertaining to class. The basic structure is set up in the double analepsis that opens the novel, where the servant's story frames the mistress's. Despite the significant formal differences between the two narratives—Germinie's tale is, at least initially, cast in a choppy, first-person narrative, riddled with aposiopeses, whereas Mlle de Varandeuil's biography is recounted in a seamless, masterful mode—they are in their content strikingly similar: both rehearse the victimage of women in patriarchy. Against the pathos of Germinie's tale of rustic squalor and urban rape is set the story of Mlle de Varandeuil, the daughter of a nobleman who survives the French Revolution in part by reducing his daughter to a state of domesticity:

> The daughter continued to act as servant to her father and her brother. Gradually Monsieur de Varandeuil had grown used to considering her as no more than the servant her clothes and occupations suggested. He no longer had the eyes of a father for the person beneath the servant's apron.[3]

> La fille continuait à servir son père et son frère. M. de Varandeuil s'était peu à peu accoutumé à ne plus voir en elle que la femme de son costume et de l'ouvrage qu'elle faisait. Les yeux du père ne voulaient plus reconnaître une fille sous l'habit et les basses occupations de cette servante. (p. 39)

Servitude is then not a matter of class, but rather of sex. Indeed, of sexual marketability, for female servitude are the wages of ugliness. More than anything else it is Mlle de Varandeuil's deviance from an aesthetic norm that consigns her to the status of servant in her father's house:

> The little girl born of this marriage in 1782 was sickly and ugly with her father's big nose, absurd in a face as round as a fist. She had none of those qualities her parents' vanity would have wished for her. After having come to grief at the forte-piano when she was five, at a concert given by her mother in her *salon,* she was banished to the servants' quarters.

> La petite fille, née de ce mariage en 1782, était de pauvre santé, laide avec un grand nez déjà ridicule, le nez de son père, dans une figure grosse comme le poing. Elle n'avait rien de ce qu'aurait voulu d'elle la vanité de ses parents. Sur un fiasco qu'elle fit à cinq ans au forté-piano, à un concert donné par sa mère dans son salon, elle fut reléguée parmi la domesticité. (p. 6/35)

As for Germinie her ugliness borders on the animalistic:

> Germinie was ugly . . . The greatest defect of her face was the excessive distance between nose and mouth. This disproportion gave an almost Simian character to the lower part of her head . . .

> Germinie était laide . . . La plus grande disgrâce de ce visage était la trop large distance entre le nez et la bouche. Cette disproportion donnait un caractère presque simiesque au bas de la tête . . . (p. 33/68–69)

Let us note in passing that Germinie is not the only monkey-like woman in the novel; Mlle de Varandeuil views her black sister-in-law as "neither more nor less than a monkey" ("absolument comme une singesse" [p. 16/48]). Naturalized woman is by definition an aesthetic monstrosity. It is a measure of Zola's adherence to mythical rather than naturalist codes of description that Nana is beautiful. Yet, at the same time, it is a measure of his fundamental allegiance to the codes of naturalism that Nana ends up by reverting, as she does, to a primeval ugliness.

Bound together by their sex-determined domesticity, Germinie and her mistress share an even more compelling female bond: the quasi-maternal relationship they enjoy. Thus, what is first and foremost an economic relationship involving an employer and an employee is transformed into a pseudo-familial one, sublimating the economic into the affective: "she's not a maid, she's not a servant to me, this girl: she's practically the family I never had" ("ce n'est pas une bonne, ce n'est pas une domestique pour moi, cette fille-là: c'est comme la famille que je n'ai pas eue!" [p. 178/224]). As for Germinie, her efforts to keep Mlle de Varandeuil in the dark about her tawdry sex life are inspired by a "a pious, almost religious sentiment, like that felt by a daughter lying to her mother's face" ("un sentiment pieux, presque religieux . . . pareil au sentiment d'une fille mentant aux yeux de sa mère" [p. 116/158]).

It would appear then that the naturalization of woman is predicated on the denial of class difference, as well as on the breakdown of difference between the animal and the human. But the difference that is denied on one axis reappears on the other, splitting the female subject along class lines, with the pure and undefiled half represented by the aristocrat and the sullied, pathological half represented by the peasant. Commenting on the mistress/maid relationship, Cixous writes in *La jeune née:* "The maid is the mistress's repressed."[4] And *Germinie Lacerteux* certainly stages that topical relationship with exemplary clarity in the very theatrical scene where Mlle de Varandeuil listens to Germinie talk in her sleep, giving voice to "that unconscious mind talking all by itself, that voice which could not hear itself" ("cette pensée sans connaissance qui parlait toute seule, cette voix qui ne s'entendait pas elle-même" [p. 128/171]).

Whether Germinie is viewed as acting out Mlle de Varandeuil's repressed sexuality or, in less analytical terms, as serving as a foil for the noble *vieille fille,* she is the paradigmatic naturalized female protagonist. Her entire fictional destiny is determined by her supposedly innate disposition to sexual degradation and that disposition, in turn, somehow justifies her social inferiority. Never is the disoriginated voice of the doxa more audible than in those passages where what is at stake is the legitimation of a new type: *la femme du peuple.* It is at these moments that one can best appreciate how class difference leans up against sexual difference, by in effect masquerading as a difference within that difference. A case in point is the opening of the chapter devoted to Germinie's fleeting religious fervor:

> Those who see the Catholic Church as ending in our times do not realise what strong and infinite roots it still thrusts out deep among the people. They do not realise the secret and delicate ramifications it has for *a woman of the people* . . . In the priest who listens and whose voice comes to her with gentleness, *the woman of labour and suffering* sees not so much the minister of God . . . as the confidant of her sorrows and the friend in her hardships. However coarsened she may be, there is always something of fundamental *woman* in her, something feverish, shuddering, sensitive and wounded, an agitation and, as it were, a sick person's breathing, which calls for the caresses of speech just as a child's bruises demand a nurse's crooning. She, just as much as a *woman of society,* needs the relief that is to be had from expansiveness, confidences, outpourings. For it is of the nature of her sex to desire to expand and be supported.

> Ceux qui voient la fin de la religion catholique dans le temps où nous sommes, ne savent pas quelles racines puissantes et infinies elle pousse encore dans les profondeurs du peuple. Ils ne savent pas les enlacements secrets et délicats qu'elle a pour *la femme du peuple* . . . Dans le prêtre qui l'écoute et dont la voix lui arrive doucement, *la femme de travail et de peine* voit moins le ministre de Dieu . . . que le confident de ses chagrins et l'ami de ses misères. Si grossière qu'elle soit, il y a toujours en elle un peu du fond de *la femme,* ce je ne sais quoi de fiévreux, de frissonnant, de sensitif et de blessé, une inquiétude et comme une aspiration de malade qui appelle les caresses de la parole ainsi que les bobos d'un enfant demandent le chantonnement d'une nourrice. Il lui faut, aussi bien qu'à *la femme du monde,* les soulagements d'expansion, de confidence, d'effusion. Car il est de la nature de son sexe de vouloir se répandre et s'appuyer. (p. 28/ 62; emphasis added)

The new literary type that is *la femme du peuple* is thus naturalized by being grafted onto a code already well established, the code of femininity which equates femininity with illness and infantilism. Even as class difference cleaves the female subject, the eternal feminine is reinscribed.

But our schema is too simple, for it fails to take into account a split that exists within Germinie herself. Indeed, by the end of the novel, we are told that Germinie has evolved. There is in her masochistic relationship to Jupillon a literary dimension which raises her above the women of her class; she is not, in fact, a typical *femme du peuple:* "Round about her there seemed to be nothing like this, among the women of her sort. None of her sort with whom she conversed brought to a liaison the intensity, bitterness, torment, the happiness in suffering, which she found in hers" ("Autour d'elle, rien ne lui semblait exister de pareil parmi les femmes de sa condition. Aucune des camarades qu'elle approchait ne mettait dans une liaison l'âpreté, l'amertume, le tourment, le bonheur de souffrir qu'elle trouvait dans la sienne" [p. 117/160]). Furthermore, Germinie's difference involves her superior mastery of the language. She is a sort of cross between a Madame Bovary figure and that recurrent figure of the *déclassé* in Zola's fiction, the half-educated autodidact:

> Germinie was not a domestic beast of burden with nothing in her head but her work . . . she had often surprised Mademoiselle de Varandeuil by the vivacity of her understanding, her promptitude at catching things half-said, the felicity and ease with which she found the words a good talker would have used . . . She understood a play on words . . . She had also that store of confused knowledge which the women of her class have when they read.
>
> Germinie n'était pas la bête de service qui n'a rien que son ouvrage dans la tête . . . Elle était arrivée à surprendre souvent Mlle de Varandeuil par sa vivacité de compréhension, sa promptitude à saisir des choses à demi dites, son bonheur et sa facilité à trouver des mots de belle parleuse . . . Elle comprenait un jeu de mots . . . Elle avait aussi ce fond de lectures brouillées qu'ont les femmes de sa classe quand elles lisent. (pp. 148–149/192)

Nowhere is Germinie's somewhat implausible, even uncanny command of the logos more in evidence than in the scene alluded to earlier where Mlle de Varandeuil listens to her talk in her sleep. The voice that emerges from Germinie's Other is the voice of the people miraculously chastened of all impurities, of all vulgarity, a kind of idealized popular discourse:

> And as she spoke, her speech became as unrecognizable as was her voice, transposed into the tones of the dream. It rose above the woman, above her everyday accents and expressions. It was a sort of popular speech purified and transfigured by passion.

> Et à mesure qu'elle parlait son langage devenait aussi méconnaissable que sa voix transposée dans les notes du songe. Il s'élevait au-dessus de la femme, au-dessus de son ton et de ses expressions journalières. C'était comme une langue du peuple purifiée et transfigurée dans la passion. (pp. 128–129/171)

When one recalls that in the celebrated preface to *Germinie Lacerteux,* the Goncourt call for an extension of the space of representation to include the lower classes, the significance of Germinie's alienation becomes apparent: under the guise of giving the people *voix au chapitre,* what the Goncourt in fact do is to give the people the voice of the bourgeoisie. Germinie's mastery of discourse is obtained only at the cost of speaking the master's discourse.

In the light of this analysis, the by now familiar question, *qui parle?* takes on a new urgency: for it would appear that in *Germinie* the disorigination of doxal discourse on femininity is accompanied by another mode of loss of origin: the disorigination of the *femme du peuple*'s own discourse. I would read this remarkable scene as an allegory of the naturalization of woman: *la femme du peuple* is brought onto the scene of representation as an actress—Mlle de Varandeuil compares Germinie's performance to Rachel's—an actress mouthing a script she did not write and whose author is nowhere to be found. Indeed, I would suggest that the culmination of this scenario occurs in *Nana,* where Nana's final appearance on stage is marked by a spectacular silence:

> She didn't say a word; the authors had even cut the line or two they had given her, because they were superfluous. No, not a single word: it was more impressive that way, and she took the audience's breath away, by simply showing herself.

Elle ne disait pas un mot, même les auteurs lui avaient coupé une réplique, parce que ça gênait; non, rien du tout, c'était plus grand, et elle vous retournait son public, rien qu'à se montrer.[5]

In guise of a conclusion a brief and difficult question: if the disorigination of discourse that constitutes *écriture* not only naturalizes *la femme du peuple,* but also legitimizes the theft of her language, the question arises: is modernity good for women? The question remains open.

8

Unwriting *Lamiel*

Basing herself on Roland Barthes' high structuralist assumption that a novel is structured like a sentence Nancy Miller, in her book *The Heroine's Text,* has shown that eighteenth-century feminocentric novels can be read as expansions of a a single maxim: "Il n'y a que le premier pas qui coûte" ("The first step is the hardest").[1] The question then arises: what becomes of this "female plot" in nineteenth-century feminocentric fiction? Is the fate of the nineteenth-century female protagonist also ruled by the logic of the misstep? In her epilogue Miller eloquently makes the case for the essential permanence of the "stereotypes of literary femininity," concluding that in spite of the undeniable opening out of the scene of representation in the nineteenth-century novel, "experience for female characters is still primarily tied to the erotic and familial. The sexual faux pas is still a fatal step" (p. 157).

I will want to argue here that this very real and significant continuity—the unchanging restriction of woman's sphere to the sexual and the domestic—masks a subtle yet crucial discontinuity which flies in the face of our own legacy from the eighteenth century: the belief in the inevitability of progress. For what distinguishes the nineteenth-century French heroine from her immediate predecessors, what seals the degradation of the feminine in nineteenth-century French fiction is the devastating fact that the post-Revolutionary female protagonist is consistently deprived of the minimal attribute of subjecthood, which is not, or not merely, the faculty of speech, the capacity to produce signs, but rather the power of locomotion, the right to move about freely. Indeed, it will be recalled that the jubilation the Lacanian infant experiences in front of the mirror results from the illusory command of his *motor* functions the mirror provides. In contrast to the eighteenth-century heroine who is imagined as free to take that first fatal step, the nineteenth-century heroine is figured as so restricted in her movements that for her the very act of taking a step becomes problematic. Put another way: whereas in the eighteenth century the "step" can be taken both figuratively and literally because the logic of the misstep rests on a representation of woman as essentially mobile, in the nineteenth century, the step is a trope and nothing more. The nineteenth-century heroine is condemned to a purely rhetorical mobility, for in the world of the referent she is a cripple, the victim of as great (if not greater) a "lockup" as the mad in the age of Classicism. The case of Emma Bovary is in this respect—as in so many others—exemplary: on the one hand, as Michael Riffaterre has recently shown, Emma's entire trajectory is determined by the inexorable logic of the faux pas,[2] while on the other, Flaubert codes her dissatisfaction with woman's estate in terms of locomotion:

> . . . and this idea of having a male child was like an expected revenge for all her impotence in the past. *A man, at least, is free;* he can explore all passions and all countries, overcome obstacles, taste of the most distant pleasures. But *a woman is always hampered.* Being inert as well as pliable, she has against her the weakness of the flesh and the inequity of the law. Like the veil held to her hat by a ribbon, her will flutters in every breeze; she is always drawn by some desire, restrained by some rule of conduct.

> . . . et cette idée d'avoir pour enfant un mâle était comme la revanche en espoir de toutes ses impuissances passées. *Un homme, au moins, est libre;* il peut parcourir les passions et les pays, traverser les obstacles, mordre aux bonheurs les plus lointains. Mais *une femme est empêchée continuellement.* Inerte et flexible à la fois, elle a contre elle les mollesses de la chair avec les dépendances de la loi. Sa volonté, comme le voile de son chapeau retenu par un cordon, palpite à tous les vents; il y a toujours quelque désir qui entraîne, quelque convenance qui retient.[3]

Unlike Balzac's univocal narrative voice which serves to naturalize, that is to feminize passivity (as in *Eugénie Grandet*, see above), Flaubert's typically fetishistic narrative voice oscillates between two contradictory explanations of woman's passivity: the "anatomical" ("weakness of the flesh") and the "cultural" ("inequity of the law"). In Flaubert anatomy is and is not destiny. Hence the double motivation of woman's paralysis: in the sentence that begins, "inert as well as pliable," Flaubert suggests that the inhibition of woman's motility is due to a *combination* of anatomical and legal restraints, whereas, in the following sentence, he implies that it is due to a *conflict* between the rival claims of desire and convention, which is not quite the same thing. Nevertheless, and however great an improvement Flaubert's partial denaturalization of woman's passivity represents over Balzac's total naturalization, this much is certain: when compared to the freedom such eighteenth-century heroines as Manon Lescaut, Marianne, and Juliette enjoy, the confinement to which Emma and Eugénie, for example, are subject represents an unquestionable step backward.

Perhaps the most persuasive illustration of the degradation of the female protagonist in nineteenth-century French fiction is the critical response to Stendhal's last, unfinished work, *Lamiel*. Unable to account for the remarkable autonomy with which Stendhal has endowed his ultimate female protagonist, in the context of the nineteenth-century French novel, the critics, especially the feminist, have repeatedly invoked eighteenth-century intertexts ranging from Sade's *Histoire de Juliette ou les prospérités du vice* to Laclos' *Liaisons dangereuses*. Lamiel has been described as a "softer" version of Juliette or a "more charming Mme de Merteuil."[4] If Lamiel is seen as an eighteenth-century heroine struggling to break out of the nineteenth-century novel in which she has somehow become trapped, this tells us something about the difference between the fictional— not to say historical—status of women before and after the French Revolution.

If we turn now to *Lamiel*, we find that the question of locomotion is absolutely central to Stendhal's portrayal of his remarkable female protagonist. From the very first outline of the novel, Lamiel, who is still called Amiel, is conceived of as excessively mobile:

> Amiel, tall, well-built, a bit skinny, with good colour, very pretty, well dressed in the manner of the rich country bourgeoisie, walked too fast in the streets, stepped over gutters, jumped on the sidewalks.
>
> Amiel, grande, bien faite, un peu maigre, avec de belles couleurs, fort jolie, bien vêtue comme une riche bourgeoise, marchait trop vite dans les rues, enjambait les ruisseaux, sautait sur les trottoirs.[5]

The body in Stendhal is, as we well know, the site of an intense struggle between nature ("le naturel") and culture ("hypocrisie"). The worldly success of the Stendhalian protagonist can only be obtained by acquiring complete mastery over the body and its involuntary language. And yet, at the same time, it is the irruption of the semiotic in the symbolic that sets the Stendhalian hero or heroine above and apart from the other members of society. Now, whereas Julien Sorel must learn to control his eyes, Lamiel, often called a "female Julien,"[6] must learn to pace herself. In other words, whereas the male protagonist must learn to mask his affectivity, the female must learn to conceal her energy. And yet, just as Julien owes his success in the world as much to his failures at acculturation as to his triumphs, Lamiel wins the affection of the snobbish Duchesse de Miossens whose reader she is by the inadvertent display of her animal spirits:

> Lamiel had too much energy and vivacity to walk slowly and with eyes lowered, or at least so levelled as to let but an insignificant glance at the magnificent carpet in the Duchess' salon escape her. The charitable warnings of the chambermaids had caused her to adopt a curious gait; she walked slowly, to be sure, but she looked like a *chained gazelle;* a thousand little impulsive movements betrayed her country habits. She had never been able to acquire that conventional social bearing which must suggest the ultimate effort of a nature whose ideal is never to make the slightest move. The moment she was not directly under the stern glance of some old chambermaid, she would frisk through the rooms leading to the Duchess' salon. Informed of it by talebearing chambermaids, the great lady had a mirror placed in a salon in order to watch this gaiety from her armchair. Although Lamiel was lightness itself, everything was so quiet in the vast château that the shaking of the furniture as she bounded along was everywhere audible. All the servants were much shocked at this behavior which, in the end, caused the fortune of the young villager. When the Duchess was sure that she had acquired a little girl who did not affect the airs of a lady, she gave her inclination for Lamiel free play.

> L'Amiel avait trop de vivacité et d'énergie pour marcher lentement et les yeux baissés ou du moins ramenés à un regard insignifiant sur le magnifique tapis du salon de la duchesse. Son allure était des plus singulières: elle marchait lentement, il est vrai, mais elle avait l'air d'une *gazelle enchaînée;* mille petits mouve-

ments pleins de vivacité trahissaient ses habitudes campag-
nardes. Dès qu'elle n'était pas immédiatement surveillée par les
regards sévères de quelqu'une des vieilles femmes de chambre,
elle parcourait en sautant la suite des pièces qu'il fallait traverser
pour arriver à celle où se tenait la duchesse. Avertie par les plaintes
de ses femmes, la grande dame fit placer une glace pour voir
cette gaieté de son fauteuil. Rien pourtant n'eût dû paraître plus
choquant aux yeux de la grande dame. Quoique L'Amiel fût la
légèreté même, tout était si tranquille dans ce vaste château que
l'ébranlement causé par ses sauts s'entendait de partout. Tout le
monde en parlait, et c'est ce qui décida la fortune de L'Amiel.
Quand la duchesse fut bien sûre de n'avoir pas fait l'acquisition
d'une petite fille se donnant des airs de demoiselle, elle se livra
avec bonheur au vif penchant qu'elle sentait pour elle. (pp. 73–
74/35–36; emphasis added)

Placed strategically off-center in the Duchess' salon, the mirror fulfills
a double function: first, like the mirror in the Bishop d'Agde scene in *Le
Rouge et le noir,* it serves as an instrument of revelation, making manifest
to a hidden observer precisely that which the reflected subject strives to
dissimulate, which is in both cases on the order of spontaneity, here its
excess, there its lack. At the same time, the mirror functions abysmally,
placing the reader in the voyeur's position, and refracting not the character's but the text's duplicity, for what is ultimately noteworthy about
this scene is its display of the alternate containment and release of Lamiel's energy, a tension concretized by the oxymoronic expression: "chained
gazelle" ("gazelle enchaînée").

Lamiel's singular gait will continue to draw attention throughout the
novel. Thus, at the outset of her stay in Paris, Lamiel asks her hostess,
Mme Le Grand, if she may engage a dancing master, saying: "I feel I do
not walk or enter a room like other people" ("Je sens que je ne marche
pas, que je n'entre pas dans un salon comme une autre" [p. 253/109–
110]). The Comte d'Aubigné, the dandy lover she takes in Paris, is titil-
lated at the prospect of taming, which is to say encaging the young gazelle: "Careful, d'Aubigné, it's a young gazelle you are trying to put in a
pen; she must not jump over the barriers" ("Attention, d'Aubigné, c'est
une jeune gazelle que je veux mettre en cage, il ne faut pas qu'elle saute
par-dessus les barrières" [p. 265/117–118]).

In the end, Lamiel never does learn to walk in a socially acceptable
fashion. Her loping gait continues to function as the place of inscription

of her naturality. Unlike Flaubert's Salammbô who succeeds only fleetingly in *breaking the chain* that binds her movements, Lamiel succeeds only fleetingly in fettering her walk: beneath the measured steps of the would-be lady, the lithe movements of the gazelle constantly show through. The question then becomes: what connection if any is there between Lamiel's peculiar walk and *Lamiel's* incompletion, for *Lamiel* is, as we know, a notoriously fragmentary text, riddled with gaps, maddeningly repetitive, totally inconclusive, and, in the eyes of more than one critic, a failure.

Critics have long speculated about the reasons for the incompletion of *Lamiel,* a manuscript whose writing was abruptly cut off by Stendhal's sudden death. Two interlocking questions have dominated these speculations: first, are the reasons for the incompletion of *Lamiel* similar to those of the incompletion of other Stendhal manuscripts, notably *Lucien Leuwen?* Second, would Stendhal have completed *Lamiel* had he lived?

Before one can begin to answer these questions, it is necessary to recall the history of the publication of *Lamiel.* I will summarize here the admittedly partial account of this history provided by Victor Del Litto in the "Preface" to his edition, which is the best we now have. As he reminds us, there have been to date three major editions, including his own. The first was brought out some fifty years after Stendhal's death (1889) by Casimir Stryienski. According to Del Litto, Stryienski's main concern was to organize the disparate elements of the manuscript in order to present to the readers "a text as complete and coherent as possible" (p. xii). Which he succeeded in doing but only at the cost of taking tremendous liberties with the manuscript. The next edition of *Lamiel*—the one most often reprinted and familiar to the majority of readers—is the 1928 Divan edition by that great Stendhalian Henri Martineau. Martineau, Del Litto notes, is highly critical of Stryienski in his preface, and yet, claims Del Litto, in the final analysis there is not all that much difference between the Stryienski and Martineau editions, when it comes to respect for the original manuscript as it is to be found at the Municipal Library of Grenoble. Indeed, according to Del Litto—for whom the great rival is clearly Martineau and not the hapless Stryienski—Martineau went even further than Stryienski in his effort to weld the fragments of the *Lamiel* manuscript into a seamless web. Concluding his comparison of the two editions, Del Litto writes: "Stryienski was guilty, of course, but Martineau is even more so [. . . .] He thought it advisable, and wrongly, to denounce his predecessor. He in turn is vulnerable to criticism, because his edition in fact deceives and constantly misleads the reader" (p. xvii). For Del Litto the question then becomes how not to repeat the errors of his predecessors. In keeping with the aesthetic and epistemological preferences of the age, he concludes that the only way "to respect the letter and the spirit of such a tortured novel" is to publish the full contents of the *Lamiel* manuscripts *in their chronological order:* "It is absolutely necessary to place before the reader all the brute materials, with all their repetitions, contradictions, incoherencies, to allow him to arrive at his own understanding of the laborious gestation of *Lamiel*" (p. xviii).

The Del Litto edition is then the edition of our age of the fragment: instead of attempting to paper over the gaps, breaks, and false starts that characterize the manuscript of *Lamiel,* Del Litto leaves them in their unreconstructed state. "The result of Del Litto's treatment," writes Dennis Porter, "is that what has long been recognized as Stendhal's wildest and most enigmatic novel achieves a new kind of exemplary status. Paradoxically, the consequences of scientific editorship are in this case a work of fiction calculated to appeal to post-modernist sensibility."[7] Porter—adding paradox to paradox—thereupon elects to read Del Litto against the grain, reducing the scandal of the text's morcellization by reassembling the *membra disjecta* and teasing out of them the morphology of a reassuringly familiar folktale: beauty and the beast.

Reduced scandals are notoriously resilient. The glimpse Del Litto affords us into the genesis of *Lamiel* suggests, however, that the irreducible scandal of the text is not its fragmentariness, its discontinuity, rather its failure to sustain its initial impetus, to bring to completion the narrative of Lamiel's self-education in the ways of love and geometry. What the Del Litto edition reveals is not so much the writing as the *unwriting* of *Lamiel.* For what is placed before the reader is a double and even triple text, consisting of an initial core narrative centered on Lamiel *(Lamiel I),* succeeded by a second narrative *(Lamiel II),* centered on the hunchback doctor-*philosophe,* Sansfin, which is in turn followed by several other increasingly brief fragments. The question the Del Litto edition raises is why, when Stendhal resumed work on the manuscript of *Lamiel,* did he in effect proceed to unwrite what he had written?[8] The answer is disarmingly, deceptively simple: *Lamiel,* or rather, *Lamiel I* is an *unwritable text.* What then is an unwritable text? The unwritable text is not literally a text which cannot be written (any more than Barthes' "writerly" text is a text that *can* be written), rather it is a text which cannot but be unwritten, a text which contains within it the principles of its own nonclosure, its own undoing. For all the eighteenth-century models available to him, Stendhal was a nineteenth-century novelist bound by the constraints peculiar to then nascent representational realism. What the incompletion of *Lamiel I* testifies to is the fundamental impossibility of representing, or representing in any sustained sort of fashion, a mobile, fully empowered female protagonist within the limits of realism, at least in its French modality. (Obviously the logic of my argument entails two consequences: the case of *Lamiel* cannot be assimilated to that of *Lucien Leuwen* and Stendhal's death cannot be invoked as an explanation for the text's state). If *Lamiel I* is constitutively in-terminable it is not because reality failed to provide models of free female subjects, rather because the production of realist fiction depends to an unsuspected degree on the binding of female energy. Unchain the gazelle and let her roam free and the nineteenth-century French novel collapses.

So inexorable is this law that the binding of female energy is to a very large extent independent of and unrelated to an author's ideology. This would explain a paradox contained in Simone de Beauvoir's celebrated chapter in *The Second Sex* praising Stendhal's feminism, where she notes: "Clearly Stendhal's sympathy for his heroines is the greater the more closely they are confined."[9] Stendhal's delight in imagining both interior and exterior obstacles against which his female protagonists must strain in order to achieve their "authenticity" is accountable not to some Stendhalian notion of pathos—as de Beauvoir would have it—rather to a more general and terrible law of textual production. It is, of course, precisely because Stendhal is a feminist that his predilection for imprisoned women is so very telling. My claim here is large: representation in its paradigmatic nineteenth-century form depends on the bondage of woman. Just why this should be so one can only speculate, but these speculations are grounded in verifiable trends and events. I would single out four overdetermining factors; the first two are gender-specific, the other two, not: 1) the tremendous loss of power inflicted on women by the French Revolution and ratified by the Napoleonic Code; 2) the disciplining of the female body Michel Foucault terms "hysterization"; 3) the generalized "fear of desire" Leo Bersani has shown to be characteristic of realism, and 4) the increasing concern with entropy and the exhaustion of non-renewable sources of energy.[10]

Lamiel II is then not so much a rewriting, as an unwriting of *Lamiel I*, a clumsy and desperate attempt to restart the grounded textual machine by recontaining the unleashed forces of female energy. This recontainment takes the form of a *double framing:* the story of Lamiel is inserted in the framework of the story of the noble Duchess de Miossens and the bourgeois Sansfin, which is itself embedded in the first-person narration of an entirely new character: the notary's son who narrates the first three chapters and then, after a valedictory address to the "benevolent reader," bows out. In unwriting *Lamiel I* Stendhal reveals the obverse side of the eighteenth-century model of heroinism: the pedagogical relationship which subsumes a female disciple to a male master. The displacement of Lamiel by Sansfin as the main protagonist goes hand in hand with the putting into place of one of the standard plots of female subjection (and often subversion): what we might call the pedagogical plot.[11] From an autodidact with multiple masters, Lamiel is transformed into the brilliant pupil of a single professor of cynicism: Sansfin. In the end, in the last fragment but one, *Lamiel III* or *IV*—one begins to lose count as the sputtering narrative splinters into ever smaller sections—Stendhal unwrites the most radical episode in the original text—Lamiel's sexual initiation by hire, the ultimate role reversal—by reinscribing Lamiel in the circuit of homosexual exchange from which he had initially so miraculously exempted her. In the final fragment then, upon hearing that Lamiel had paid the upholsterer Fabien 40 francs to assuage her "doubts" about what is known as virginity, Sansfin goes into a jealous rage and meeting Fabien tries to stab him. In the very last fragment of the manuscript, Lamiel has completely disappeared and only Fabien and Sansfin remain, locked into the eternal embrace of male rivals.

But the unwriting of *Lamiel I* does not stop with the Del Litto edition. It continues in the modern-day pastiche of Stendhal, Jacques Laurent's *La Fin de Lamiel*, about which Gérard Genette writes: "All this seems to be very well done and more Stendhalian in spirit then Stendhal himself."[12] This out-Stendhaling of Stendhal brings the unwriting of *Lamiel* to its inevitable conclusion.

What is most remarkable about Laurent's sequel is that it confirms a contrario the link I have been positing between female bondage and realism in all its nineteenth-century modulations. In a scene completely invented by Laurent, he describes a painting of Lamiel by her painter-lover, Cruz:

He had undertaken, imagining that he was acting on an artistic impulse, a painting where Lamiel was represented bound hand and foot and almost naked. He claimed that this "Young Greek slave tormented by the Turks" would make his fortune at the next Salon.

Il avait entrepris en s'imaginant qu'il cédait à une impulsion d'artiste un tableau où Lamiel était représentée pieds et poings liés et presque dévêtue. Il prétendait que cette "Jeune esclave grecque tourmentée par les Turcs" ferait sa fortune au prochain salon . . .[13]

Laurent is nothing if not crafty in his presentation of this scene. By stressing the painter's denegation of his true motives for depicting Lamiel in this humiliating position—on the following page we learn that Cruz experiences sexual gratification only by submitting proud women to his will—Laurent adroitly transfers the responsibility for this representation onto a fictional scapegoat. Unfortunately for Laurent, at the same time as the painter represents the bound Lamiel, the narrator presents her posing:

The next day, as though it were perfectly natural, as soon as she arrived at Cruz's she got ready to resume the pose. She even asked to be bound as before so that the resemblance would be perfect.

Le lendemain, comme si la chose allait de soi, à peine chez Cruz, elle se mit en état de reprendre la pose. Elle exigea même d'être liée comme autrefois afin que la ressemblance fût parfaite. (p. 251)

The unwriting of *Lamiel* culminates by the inescapable logic of realism in a scene where Lamiel legitimates her oppression by asking her sadistic lover to tie her up: this is not parody, this is pornography—or better yet a parody of a bondage fantasy: it is as though one imagined Galatea begging Pygmalion to turn her to stone, which may well be the nineteenth-century male writer's ultimate fantasy.

That *Lamiel* serves as the paradigm of the unwritable text should not surprise us, for, as I have tried to show, realism, far from excluding woman from the field of representation draws its momentum from the representation of bound women, and that binding implicitly recognizes woman's energy and the patriarchal order's dependence on it for the production of Literature. The necessary link between woman and representation serves to explain why the nineteenth-century novel—and not just in France—is so overwhelmingly feminocentric, even as the female protagonist is represented as forbidden to experience sexual pleasure, fulfill her ambitions, and move about freely.

A final question arises: can one speak of realism without taking into account the plural writing practices that singular term covers? To raise that question is to suggest that the relationship of representation and the female in nineteenth-century France was decisively marked by the triumph of Balzacian realism over the Stendhalian, a triumph whose consequences have perhaps never been fully measured. As Balzac in his celebrated homage to the author of *La Chartreuse de Parme* recognizes, and as Lukács underscores in his essay on that historic encounter,[14] Stendhal and Balzac name the split *within* realism, a split of which *Lamiel* may well be the only trace. Let us recall some further facts regarding the genesis of *Lamiel*. In the yearlong interval between the writing and the unwriting of *Lamiel*, Balzac's article appeared, urging Stendhal to rewrite *La Chartreuse*, a project Stendhal actually entertained. The unwriting of *Lamiel* participates then in Stendhal's attempt to "Balzacize" his fiction. Now if, according to Barthes, the "Flaubertization" of Literature marks the beginning of our modernity, I would like to suggest that its "Balzacization" marks the divorce between women and modernity which is only now beginning to be healed.

One of the major objectives of feminist literary criticism has been the reshaping of the canon, especially by opening it up to accomodate works by women writers. I believe a complementary and perhaps more insidious revisionism is called for as well, one which would take the form of subtle displacements within the canon we have inherited from Lanson and company and transmitted more or less unexamined for decades. My revisionist literary history of nineteenth-century French fiction would involve three substitutions which would do much to denaturalize an all too familiar landscape. First, Chateaubriand's *Atala* would displace his *René* as the founding text of nineteenth-century French literature, for it is in the former that the enchaining of the female protagonist is explicitly staged, as Atala is transformed from the mobile liberatrix of the male captive with whom she falls in love to a suicide who dies ruing the vow her mother made forbidding her daughter from ever knowing jouissance. Second, at the other end of the diachronic axis, Villiers de l'Isle-Adam's *L'Eve future* would displace J-K. Huysmans' *A Rebours* as the ultimate text of post-realism, for Villiers' futuristic fantasy of a female android is the logical conclusion of a century of fetishization of the female body. And, finally, Stendhal would displace Balzac as the paradigmatic realist novelist. The degree to which this history appears outlandish and even outrageous is a measure of the work that remains to be done.

III
THEORY'S BODY

9

Female Paranoia:
The Case for Psychoanalytic Feminist Criticism

One can speak in general terms of the "schizoid," but not of "the paranoid" in *general*. Paranoia is always masculine or feminine . . .

Philippe Sollers

As a substitute for penis envy, identification with the clitoris: neatest expression of inferiority, source of all inhibitions. At the same time [in Case X] disavowal of the discovery that other women too are without a penis.

Sigmund Freud

Even if, under the impact of recent developments in France, a growing number of American feminists have ceased to view Freud as one of womankind's prime enemies and psychoanalysis as a movement to be relegated to the junk heap of history, the theoretical foundations of psychoanalytic feminist literary criticism remain extremely shaky. I would ascribe this theoretical instability to a rather simple but far-reaching situation: those theoreticians who have contributed to articulating psychoanalysis and feminism are not necessarily or primarily interested in literary criticism (Mitchell, Dinnerstein, Irigaray); conversely, those who have contributed to articulating psychoanalysis and literature are not necessarily or primarily feminists (Felman). This leaves those who are attempting to read texts in a psychoanalytic perspective and with a feminist consciousness in something of a theoretical vacuum, straddling two approaches: on the one hand, a psychoanalytic feminist *thematics,* centering on the oedipal relationships (mother-daughter and, less frequently, father-daughter) as they are represented in works of literature; on the other, a psychoanalytic feminist *hermeneutics,* involving close readings of nonliterary texts, essentially those of Freud, Lacan, et al., using the techniques of literary analysis (Irigaray, Cixous, Gallop). In what follows I shall attempt—in an admittedly, indeed deliberately sketchy fashion—to outline a new feminist thematics grounded in feminist hermeneutics. In other words: basing myself on a respectful but, literally, perverse reading of one of Freud's minor essays on femininity, I shall propose a psychoanalytic feminist hermeneutics which turns to account the specific contribution of women to contemporary theory, that is, their militant materialism. Finally, I shall illustrate my approach through a reading of Poe's *The Mystery of Marie Roget.* My progress from Freud to Poe is, of course, not innocent: it is, as we shall see, a return to the scene of the crime.

FEMALE PARANOIA

(Female) Paranoia as (Female) Theory

At first glance Freud's essay "A Case of Paranoia Running Counter to the Psychoanalytic Theory of the Disease" may seem like a particularly unpromising Freudian text to enlist in the elaboration of a theoretical model for feminist psychoanalytic criticism, for it bears blatant witness to precisely that aspect of Freud's writings which has most angered his feminist critics: the unexamined priority and primacy of the male paradigm. As we soon discover, this contradictory case *(eines . . . widersprechenden Falles)* is a case of female paranoia which seems at first to call seriously into question the universal validity of the theory of paranoia derived from the analysis of a male paranoiac (Schreber). Freud, however, goes to great lengths to demonstrate that despite its apparent irregularity, when subjected to rigorous psychoanalytic investigation, even this contrary case conforms to the masculine model. This reduction of the atypical female exception to the prototypical masculine rule is a gesture of "normalization" too familiar to Freud's feminist readers to be belabored here. What needs to be stressed is the fact that not only does this perplexing case, as we shall soon see, appear to threaten a dogma central to Freud's theory of paranoia—namely that the persecutor is, in fact, the object of a re-pressed homosexual desire—but that, in so doing, it threatens theory it-self. By bringing the seemingly aberrant case of female paranoia under the sway of psychoanalytic theory, Freud is seeking to make the world safe for that theory which has, as he repeatedly states, deep affinities with paranoia. Thus, at the end of his analysis of the Schreber case, Freud writes: "It remains for the future to decide whether there is more delusion in my theory than I should like to admit, or whether there is more truth in Schreber's delusion than other people care to believe";[1] similarly, in his late article "Construction in Analysis," he remarks: "The delusions of pa-tients appear to me to be the equivalents of the constructions which we build up in the course of analytic treatment—attempts at explanation and cure."[2] But it is Freud's oft-cited comparison of paranoiacs and philoso-phers—"the delusions of paranoiacs have an unpalatable external similar-ity and internal kinship to the systems of our philosophers"[3]—which has led many of his French readers to simply equate paranoia and theory, thereby minimizing—as Freud invites us to do—the differences between socially acceptable and deviant forms of system-building.

Female Paranoia vs. Male Paranoia

What is, then, at stake in Freud's text is the accuracy of his diagnosis: is there in fact such a clinical category as female paranoia? In other words: the urgent question posed by this case is not so much: does female par-anoia corroborate the psychoanalytic theory of the disease, rather: can fe-males theorize, albeit in the caricatural mode of the mad? Does the ho-mology between male and female paranoia include the prestigious intellectual (hyper-)activity associated with the male model? This may strike some readers as a rhetorical question, since the very writing and publi-cation of this theoretical text attests to my belief in women's ability to theorize; nevertheless, it must be raised. For while most authors dealing with the subject seem to agree that there are female paranoiacs—indeed Phyllis Chesler lists paranoia among the "female diseases"[4]—at least one prominent Freudian has suggested that the typical form of female para-noia is decidedly less systematic and elaborate than the typical male form of the disease:

151

The usual persecutory paranoia, with its elaborate ideation, its excessive intellectuality, and its occurrence in individuals with a high power of sublimation, is essentially a highly organized and masculine psychosis, and is, as a matter of fact, much more common in men than in women . . . I should like at this point to make a possible differentiation between two of the types of true paranoia, the jealous and the persecutory. The latter, as we have seen, is an elaborate psychosis of an essentially masculine nature, and is the commonest form of paranoia in men. The jealous form, on the other hand, is par excellence the paranoia of women . . . In contradistinction to the philosophic, systematizing persecutory paranoia, the delusional jealousy is both feminine and rudimentary and, as it were, closer to the normal and the neurotic.[5]

These remarks are drawn from an essay entitled "The Analysis of a Case of Paranoia" (1929), which Freud cites in "Female Sexuality" (1931); its author is Ruth Mack Brunswick, Freud's favorite female disciple in his later years. Though this essay was written some fourteen years after the Freud essay under discussion, and has no direct bearing on it, it cannot go unmentioned, for it indicates the tremendous difficulties and dangers inherent in defining a specifically female form of paranoia, that is, as I will maintain throughout, of theory.

The Case for Psychoanalytic Feminist Criticism

At the outset Freud's case history is cast in the traditional narrative mode—"Some years ago . . ."[6]—but this innocuous opening is almost immediately belied by the unfolding of a complicated twice-told tale. In the course of their first meeting, the patient presents her case to Freud, indeed the entire text turns on a pun on the word case, *Fall*, which means both legal and medical case: the patient belongs to that class of paranoiacs known as *quérulants*, and she is referred to Freud not by another doctor, but by a lawyer. The facts of her *case*, as she recounts them during her first interview with Freud, are as follows: a fellow worker in the office where she had worked for years—the patient is a "singularly attractive and handsome" (p. 151) thirty-year-old woman—had become interested in her and had invited her up to his place. Although she had never been interested in men and lived quietly with her old mother, and although her suitor could not offer marriage, the young woman agreed to visit his place in the daytime. There, as they were embracing, "she was suddenly frightened by a noise, a kind of knock or tick" (ibid.). The young man assured her that the sound came from a small clock on a nearby writing desk. As she was leaving the house she met two men on the stairs. "One of the strangers was carrying something which was wrapped up and looked rather like a box" (p. 152). On arriving home the young woman decided that this box-like object was a camera and that the sound she had heard was that of a shutter clicking. She thereupon became convinced that her lover had been trying to blackmail her and began to pursue him with her reproaches. Finally she went to consult the lawyer, who brought her to Freud.

For Freud the question posed by the patient's narrative is: does she *have* a case or *is* she a case? What prevents Freud from making up his mind is the fact that contrary to the psychoanalytic theory of paranoia, the persecutor—that is the young man—is not of the same sex as the victim: "there was no sign of the influence of a woman, no trace of a struggle against a homosexual attachment" (p. 153). Confronted with this difficulty, rather than conclude that his theory needed to be revised or that the patient did indeed have a legitimate case, Freud hypothesized that if the case did not fit the theory, then perhaps the case history was incomplete. He asks for and is granted a second interview with the young woman, who thereupon produces Narrative II, in which she reveals that she had visited the young man not once but twice. The insistent doubling in this text—there are the double frame of reference, the lawyer and the analyst, the two strangers, the double delusion—is hardly accidental, as doubling is a characteristic feature of paranoia, the persecutor always being in some sense the victim's double, if only as a projection effect. Now what is significant about the disparity between Narrative I and Narrative II is not so much the fact that there are two visits, as the fact that something crucial occurred in the interval separating the two encounters. The doubling of the visit opens up another time frame, precisely the one during which the missing event took place: the day after the uneventful first rendezvous, the young woman saw her would be lover talking to her supervisor, an elderly woman whom she describes as having white hair and looking like her mother. When she saw the two in conversation, she became convinced that they were speaking of her visit, further, that the elderly supervisor and the young man were lovers. She confronted her suitor with these suspicions, but he was so successful in allaying them that she consented to a second meeting. The conflation of the supervisor and the mother provided Freud with the information he needed to confirm his theory; beneath the male persecutor stood a female persecutor and one resembling the victim's mother: "The *original* persecutor . . . is here again `not a man but a woman" (p. 155). Indeed the daughter's homosexual bond with her mother makes it difficult, not to say impossible, for her to enjoy a satisfactory heterosexual relationship.

Having successfully surmounted the principal difficulty posed by this perplexing case, Freud proceeds in the second half of the paper to turn his attention to what turns out to be by far the most striking and enigmatic aspect of the case, the nature of the sound heard by the patient. This part of the text can itself be divided into two parts: in the first, Freud seeks to demonstrate that there was nothing accidental about the noise; rather than triggering the delusion, the delusion latched on to the noise, because noise is an intrinsic component of the primal scene: "The accidental noise is merely a stimulus which activates the typical phantasy of eavesdropping, itself a component of the parental complex" (p. 157). And, according to Freud, what we have here is a reenactment of the primal scene, with the patient coming to occupy the mother's place.[7]

But Freud does not stop there: in the second part of his discussion of the troublesome noise, in a dramatic though not atypical change of venue, he offers a hypothesis which renders the entire discussion of the order of events academic: "I might go still further in the analysis of this apparently real 'accident.' I do not believe that the clock ever ticked or that any noise was to be heard at all. The woman's situation justified a sensation of throbbing [*Klopfen*] in the clitoris. This was what she subsequently projected as a perception of an external object" (pp. 158–159).

FEMALE PSYCHOANALYTIC THEORY IS A MATERIALISM

If we take Freud's patient as a paradigmatic female paranoiac and her delusion as an exemplary case of female theorizing, then the implications of Freud's audacious and quite possibly mad hypothesis must be articulated and examined in some detail. The first of these implications can be stated quite simply: female theorizing is grounded in the body. Indeed it may well be that female theorizing involves at least as much asserting the body's inscription in language, as demonstrating the female body's exclusion from language, a more widely held view. As Guy Rosolato notes in his analysis of the Freud text: "We must take another look at Freud's previously cited case, in order to emphasize *the very important part the body plays in it.* Freud views the projection as emanating only from the corporeal excitation and from nothing else. His construction presupposes it."[8]

The question then becomes: is there any evidence to support my hypothesis that female psychoanalytically based and oriented theory is, by definition, a materialism riveted to the body, its throbbing, its pulsations, its rhythms? My question is here a rhetorical one, because by its very phrasing it contains its own affirmative answer: by linking up throbbing with the larger semantic field of rhythm, I am alluding to the critical vocabulary of the major French female theoretician of the past decade, Julia Kristeva. I am alluding in particular to her insistent valorization of what she terms the *semiotic*—in contradistinction to the *symbolic*—and which she defines as follows:

> It is chronologically anterior and synchronically transversal to the sign, syntax, denotation, and signification. Made up of facilitations and their traces, it is a provisional articulation, a non-expressive rhythm. Plato *(Thaetetus)* speaks of a chora, anterior to the One, maternal, having borrowed the term from Democritus' and Leucippes' "rhythm" . . . The semiotic is a distinctive, non-expressive articulation; neither amorphous substance nor meaningful numbering. We imagine it in the cries, the vocalizing, the gestures of infants; it functions, in fact, in adult discourse as rhythm, prosody, plays on words, the non-sense of sense, laughter.[9]

Now although the semiotic is in Kristeva's words "connoted" as maternal and coextensive with the preoedipal, to take it for the specificity of women's writing *(écriture féminine)* would constitute a gross misunderstanding of Kristeva's theory. As she demonstrates repeatedly throughout both *Révolution dans le langage poétique* and *Polylogue,* semiotic breaks in and primacy over the symbolic characterize the avant-garde texts of such writers as Mallarmé, Lautréamont, and Artaud. This is not to say that the feminine does not enjoy a privileged relationship with the semiotic, for it does, but only in nonartistic, nontextual forms: for Kristeva, pregnancy and childbirth have been historically, in our culture, the female equivalent of (avant-garde) art: "The speaker reaches this limit, this requisite of sociality, only by virtue of a particular, discursive practice called 'art'. A woman also attains it (and in our society, *especially*) through the strange form of split symbolization (threshold of language and instinctual drives, of the 'symbolic' and the 'semiotic') of which giving birth consists."[10]

What Kristeva elaborates then is not a theory about the female imagination (or imaginary), rather—and therein lies her unique contribution to feminist theory—a specifically female theory, one which must be seen as a response and an alternative to the most pervasive and insidious form of idealism in our time: structuralism. In the face of a powerful ideology of scientific neutrality, of an eerily disembodied, neutered linguistics, Kristeva proclaims the indelible imprint of the body on or in language, and in so doing, associates the practice of a feminist psychoanalytic criticism with a return to Freud potentially more radical than Lacan's. Whatever Kristeva's own misgivings about paranoia—she generally equates it with male homosexuality and "logical unity,"[11] though in her more recent writings she has stressed the part played by the repression and recuperation of female paranoia in the history of religion—[12] her own writings offer an impressive and precious confirmation of the connection between female paranoia and the body dramatized by Freud's patient.

THE VAGINAL VS. THE CLITORAL

Let us now return to Freud's text. As I noted above, Freud's startling hypothesis—the noise allegedly heard by the patient was nothing but a projection of the throbbing of her clitoris—is rich in implications; we have examined, however briefly, one of these implications—female theory is grounded in the body. Now, what of the others? The second is both more obvious and more problematic than the first: it is that female theory is clitoral. The distinction between body and clitoris is not, I would emphasize, merely a heuristic device enlisted to facilitate my discussion of Freud's text; it is fundamental to my understanding of that text and to the privilege I accord it in the elaboration of my own theory. As Rosolato remarks: "The faintly perceived clitoral excitation remains isolated, enigmatic in its suspension, *separate*."[13]

With the clitoris we enter the realm of speculation, for no *evidence* (leaving behind the scopic economy so inimical to women) can be marshaled in support of my provocative extrapolation from Freud's unconfirmed interpretation of the patient's delusion—a sort of paranoia in the third power—with its distinctly clinical overtones. In the absence of a Masters and Johnson type of study of text pleasure, how can one hope to distinguish between the "vaginal" and the "clitoral" schools of feminist theory? And what is to be gained by adopting this distinction? Before venturing into this truly "dark continent," I would like to take two steps backward, to situate my enquiry, and thereby to mitigate—if I can—its outrageousness. The notion that there might be something like an erotics of theory flows naturally from Roland Barthes' notion of "the pleasure of the text": thus, to some extent, the vaginal/clitoral paradigm may be said to be modeled on Barthes' pleasure/jouissance opposition. Now both Kristeva and Irigaray confidently and repeatedly assert that female theory is intimately bound up with jouissance, that is, with the most intense form of sexual pleasure. In one of the rare passages where Kristeva comments explicitly on the specific vocation of female theoreticians, she writes:

> It is perhaps not indifferent that it is left up to a woman subject to maintain here—and elsewhere—this frustrating discourse of heterogeneity. Since everyone knows that it is impossible to know what a woman wants, since she wants a master, she comes to represent that which is negative within the homogeneity of the community: "the eternal irony of the tribe." She is able to ironize communal homonymy because: "in her vocation as an individual and in her pleasure, her interest is centered on the universal and remains alien to the particularity of desire." Psychoanalysis would say that this means that she is bound up with jouissance (the "universal"—the impossible) which she distinguishes from the body ("particularity," the locus of "desire" and "pleasure"), all the while knowing that there is no jouissance other than that of the body ("particularity"). In other words, her knowledge is the knowledge of jouissance ("centered on the universal"), beyond the pleasure principle (the pleasure of the body, be it perverse).[14]

The question then becomes: does jouissance designate female orgasm in general, clitoral as well as vaginal, or rather strictly the vaginal, which has, at least since Freud, been held to be the specifically female form of orgasm. In *Des Chinoises,* Kristeva clearly locates the mother's jouissance in the vagina; as for Irigaray, in Carolyn Greenstein Burke's words, her "fable of the generation of meaning" is "vaginal."[15] It would appear then, on the basis of this all too brief survey, that there is little or nothing in contemporary French feminist psychoanalytic theory to support my contention that female theory is clitoral; indeed, what little work has been done in this area (or zone) tends to valorize the vagina (or, as we have seen earlier, the womb). Prominent as it is, the "throbbing clitoris" in Freud's text remains enigmatic and isolated.

Or does it? Perhaps we have arrived at this impasse because we have adopted the wrong approach. In order to proceed, we must retrace our steps and rephrase our question: which is not what is the locus of jouissance—for it seems quite clear that implicitly jouissance is vaginal—but rather why recent French feminist psychoanalytic theory has tended to valorize the vagina and what are the consequences of this valorization. To these questions I would answer as follows: the valorization of the vagina is for all practical purposes bound up with a theory of production of avant-garde feminist texts, the examples of the so called *écriture féminine*. It goes hand in hand with a preoccupation with the ineffable, the unnamable, for as Eugénie Lemoine-Luccioni writes: "It is to the extent that she experiences jouissance, that she is silent. There are no words to say jouissance."[16] The dangers of this valorization of the vaginal mode of production are graphically illustrated by Lacan's evocation of Saint Theresa as represented by Bernini: "you have only to go and look at Bernini's statue in Rome to understand immediately that she's coming, there is no doubt about it. And what is her *jouissance,* her *coming* from? It is clear that the essential testimony of the mystics is that they are experiencing it but know nothing about it."[17] Finally, the vaginal theoreticians are always running the risk of seeing their writings recuperated by metaphysical thinkers like Lacan.

Now, obviously, to valorize the clitoris is also a risky enterprise; the paranoiac model is as fraught with pitfalls as the hysterical model which underlies the vaginal school of female theory. There is first and foremost the Freudian assimilation of the clitoral and the phallic (see epigraph supra) to be contended with: if French feminists—in contradistinction to American feminists and sexologists—have tended to valorize the vaginal form of jouissance, it is at least in part to lay claim to their difference, turning Freud's normative view of female sexuality into a positivity. There is further the argument that by emphasizing the clitoris one remains locked into male dichotomies: why *oppose* the clitoral and the vaginal, instead of stressing their complementarity?

To answer these important questions we must begin by considering the place of the clitoris in contemporary theory, for, however surprising this may sound to some, the clitoris lies at the heart or the center of an important polemic between Jacques Lacan and Jacques Derrida. It may be recalled that in his righting of Lacan's wrong reading of Poe's *The Purloined Letter*, Derrida points out that one of the most telling traces of Lacan's great and unacknowledged debt to Marie Bonaparte's psychobiographical analysis of that particular text involves an unmistakable allusion to a note in Bonaparte, regarding Baudelaire's mistranslation of the line describing the exact location of the purloined letter which, writes Poe, hangs "from a little brass knob just beneath the middle of the mantlepiece." First Bonaparte, then Lacan:

> Baudelaire translates: *"suspendu . . . à un petit bouton de cuivre au-dessus de la cheminée."* The imprecision of Baudelaire's translation, as far as this sentence is concerned, is obvious: in particular, "beneath" is translated by "au-dessus" ("above"), which is completely wrong.
>
> Look! Between the cheeks of the fireplace, there's the object already in reach of a hand the ravager has but to extend . . . The question of deciding whether he seizes it above the mantel piece as Baudelaire translates, or beneath it, as in the original text, may be abandoned without harm to the inferences of those whose profession is grilling [aux inférences de la cuisine].[18]

Derrida's response is that, on the contrary, the question of the correct translation is of the essence, because *"on* the mantelpiece, the letter could not have been 'between the cheeks of the fireplace,' 'between the legs of the fireplace' "[19] as Lacan states. Is Lacan's presumed rivalry with Bonaparte a sufficient explanation of his cavalier dismissal of a question of decisive importance for his thesis? I think not. Finally, as Derrida almost inadvertently suggests, what is significant is not so much what Lacan steals from Bonaparte, as what he misses altogether. And that is the meaning she attributes to the little brass knob in a brief allusion which, notes Derrida, "the Seminar does not echo" and which reads: "We have here, in fact, what is almost an anatomical chart, from which not even the clitoris (or brass knob) is omitted."[20]

What bearing does this polemic have on our inquiry? Simply this: it demonstrates that the clitoris is coextensive with the detail. The clitoral school of feminist criticism might then well be identified by its practice of a hermeneutics focused on the detail, which is to say on those details of the female anatomy generally ignored by male critics and which significantly influence our reading of the texts in which they appear.[21] A particularly apt (but by no means unique) example of the kind of detail I am referring to is to be found in the least commented upon of the three tales that make up Poe's Dupin trilogy, *The Mystery of Marie Roget*, a tale of rape and murder which, not coincidentally I would argue, also contains Poe's most explicit theory of the detail, as indicated by its last sentence: "It may be sufficient here to say that it forms one of the infinite series of mistakes which arise in the path of Reason through her propensity for seeking truth in *detail*."[22] Which is, of course, exactly what Dupin does, emphasizing in the process two aspects of the detail:

1. its prominence: thus Dupin remarks in a sentence which could easily be superimposed on the conclusion quoted supra: "I have therefore observed that it is by prominences above the plane of the ordinary, that reason feels her way, if at all, in her search for the true" (p. 180);

2. its marginality: "experience has shown, and a true philosophy will always show, that a vast, perhaps the larger, portion of truth arises from the seemingly irrelevant." In keeping with this principle, Dupin informs the narrator, he will, "discard the interior points of the tragedy, and concentrate our attention on the outskirts" (p. 191).

This last word should be taken quite literally for, as Dupin goes on to demonstrate, the solution of the mystery of Marie Roget involves precisely drawing the correct inferences from the peculiar state of her *outer skirts:* "The dress was much torn and otherwise disordered. In the outer garment, a slip, about a foot wide, had been torn off. It was wound three times around the waist, and secured by a sort of hitch in the back" (p. 174). This detail is repeated several times in the course of the narrative, but it is only when Dupin offers his reconstruction of the events, that this detail is raised to textual (as well as referential) prominence by a combination of repetition and italicization:

> My inference is this. The solitary murderer, having borne the corpse for some distance . . . by means of the bandage *hitched* around its middle, found the weight, in this mode of procedure, too much for his strength. He resolved to drag the burden . . . With this object in view, it became necessary to attach

something like a rope to one of the extremities. It could be best attached about the neck, where the head would prevent its slipping off. And now the murderer bethought him, unquestionably, of the bandage about the loins. He would have used this, but for its volution about the corpse, the *hitch* which embarassed it, and the reflection that it had not been "torn off" from the garment. It was easier to tear a new slip from the petticoat. He tore it, made it fast about the neck, and so *dragged* his victim to the brink of the river. (p. 202)

For Dupin, the hitch (as well as the knot around the neck) serve as incontrovertible proof of the singularity of Marie's assassin: a gang would surely not have resorted to such a clumsy contrivance to transport a body. For the reader, the hitch appears as a kind of marker, a signal, in a word: a detail jutting out above the plane surface of the text, providing the would-be interpreter or literary detective with a "handle" on the text. Now this detail is quite conspicuously bound up, as it were, with the female anatomy, for as a curious slippage in the text indicates, the hitch surrounds not so much the waist, as the "loins" of the victim; indeed, the word "rape" never appears in the text, rather we find such ambiguous expressions as "brutal violence" (p. 174) or "appalling outrage" (p. 179). In this tale whose invariant might well be said to be *translation*,[23] the hitch serves, in the end, not so much as a means of moving the corpse from one place to another, as it does as a *displacement* of the sexual crime. The hitch designates the locus of violence, while at the same time the use of the word "bandage" attests to a wish to cover up and bind the wound. It is, in degraded form, the veil that male authors are forever drawing over the female sexual organs, thereby creating mysteries. The real mystery of Marie Roget lies hidden beneath the multiple circumvolutions of the text; the hitch is, to parody Freud, the navel of the tale.

In conclusion, I would suggest that if the rhetorical figure of vaginal theory is metonymy—as Irigaray would have it—or metaphor—as Kristeva would argue—the figure of clitoral theory is synecdoche, the detail-figure. It is, I would suggest further, no accident that Lacan in his re-writing of Roman Jakobson's essay on "Two Types of Language and Two Types of Aphasic Disturbance" should not only entirely do away with synecdoche (subordinated to metonymy in Jakobson's essay), but more important, offer as a privileged example of metonymy, a syntagm—"Thirty sails"—which has since antiquity served to illustrate synecdoche.[24] Clearly in Lacan's binary structural linguistics, with its emphasis on the perfect symmetry of metaphor and metonymy, there is no room for this third trope, just as in his rewriting of Bonaparte's analysis of Poe, there is no room for the knob-clitoris. Let us now praise synecdoche!

Notes

1. FOR A RESTRICTED THEMATICS

"For a Restricted Thematics: Writing, Speech, and Difference in *Madame Bovary*" started out as a lecture I gave at the Maison Française of Columbia University in 1975, as well as before the Alliance Française of New Brunswick, N.J. It was first published in *Littérature* (1976), and then reprinted in translation and with a postscript in Hester Eisenstein and Alice Jardine, eds., *The Future of Difference* (Boston: Hall, 1980).

1. In what may pass for the first such history, Jonathan Culler's *Structuralist Poetics*, the connection posited here between structural semantics and thematism is also made, albeit in an interrogative mode. In reference to the work of Greimas, Culler remarks somewhat rhetorically: "the crucial question is what claims might be made for an analysis of this sort. What is the difference, for example, between the status of the results Greimas has obtained and that of more traditional analyses of imagery as undertaken, for example, by Jean-Pierre Richard?" (p. 84).

2. Roland Barthes, *S/Z*, p. 93; Jacques Derrida, *Of Grammatology*, p. 152; Gilles Deleuze, *Proust et les signes* and *Logique du sens*. All translations unless otherwise indicated are mine (trans.).

3. Deleuze, "Table ronde," p. 91; Barthes, *S/Z*, p. 160; Derrida, *Dissemination*, p. 65.

4. Derrida, *Dissemination*, p. 65. The privileging of the textile has become something of a signature of one member of the "Yale School," J. Hillis Miller. See "Ariachne's Broken Whoof," *Georgia Review* (Spring 1977), 31:44–60.

5. Jean-Pierre Richard, *Proust et le monde sensible*, p. 221.

6. Derrida, *Dissemination*, p. 63.

7. Barthes, *The Pleasure of the Text*, p. 64.

8. Sigmund Freud, "Femininity," *New Introductory Lectures on Psychoanalysis*, in *The Standard Edition of the Complete Psychological Works of Sigmund Freud*, 22:132.

9. Jean-Paul Sartre, *L'Idiot de la famille*, 1:703.

10. Charles Baudelaire, *Oeuvres complètes*, p. 652.

11. Gustave Flaubert, *Madame Bovary*, pp. 40–41. All page numbers refer to the Norton edition. Cf. Claude Duchet, "Romans et Objets: L'Exemple de *Madame Bovary*." To Duchet's remarks about the cigar case I would add only the fol-

lowing: if in the last chapter of the first part of the novel the cigar case is opposed to the wedding bouquet, in the novel in general it is opposed not to a manifest, but to a virtual object. In effect, the textile activity of the aristocratic Penelope who wove the luxury object is opposed to that of the proletarianized Penelope, Berthe, who, it must be remembered, ends up in a "cotton-mill" (p. 255). Thus Flaubert privileges weaving both as a model of textual production and as a means of closure; the Bovary's decline and Emma's failure translate into the transformation of the silk thread into the cotton thread, i.e., into the degradation—the "Manchesterization," as Duchet would say—of the Ariadne's thread.

12. Gustave Flaubert, *Madame Bovary*, p. 91. All page numbers for the French text refer to the Garnier-Flammarion edition.

13. Richard, *Proust*. p. 8.

14. René Girard, *Deceit, Desire, and the Novel*, p. 152.

15. Flaubert, *Sentimental Education*, pp. 92–93. Cf. in *Madame Bovary* this bit of dialogue between Emma and Léon: " 'That is why,' he said, 'I especially love the poets. I think verse is more tender than prose, and that it makes one weep more easily.' 'Still in the long-run it is tiring,' continued Emma, 'and now, on the contrary, I have come to love stories that rush breathlessly along, that frighten one' " (p. 59). This superimposition valorizes the invariant relationship which in Flaubert subordinates the speech/writing, poetry/prose paradigms to the man/woman paradigm, enabling us to establish the following equivalency: woman : man :: orators : writers :: prose : poetry. Moreover, this first conversation retroactively announces their sexual relationships: Emma's masculinity vs. Léon's femininity. The genres have a sex and each sex selects, prefers the complementary or supplementary genre-sex. We will return to this notion below.

16. This "survey"—partial but motivated—obviously cannot account for all the oral manifestations in the text. Among the main characters, Léon's omission is particularly conspicuous. Let us state briefly that the relations of Emma and Léon are marked by the seal of silence; either they do not talk to each other, or their words are not recounted: "Had they nothing else to say to one another? Yet their eyes were full of more serious speech, and while they forced themselves to find trivial phrases, they felt the same languor stealing over them both; it was like the deep, continuous murmur of the soul dominating that of their voices" (p. 68); "She did not speak; he was silent, captivated by her silence, as he would have been by her speech" (p. 75); "Then they talked in low tones, and their conversation seemed the sweeter to them because it was unheard" (p. 71). All this will culminate in the coach scene. Léon is shy, and shyness is the degree-zero of speaking.

17. Claude Bremond, *Logique du récit*, p. 263.

18. Gérard Genette, "Proust et le langage indirect," p. 228.

19. Genette, *Mimologiques: Voyages en Cratylie*.

20. Hence the numerous similarities between the speech problematic in Flaubert and Constant, cf. Tzvetan Todorov, "Speech According to Constant," *The Poetics of Prose*, pp. 89–109.

21. Victor Brombert, *Flaubert par lui-même*, p. 59.

1. For a Restricted Thematics

22. Marcel Muller, *Les Voix narratives dans "la Recherche du temps perdu,"* pp. 8, 91–175. The question of Flaubertian *irony* (or in other words, of point of view) must be raised here, a question which creates what Barthes terms "a salutary discomfort of writing . . . for the very being of writing . . . is to keep the question *Who is speaking?* from ever being answered" (Barthes, *S/Z,* p. 140).

23. Girard, p. 149. Does the problematic case of Rodolph require the insertion of a new combination, a combination between types 1 and 3: encoding +, decoding +/−?

24. Girard, p. 9 and passim.

25. Obviously this sentence was written before Sandra M. Gilbert and Susan Gubar framed the question "Is a pen a metaphorical penis?" (*The Madwoman in the Attic,* p. 3), thereby boldly inaugurating a new era in the study of the relationship between writing and sexual difference. This being said, the phallus is not a penis, however metaphorical—rather it is a symbol of the phallocentric order. Much of the difficulty feminists have in accepting the distinction Lacan makes between the penis and the phallus—which underlies the privilege he accords the phallus as lynchpin of the symbolic order—has to do with the fact that the penis/phallus relationship appears to be more iconic (Peirce) than purely symbolic.

26. Barthes, *The Pleasure of the Text,* p. 9. What I am suggesting here is that *Madame Bovary* stages the scene of its own production, a production which inextricably links writing to death. On the relationship of the corpse to figuration in Flaubert, see Eugenio Donato, "The Crypt of Flaubert," in Schor and Majewski, eds., *Flaubert and Postmodernism,* pp. 30–45.

27. See Raymonde Debray-Genette, "Les Figures du récit dans *Un coeur simple.*"

28. For a discussion of the diverse symbolic readings of the blind man see P. M. Wetherill, *"Madame Bovary's* Blind Man: Symbolism in Flaubert."

29. Luce Irigaray, *Speculum de l'autre femme,* p. 106.

30. See Genette, *Figures III,* pp. 246–41, and Jacques Neefs, "La figuration réaliste," p. 472.

31. To footnote "jouissance" is at this belated poststructuralist moment to perform a highly ritualized gesture. This then is the obligatory metatextual note on jouissance. The difficulties in finding a suitable English equivalent to the French *jouissance* were to my knowledge first articulated by Roland Barthes' translators; see Richard Howard, "Notes on the Text," in Barthes, *The Pleasure of the Text,* and Stephen Heath, "Translator's Note," in Barthes, *Image-Music-Text.* In the first instance the translator has chosen to translate the untranslatable word throughout by "bliss," a decision criticized by Heath, who adopts a more complex strategy which involves resorting to "a series of words which in different contexts can contain at least some of [the] force" (p. 9) of the original French term. I have opted for yet another unsatisfying solution, that favored by other (feminist) translators (Michèle Freeman, Alice Jardine, Parveen Adams): the nontranslation of the untranslatable. Thus, for example in her "Translator's Note," Jacqueline Rose explains that she has left such terms as *signifiance, objet a,* and *jouissance* "in

the original . . . in order to allow their meaning to develop from the way in which they operate." *Feminine Sexuality: Jacques Lacan and the 'école freudienne,'* Juliet Mitchell and Jacqueline Rose, eds., p. 59. For an illuminating and pertinent study of the peculiar linguistic status of jouissance, see Jane Gallop, "Beyond the Jouissance Principle," *Representations* (1984), no. 7: 110–115.

32. See Genette, "Silences de Flaubert," *Figures*.

33. For a magnificent demystification of this entire passage the reader should consult Sartre, *L'Idiot*, 1:454–61.

34. Flaubert, *Extraits de la correspondance*, p. 71.

35. See Barthes, "Flaubert and the Sentence," in *A Barthes Reader*, p. 302.

36. Sartre, *L'Idiot*, 2:1618.

37. Flaubert, *Extraits de la correspondance*, p. 30.

38. Genette, "Table ronde," pp. 91–92.

2. SMILES OF THE SPHINX

A much abbreviated version of this text was presented at the First Colloquium in Nineteenth-Century French Studies held at SUNY at Fredonia; it appeared in the Special Issue of *Romantisme* entitled "Mythes et Représentations de la Femme" (1976).

1. The quotation is from Michel Serres, *Feux et signaux de brume: Zola*, p. 254; the allusions are to, in the order of their appearance: Jean Borie, *Zola et les mythes* and *Le tyran timide*; Chantal Jennings, "Zola féministe?" *Les Cahiers naturalistes* (1972), 44:172–187 and (1973), 45:1–22; and Anna Krakowski, *La condition de la femme dans l'oeuvre d'Emile Zola* (Paris: Nizet, 1974). For a further elaboration of some of these introductory remarks, see my review article on *Le tyran timide* and *La condition de la femme* entitled "Mother's Day: Zola's Women," *Diacritics* (Winter 1975), 5:11–17.

2. Sigmund Freud, "Femininity," in *The Standard Edition of the Complete Psychological Works of Sigmund Freud*, 22:116. All future references will be in the text and give volume and page numbers. For more on the pre-Oedipus and its relationship to Lacan's Imaginary, see note 2 of chapter 5.

3. I am drawing here on some remarks by Otto Rank regarding the Sphinx, in *The Trauma of Birth*, p. 144. In what concerns the (bi-) sexuality of the Sphinx—an important issue which must be raised—I find these remarks by Gilbert Durand particularly useful: "Among the Carribeans and the Iroquois, femininity is linguistically relegated to the side of the animal; it is semantically coextensive with animality. Similarly mythology feminizes such animalistic monsters as the Sphinx and the Sirens," *Les Structures anthropologiques de l'imaginaire*, p. 114. All translations are mine except where otherwise noted. See also Claude Lévi-Strauss, "The Structural Study of Myth," in *Structural Anthropology*, note 6, pp. 227–228, re the femininity of the Sphinx. Lévi-Strauss, following Marie Delcourt to whom he refers and defers, describes the Sphinx as a "female monster," and further, as a "phallic mother par excellence." Unrelated to the above, but in connection with my approach I would cite Philippe Hamon's congruent observation that "the

2. Smiles of the Sphinx

'Sphinx-like young girl' " is "an obsessive theme in Zola," "Du savoir dans le texte," p. 493.

4. Emile Zola, *Oeuvres complètes*, 12:701.

5. René Girard, *Violence and the Sacred*, p. 49 et passim. For more on the crisis of distinctions, see note 2 of chapter 4.

6. The proliferation of narratives featuring these borderline cases is matched by an equal number of critical texts of which Roland Barthes' *S/Z* remains the privileged example. Other critical commentaries dealing with these forms of problematic sexuality include: Pierre Albouy, "Le mythe de l'androgyne dans *Mademoiselle de Maupin*," *Revue de l'histoire littéraire de la France* (1972), 72:600–608, and Maurice Laugaa, "Polygraphe hermaphrodite," *Digraphe* (1974), 4:89–102.

7. Angus Wilson, *Emile Zola*, p. 58.

8. Emile Zola, *Zest for Life*, p. 36; *La Joie de vivre* in *Les Rougon-Macquart*, 3:838. All future references to the *Rougon-Macquart* will be to the Pléiade edition.

9. Luce Irigaray, *Speculum de l'autre femme*, p. 7 et passim.

10. Roland Barthes, *The Pleasure of the Text*, p. 32.

11. Roland Barthes, *S/Z*, p. 32.

12. Emile Zola, *Nana*, p. 24. All references to the English translation of *Nana* are to the Penguin edition.

13. Emile Zola, *A Page of Love*, 1:110.

14. Philippe Hamon, "Zola, romancier de la transparence," *Europe* (1968), 468–469: 386. On one level this article serves as an intertext to my study of Zola and the riddle of femininity. Our dialogue is pursued further in Hamon, *Le Personnel du roman: Le système des personnages dans les Rougon-Macquart d'Emile Zola* (Geneva: Droz, 1983), in particular, pp. 296–302.

15. Cf. Madame de Merteuil's celebrated phrase in Letter LXXXI: "I did not desire to enjoy, I wanted to know," Choderlos de Laclos, *Dangerous Acquaintances: Les Liaisons dangereuses*, p. 224.

16. Let us note that in this scene ignorance is contagious, thus when Henri, who is mystified by this rendezvous agreed to by Hélène at the very point at which he had given up on possessing her, asks: "But why this letter? . . . where are we?" Hélène answers: "Don't ask me any questions, don't ever seek to find out" ("Mais pourquoi cette lettre? . . . où sommes nous?"—"Ne m'interrogez pas, ne cherchez jamais à savoir" [2:1021]).

17. Cf. "mère Fétu": "Perhaps I've been poisoned . . . There is a woman in the rue de l'Annonciation whom a pharmacist killed by giving her the wrong drug" ("Je suis peut-être bien empoisonnée . . . Il y a une femme, rue de l'Annonciation, qu'un pharmacien a tuée en lui donnant une drogue pour une autre" [2:828]).

18. The implications of this feminist critique of Barthes' patriarchal poetics—which have been accepted uncritically by many otherwise canny male critics—are at least threefold: first it signifies that, as we argue here, the hermeneutic code is "inapplicable" to male-authored texts centered on the preoedipal mother-daughter relationship. Second—and a fortiori—that it cannot be applied to women's writing in general without risking missing its specific modes of plotting altogether.

2. Smiles of the Sphinx

On female plotting, see Nancy Miller, "Emphasis Added: Plots and Plausibilities in Women's Fiction." Finally, the unmasking of the masculinist bias in Barthes' notion of the hermeneutic code lends credence to the argument that reader response is gender-specific. Hélène's jouissance in delaying the moment of closure of her reading of *Ivanhoe* would make of her a typical female reader. Thus in an interesting study on TV soap operas by Tania Modleski, "The Search for Tomorrow in Today's Soap Operas: Notes on a Feminine Narrative," Modleski argues that women's text-pleasure, unlike men's, does not privilege climax and closure, rather deferral and interminability.

19. Victor Brombert, *Flaubert par lui-même*, p. 83.

20. Gustave Flaubert, *Salammbô*, p. 351, and *Salammbô* (Garnier-Flammarion), p. 296.

21. Honoré de Balzac, *The Wild Ass's Skin*, p. 125; and *La Peau de chagrin*, p. 160. All future references will be included in the text.

22. Hélène Cixous, "The Laugh of the Medusa."

23. This study would be incomplete if mention were not made of what is most probably the finest example of hieratic fiction in nineteenth-century French literature, the novel which inspired Flaubert to write *Salammbô*, Théophile Gautier's *Roman de la momie*. It is, incidentally, in part to this text that I owe the title of this chapter, for the mummy's mask is described as "smiling with an indescribable sphinx-like smile," *The Romance of a Mummy*, in *Works of Gautier*, 3:51. Discovered at the conclusion of arduous excavations which lead the archeologists (here the archetypal representatives of imperialist masculine knowledge) to wander about in a veritable underground labyrinth, swaddled in a series of "envelopes" (sarcophagus, casket, casing, wrappings), the mummy exemplifies the insistence of the enigma, as well as the imbrication of the woman of stone and the palimpsest. Thus, below the layers of secrets, the archeologists uncover not only a mummy, but above all a manuscript: "Suddenly a papyrus roll concealed between the side and arm of the mummy caught the doctor's eye" (p. 64). This *supplement* is supposed to reveal the mummy's secret, but it turns out to be a particularly twisted snare. In keeping with the laws of the hieratic code we have articulated, the final chapter only foils our expectations by starting the inquiry instituted in the Prologue all over again; despite the rape whose victim it is, the mummy preserves its most intimate secret from hermeneutic appropriation: "Was it Pharaoh or Poëri she regretted? Kakevou the scribe does not tell us, and Dr. Rumphius, who translated the hieroglyph of the Egyptian grammat, did not venture to settle the question" (p. 295). Cf. Ross Chambers, "Gautier et le complexe de Pygmalion," *Revue d'histoire littéraire de la France* (1972), 72:641–658, in particular pp. 643–644, and Michael Danahy, "Le roman est-il chose femelle?" in particular p. 89.

24. At least that is what I argue in an article entitled "Mythes des origines, origine des mythes: *La Fortune des Rougon*," *Les Cahiers naturalistes* (1978): 124–134, as well as in the initial chapter of my book, *Zola's Crowds*, from which this article is adapted.

25. See Auguste Dezalay, "Les Mystères de Zola."

3. UNE VIE OR THE NAME OF THE MOTHER

"Une Vie or the Name of the Mother," was never delivered as a lecture. It first appeared in *Littérature* (1977).

1. Jacques Derrida, *Dissemination*, pp. 262–264.

2. Jean Paris, "Maupassant et le contre-récit," *Le Point aveugle*.

3. Guy de Maupassant, *Mont-Oriol*, p. 134. All references to the French text refer to the Bibliothèque Marabout edition. *Complete Works of Guy de Maupassant*, 8:144–145. For the English text, the references are to the Brainard edition.

4. "He found it in a novel by Léon Cladel, *Ompdrailles ou le tombeau des lutteurs*. In that work it is the name of one of the characters." Critical Appendix, *Mont-Oriol*, p. 179.

5. Cf. the etymology of the name Obardi: "Her real name, her maiden name—for she has remained a maid except on the score of her innocence—is Octavie Bardin from which Obardi is derived by keeping the first letter of her name and dropping the last one of her surname." *Yvette*, in Maupassant, *Contes et nouvelles*, 2:483. All references to Maupassant's short stories refer to the two-volume Albert-Marie Schmidt edition. Translations are mine except where otherwise noted.

6. Jean-Pierre Richard, "Céline et Marguerite," p. 934.

7. For an extended reflection on the name of the mother and the writer's signature, see Jacques Derrida, *Glas* (Paris: Galilée, 1974), the Genet column. A "biographeme" is perhaps here not entirely inappropriate: as for Maupassant, the syllable *or* is for me highly cathected. It both figures in my patronym and refers to the privileged material of the parental art and craft: goldsmithing.

8. See Philippe Hamon, "Un discours contraint," pp. 426–427.

9. See Pierre Fauchery, *La Destinée féminine dans le roman européen du dix-huitième siècle, 1713–1807: Essai de gynécomythie romanesque* (Paris: Armand Colin, 1972). The overwhelming femininity of biographical fiction in the French nineteenth-century novel is rooted in the biologization of woman's life: a woman's life story is the story of her/the body and thus can be charted from birth to death, whereas a man's is coextensive with his successful or failed social integration and thus doomed to premature closure. There are few grandfathers in phallocentric fiction.

10. See Hélène Cixous in Catherine Clément and Hélène Cixous, *La jeune née*, pp. 129 et passim. The play on proper/property is featured in Derrida's critique of Lévi-Strauss in the "Battle of the Proper Names" section of *Of Grammatology*, in particular p. 112.

11. Claude Duchet, "Signifiance et insignifiance: le discours italique de *Madame Bovary*," p. 362.

12. Cf. Paris' comment: "the final prophecy included in Berthe: loss *(perte)*" (*Le Point*, p. 189). Pushed to its logical extreme, one might say that all women are called Loss (Perte), since, according to Eugénie Lemoine-Luccioni, loss is woman's lot: "Rather than the anxiety of castration, woman experiences the anx-

3. Une Vie *or the Name of the Mother*

iety of *partition*. She truly lives under the sign of abandonment: mother, father, children, husband, penis, all leave her" (*Partage des femmes*, p. 71).

13. Maupassant, *Une Vie*, p. 22; emphasis added except where otherwise noted. All references to the French text are to the Livre de Poche edition. *A Woman's Life*, p. 17. The English references are to the Penguin edition.

14. Cf. this passage from a short story entitled *Un Vieux*. "He had, moreover, a special way of emphasizing personal pronouns referring to all the parts of his person or even to things that belonged to him. When he said: 'My eyes, my legs, my arms, my hands,' it was clear that one should make no mistake about it: these organs were not just anybody's. But this distinction stood out particularly when he spoke of his doctor: '*My doctor.*' You would have thought this doctor belonged only to him, had been created for him alone, to take care of his illnesses and nothing else, and was superior to all other doctors in the universe without any exception."

15. Maupassant, *Pierre et Jean*. All references to the French text are to the Livre de Poche edition. Maupassant, *Pierre and Jean*, in *Complete Works*, 4:27. All references to the English text are to the Brainard edition.

16. On this point I am in agreement with André Vial who writes: "*Une Vie* visibly combines the formula and the tonality of *Un Cœur simple* and those of *L'Education sentimentale*, but reduced to the strictly individual element . . . From *L'Education sentimentale*, *Une Vie* adopts the idea and the execution of a gradual elaboration of the intimate structures of a moral constitution . . ." *Guy de Maupassant et l'art du roman*, p. 356 and 357, respectively.

17. It is important to recognize that the pleasant *(dulce)* and useful *(utile)* constitute categories of Maupassant's thought. Thus woman is considered an object with two mutually exclusive purposes: "He considered woman as a *useful institution* for such men as required a well-kept house and children, *or* as a *pleasant toy* for such as desired the pastime of lovemaking" ("Il considérait les femmes comme un *objet d'utilité* pour ceux qui veulent une maison bien tenue et des enfants, comme un *objet d'agrément* relatif pour ceux qui cherchent des passe-temps d'amour"). *Notre Cœur*, 7:39/p. 57. It follows that there exists for woman as well as for man, a double standard: "Marriage and love have nothing to do with each other . . . Marriage, you see, is a law, whereas love is an instinct which drives us now to the left, now to the right" ("Le mariage et l'amour n'ont rien à voir ensemble . . . Le mariage c'est une loi, vois-tu, et l'amour c'est un instinct qui nous pousse tantôt à droite, tantôt à gauche"). *Jadis* in *Contes*, 1:599. Let us note that, though immutable, this binary opposition is not without mediating instances: such as the female breast (metonym for femininity) in the *Dictionary of Medical Sciences* definition quoted and commented upon by one of Maupassant's characters: " 'Woman's breast can be considered an object of *both* use and pleasure.' Let us drop the notion of usefulness and retain only that of pleasure. If it were solely destined to nurture the young would it have that adorable shape which calls irresistably for caresses" (" 'Le sein peut être considéré chez la femme comme un objet en même temps d'utilité et d'agrément'. Supprimons, si vous voulez, l'utilité et ne gardons que l'agrément. Aurait-il cette forme adorable qui appelle irrésistiblement la caresse s'il n'était destiné qu'à nourrir les enfants"). *La Caresse, Contes*, 1:624.

3. Une Vie *or the Name of the Mother*

18. Cixous, *La jeune née*, p. 276.

19. Maupassant, *Notre Cœur*, p. 18. Cf. *Enragée? Contes*, 2:880–887. To get some idea of the place wedding nights occupy in male fantasies of the period, it is interesting to read Wladimir Granoff's analysis of the young Freud's "deflo-ration fantasies" in *La pensée et le féminin*, pp. 335–340.

20. Loving and drinking are equivalent in Maupassant (cf. the proverb: "Once a drunkard, always a drunkard—once a lover, always a lover" ["Qui a bu boira—qui a aimé aimera"], *La Rempailleuse, Contes*, 1:650), when they are not contig-uous: thus the topography of the brothel *(La Maison Tellier, Le Port)* insures the repeated passage from café to bed.

21. Once again I am in agreement with Vial who writes that Rosalie "reap-pears at the very moment when Tante Lison's body is swallowed up by the grave" *(Maupassant, p. 516)*.

22. To this exception which confirms the rule one should add another: *La Chevelure*, where instead of a scriptural relic the narrator discovers a mass of hair, that is a fetish-relic: "I would lock myself up alone with it to feel it against my skin, to sink into it, to kiss and bite it. I would roll it around my face, I drank it, I plunged my gaze in its golden waves, to see the daylight filtered through it" ("Je m'enfermais seul avec elle pour la sentir sur ma peau, pour enfoncer mes lèvres dedans, pour la baiser, la mordre. Je l'enroulais autour de mon visage, je la buvais, je noyais mes yeux dans son onde dorée, afin de voir le jour blond, à tra-vers"). *Contes*, 2:940–941. *La Chevelure* is, of course, the story of a madman put away for "morbid erotomania" *(ibid., p. 935)*: it is then only within the ulti-mately reassuring framework of the madhouse that Maupassant can give free reign to his necrophiliac fantasy.

23. Can one do without biographical information when one uses a "psycho-critical approach"? This nagging question returns insistently after its long repres-sion. At the very least it seems imperative to take into account all manner of au-tobiographical texts (diaries, journals, letters, etc.)—which we now know to be as fictional as fiction is true—while respecting the self-sufficiency of the fictional text. A preamble to this very brief quotation from one of Maupassant's letters to his mother: "Try to find me short story subjects." *Correspondance inédite de Guy de Maupassant*, p. 16.

24. Lemoine-Luccioni, *Partage*, p. 40.

25. See Michael Danahy, "Le roman est-il chose femelle?" *Poétique*, pp. 91 and 95–96.

26. For an exhaustive account of the features that allow one to measure the importance of a character, see Philippe Hamon, "Pour un statut sémiotique du personnage."

27. Jean Borie, *Zola et les mythes*, pp. 87–94.

28. Jean-Louis Bachellier, "Sur-Nom," p. 70. A note in the same article, inci-dentally, admirably corroborates my hypothesis concerning the Name of the Mother, while at the same time making explicit the theoretical issues raised by this notion: "whence, on another level, the letter i which scans the first and last names of the female characters in the M.P. *[Les Mystères de Paris]*. That this letter

also scans the name of Eugène Sue's mother (Marie-Sophie Tison de Reilly) should force us to rethink the articulation of the so-called biographical text and the text itself. Significant locuses of the mother's desire."
29. Hamon, p. 145.

4. L'ENSORCELÉE: THE SCANDALIZED WOMAN

"*L'Ensorcelée:* The Scandalized Woman" was commissioned for the "Perspectives in Mimesis" issue of *Modern Language Notes*, dedicated to René Girard (1979); it was also delivered in a 20-minute-paper form at the Fourth Annual Colloquium in Nineteenth-Century French Studies held at the University of Michigan, East Lansing in 1978.

1. Barbey d'Aurevilly, *Bewitched*, p. 109; *L'Ensorcelée* (Paris: Garnier-Flammarion, 1966), p. 121. All subsequent references to these will be included in text, Harper and Garnier-Flammarion editions respectively.

2. This is an "adaptation" of the triple schema René Girard provides in *Des Choses cachées depuis la fondation du monde*, p. 166. All further references to this text will be included in the text. All translations mine except where otherwise noted. Girard's fullest account of the basic syntax of sacrifice appears in *Violence and the Sacred*. For Girard violence and the sacred are inseparable, indeed religion is a sublimated violence and that sublimation takes the form of a sacrificial ritual. It is possible to tease out of *Violence and the Sacred* the following reconstruction of the sacrificial scenario. In a first stage, sacrifice (of an animal or a human victim) functions smoothly as an efficacious means of catharsis for a community rent by aggression and conflict. Then, in a second stage, the sacrificial system breaks down. This "sacrificial crisis" consists in the collapse of those very distinctions which constitute the social order: e.g., the differences between man and god, man and beast, parent and child (incest), and, perhaps the most devastating of all, what Freud called the "small differences" between man and man (doubling). The sacrificial victim whose expulsion by death or exile brings an end to the rampant reciprocal violence of the sacrificial crisis is a *surrogate-victim:* the *pharmakos* or scapegoat is no more or less guilty than any other member of the community, and must be drawn from the margins of society to preclude a new outbreak of reciprocal violence in the form of revenge. Unanimously carried out by the community, the scapegoat's expulsion ushers in a new era of peace and harmony. This account is a summary of Girard's thesis that I provide in my *Zola's Crowds*, pp. 5–8.

3. Girard, pp. 139–145. I am using this expression in its widest application, following Girard's remark: "I am proposing . . . to extend to mythology properly speaking the type of interpretation universally accepted for persecution-texts only."

4. Hélène Cixous, in Catherine Clément and Hélène Cixous, *La jeune née*, p. 125.

5. Michel Serres, *Hermès IV: La Distribution*, p. 243; see pp. 240–251. If, as Serres emphasizes, the heath is a "space from before meaning" (p. 242)—I would argue that it constitutes a veritable protocol for plural readings—to read this text

4. L'Ensorcelée: *The Scandalized Woman*

in my perspective is to traverse this presemantic literary space in a direction different from Serres'. But, let us note, to the extent that this is a "non-Euclidean" space (p. 250), the intersection of "parallel" readings is plotted out in advance, indeed inevitable.

6. To be convinced of the violence of the specular—when it is not the specularity of violence—in *L'Ensorcelée*, one need only compare this episode to another which is inserted in a flashback that fills us in on Jeanne's genealogy. One day, Jeanne's mother, then a very young girl, is alone in the castle. A beggar comes to ask for alms. As she is going to get him something to eat, she sees in a "mirette" the false beggar preparing to murder her. Warned by the mirror, she forestalls the robber, thereby earning the nickname: Louisine-à-la-hache (Louisine-of-the-Hatchet) (pp. 101–104).

7. This Girardian paradigm is drawn from the "Interview" which appears in *Diacritics* (Spring 1978).

8. Barbey d'Aurevilly, *Un Prêtre marié*, p. 129.

9. Michael Riffaterre, *Essais de stylistique structurale* (Paris: Flammarion, 1971); A. J. Greimas, ed. *Essais de sémiotique poétique* (Paris: Larousse, 1972), pp. 18–19; Sigmund Freud, *The Interpretation of Dreams* (London: Hogarth, 1953), vol. 4–5; and Leo Spitzer, *Linguistics and Literary History: Essays in Stylistics* (Princeton: Princeton University Press, 1948), p. 19. Let us note that while according the same *status* to the detail as Spitzerean stylistics, Riffaterrian stylistics does not assign it the same *function:* see in Riffaterre, *Essais*, pp. 6, 45, and 120–121.

10. In a recent feminist critique of what she terms the "proud, patriarchal, and oppressively monolithic theory" of René Girard, Toril Moi has argued that, "Girard's theory of mimetic desire cannot account for feminine desire" ("The Missing Mother: The Oedipal Rivalries of René Girard," *Diacritics* [1982], 12:29, 21), because of Girard's evacuation of the mother from the oedipal triangle as well as of the preoedipal stage, presided over by the mother. Unquestionably, there is nothing specifically feminine about the desire fostered by Jeanne's imitation of Jehoël. On the contrary, one might even go so far as to maintain that when, as in this case, female desire is mediated by male desire, that female desire is ipso facto masculine and masculinizing. If Girard's model "works" so well for Jeanne, it is precisely because she is characterized as "virile."

11. Cf. in Nancy Miller's article, "Novels of Innocence: Fictions of Loss," the analysis of the destructive power of female innocence. The hypothesis that for Barbey the dissemination of scandal is the specifically feminine means of revenge is confirmed by one of the short stories that make up *Les Diaboliques*, "La vengeance d'une femme," where a noble woman revenges her husband's cruelty to her by becoming a prostitute and dragging his name in the mud.

12. Such is at least the meaning I attribute to the shepherd's ambivalent gesture: "before disappearing, the horrible shepherd had accomplished one of those deeds which, when they are not a pious duty, are a sacrilege. He had cut Jeanne's hair" ("avant de disparaître, l'horrible pâtre avait accompli sur le cadavre un de ces actes qui, quand ils ne sont pas un devoir pieux, sont un sacrilège. Il avait

4. L'Ensorcelée: *The Scandalized Woman*

coupé les cheveux de Jeanne" [pp. 207–208/199]). Cf. the outrage committed against la Clotte by the Blues: "they . . . sheared me in the market place" ("ils m'ont tousée sur la place du marché" [p. 136/143]).

13. See the "Interview" in *Diacritics,* pp. 38–43.

14. Reference is made here to the French saying: "un clou chasse l'autre," which is rendered by Harrap's as: "one memory drives out the memory of another" and "one fire drives out another's burning." The logic of the nail would then emphasize the exclusionary force of terms inscribed on the axis of substitution.

15. Jacques Lacan, *The Four Fundamental Concepts of Psycho-Analysis,* p. 188.

5. EUGENIE GRANDET: MIRRORS AND MELANCHOLIA

Madelon Gohlke graciously accepted an early version of this text for a section she chaired at the 1979 MLA, held in San Francisco. As a lecture it was presented in such diverse settings as Mount Holyoke College, the University of Vermont, the Alliance Française of Providence, R.I., and the Groupe de Travail Balzac at the Ecole Normale Supérieure in Paris.

1. I am referring here in turn to Fredric Jameson, "Imaginary and Symbolic in *La Rabouilleuse,*" *Social Sciences Information* 16 (1977): 59–81, and Jeffrey Mehlman, *A Structural Study of Autobiography.*

2. Though it is, as Jean Laplanche and J.-P. Pontalis, authors of the remarkable *The Language of Psychoanalysis,* remind us, "contrary to the spirit of Lacan's thought" to provide "strict definitions" of his key conceptual terms, because Lacan's thought, "refrains from establishing a fixed relationship between signifier and signified" ("Symbolic," *Yale French Studies,* 1972, 48:201–202, Peter Kussel and Jeffrey Mehlman, trs.), given the relative unfamiliarity of these terms and the extensive use I make of them throughout this article, a brief gloss is in order here. When I speak of the Imaginary I shall be referring to that psychic register which is synonymous with the exclusive, dual infant-mother relationship, what Freud calls the pre-Oedipus. However, as Lacan's choice of the word Imaginary indicates, his emphasis is on the prevalence of the image in the pre-Oedipus, on the manner in which the human subject's ego is constituted through a process of identification with images: the images of the other as self (mother) and of the self as other (mirror image). Because all inter- and intra-subjective relationships are rooted in narcissism and illusionism, the subject is prey to the lure of identification as well as to deathly struggles for prestige. The Symbolic register, equivalent to Freud's Oedipus, is presided over by the father and the cultural order he represents: the subject enters into the Symbolic order at the very moment when she is inscribed in the kinship system and is, as it were, reinscribed when she acquires language and, through the mediation of the father, takes her place in society. Whereas the Imaginary implies identity as well as identification, the Symbolic relies on difference, sexual (castration) as well as linguistic. The analogies I have drawn between Freud's pre-Oedipus/Oedipus and Lacan's Imaginary/Symbolic should not obscure a crucial distinction: Lacan's registers are not in any orthodox Freudian sense stages of development. Nevertheless—as the pre-

5. Eugénie Grandet: *Mirrors and Melancholia*

vailing tendency to temporalize Lacan's registers indicates—there is enough ambiguity in Lacan to make possible and perhaps even inevitable a slippage in the direction of the developmental, a slippage against which what follows struggles but to which it does occasionally succumb. The basic texts in which Lacan elaborates these notions are: Jacques Lacan, *Ecrits; Séminaire I: Les écrits techniques de Freud* (Paris: Seuil, 1975), and *Séminaire II: Le moi dans la théorie de Freud et dans la technique de la psychanalyse* (Paris: Seuil, 1978). In addition to the standard works on Lacan's thought by Anika Rifflet-Lemaire, *Jacques Lacan* (Brussels: Dessart, 1970) and Anthony Wilden, *The Languages of the Self* (Baltimore: Johns Hopkins University Press, 1968), and Jean Laplanche and J.-P. Pontalis, *The Language of Psychoanalysis,* among recent writings on Lacan I have found the following articles particularly useful: Fredric Jameson, "Imaginary and Symbolic in Lacan: Marxism, Psychoanalytic Criticism, and the Problem of the Subject," *Yale French Studies* (1977), 55/56:338–395; Gregory Ulmer, "The Discourse of the Imaginary," *Diacritics* (Spring 1980), 10:61–75; Malcolm Bowie, "Jacques Lacan" in John Sturrock, ed. *Structuralism and Since: from Lévi-Strauss to Derrida,* (Oxford: Oxford University Press, 1979), pp. 116–153, and Jane Gallop, "Lacan's 'Mirror Stage': Where to Begin," *SubStance* (1982), 37/38:118–128.

3. Shoshana Felman, *The Literary Speech Act: Don Juan with J. L. Austin, or Seduction in Two Languages,* p. 138. Cf. these remarks by Michèle Montrelay regarding the treatment by certain analysts of the "female imaginary" as a "poor relative": "Can we not ask ourselves instead whether the imaginary by giving 'consistency,' as Lacan puts it, to the symbolic which is a gap, is not just as operative, just as determining of the structure as are the real and the symbolic. To give consistency, to give body to the symbolic fractioning: that operation precedes any possible grasp of the subject in its image and that of the other. There exists a primary *imaginaire* which is not unrelated to feminine jouissance," *L'Ombre et le nom: Sur la fémininité,* pp. 155–156.

4. Honoré de Balzac, *Eugénie Grandet* (Penguin), p. 51; *Eugénie Grandet* (Garnier-Flammarion), p. 30. All subsequent references to these editions will be included in the text.

5. One might describe the mother-daughter relationship in *Eugénie Grandet* in the terms provided by Nancy Chodorow in *The Reproduction of Mothering: Psychoanalysis and the Sociology of Gender:* "prolonged symbiosis and *narcissistic overidentification* are particularly characteristic of early relationships between mothers and daughters" (p. 104; emphasis added).

6. Mehlman, *A Structural Study,* p. 25.

7. Sigmund Freud, "On Narcissism: An Introduction," in *The Standard Edition of the Complete Psychological Works of Sigmund Freud,* 14:91. All subsequent references will be indicated by the abbreviation *S.E.* and included in the text.

8. I am thinking in particular of René Girard's commentary on this aspect of Freud's essay in *Des Choses cachées depuis la fondation du monde,* pp. 391–405. For a feminist critique of Girard's reading of Freud on female narcissism see Sarah Kofman, "The Narcissistic Woman: Freud and Girard," *Diacritics* (Fall 1980): 10:36–45.

5. Eugénie Grandet: *Mirrors and Melancholia*

9. André Green, "Un, Autre, Neutre: Valeurs narcissiques du Même," p. 43.

10. Julia Mitchell, *Psychoanalysis and Feminism*, pp. 42–43.

11. *Ibid.*, p. 52.

12. Luce Irigaray, "La 'Méchanique' des fluides," in *Ce Sexe qui n'en est pas un*, p. 115.

13. Irigaray, *Speculum de l'autre femme*, p. 71. Irigaray is, of course, quoting from Freud, "Some Psychical Consequences of the Anatomical Distinction Between the Sexes," in *S.E.* 19:253.

14. On this point there is a striking convergence of Balzac's and Freud's formulations: "This was Eugénie's humble thought . . . The poor child was unjust to herself; but humility, or rather the fear of being unworthy, is one of the first awakened attributes of love" (p. 94); "it is easy to observe that libidinal object-cathexis does not raise self-regard. The effect of dependence upon the loved object is to lower that feeling: a person in love is humble. A person who loves has, so to speak, forfeited a part of his narcissism," in Freud, *S.E.* 14:98. Cf. André Green, "Un, Autre, Neutre," p. 63.

15. John Berger, *Ways of Seeing*, p. 47.

16. Irigaray, *Speculum*, p. 106.

17. In a recent article entitled, " 'Sleeping Beauty' as Ironic Model for *Eugénie Grandet*," John Gale likens Eugénie's pre-Charles state to that of Perrault's sleeping princess and observes that for Eugénie Charles' arrival "turns into a true rebirth" (p. 29).

18. The novel is, let us note, placed under the sign of Mariolatry; the name of the woman to whom it is dedicated—Maria—serves as a matrix, a master signifier of the fiction. On several occasions, Eugénie is compared to Mary (see in particular pp. 94 and 183). There are then (at least) two Christian narrative programs operative in Balzac: the Christic model (e.g., *Père Goriot*), and the Marial model (e.g., *Eugénie Grandet*), in other words, the masculine and feminine Christian novels.

19. *Speculum*, p. 78. Irigaray introduces this notion in her discussion of the little girl's response to the discovery of woman's castration. Irigaray suggests that the little girl might opt for melancholia, all the more so as Freud's description of her reaction to this unwelcome discovery bears a striking, almost point by point similarity to the symptomatology of melancholia. Implicit in this analogy is the fact that the penis belongs to that class of objects whose loss cannot be overcome through mourning work (pp. 78–84).

20. *Ibid.*, pp. 84–85.

21. Felman, "To Open the Question," pp. 8–9. In outlining the *new* psycho-analytic mode of reading she is proposing to present and practice, Felman writes: "The notion of *application* would be replaced by the radically different notion of *implication*: bringing analytical questions to bear upon literary questions, *involving* psychoanalysis in the scene of literary analysis, the interpreter's role would here be, not to apply to the text an acquired science, a preconceived knowledge, but to act as a go-between, to *generate implications* between literature and psycho-analysis—to explore, bring to light and articulate the various (indirect) ways in

which the two domains do indeed *implicate each other*, each one finding itself enlightened, informed, but also affected, displaced, by the other."

22. In their fine full-length study of *Eugénie Grandet* (*Balzac. Sémiotique du personnage romanesque: L'Exemple d' "Eugénie Grandet,"* p. 254), which appeared after this article was written, Roland Le Huenen and Paul Perron also use the word "pact" to describe the mother/daughter generic bonding.

23. Balzac is, indeed, at great pains to stress the implausibility of his fiction: "Quite often the things that human beings do appear literally incredible [littérairement parlant invraisemblables] although in fact they have done them. We might be less incredulous, perhaps, if we did not nearly always omit to throw a sort of psychological light on impulsive decisions, by examining the mysterious birth of the reasons that made them inevitable. Perhaps Eugénie's passion should be traced to the source from which its most delicate fibres sprang, its roots in the depths of her nature, and analyzed there, for it became, as would be sneeringly said in the future, a disease, and influenced her whole existence" (pp. 127–128). Gérard Genette has demonstrated in his classical essay, "Vraisemblance et motivation" *(Figures II)* that in Balzac there is the creation of an "artificial verisimilitude" which masks the "arbitrariness of the narrative." For a groundbreaking feminist reading of Genette's text, see Nancy Miller, "Emphasis Added: Plots and Plausibilities in Women's Fiction."

24. Cf. Le Huenen and Perron's Jungian analysis of the Eugénie-Charles relationship (*Balzac,* pp. 193–199). Despite our different psychoanalytic approaches—for Le Huenen and Perron, the romance of Eugénie and Charles is one of *anima* and *animus*—I concur in viewing Eugénie's attraction to Charles as rooted in an imaginary identification. According to Le Huenen and Perron, Eugénie is initially fascinated by Charles' femininity; what they exchange in the course of their relationship is nothing other than their sexual identities: Charles becomes a man, while Eugénie is feminized. Transcoded and generalized: love in the mirror stage is always homosexual.

25. Claude Lévi-Strauss, "The Structural Study of Myth," in *Structural Anthropology,* p. 207.

26. In my "Female Fetishism: The Case of George Sand" (forthcoming, *Poetics Today*), following Sarah Kofman, *L'Enigme de la femme* and Elizabeth Berg, "The Third Woman," *Diacritics,* I take woman's deliberate indecision as symptomatic of female fetishism: ultimately woman's indecision is always grounded in the refusal to decide the question of sexual difference.

27. Leo Bersani, "The Subject of Power," p. 16.

6. SALAMMBÔ BOUND

"Salammbô Bound" was written especially for the official French celebration of the centenary of Gustave Flaubert's death and presented as part of the "Journée d'Etudes: Flaubert, la Femme, la Ville," in Paris, November 1980. I wish to take this opportunity to thank Claude Duchet, who

6. Salammbô Bound

not only invited me to participate in this event, but was also instrumental in having several of my earlier efforts published. As part of his tireless efforts in behalf of nineteenth-century French studies, he has helped many young scholars get their start in the field. "Salammbô Bound" appears in French in the proceedings of the Paris colloquium, edited by Marie-Claire Bancquart, and as part of the proceedings of the University of Bielefeld Colloquium, at which it was also read, it is forthcoming in German: *Flaubert im Orient*, André Stoll, ed. (Surkamp).

1. Sainte-Beuve, Lundi du 22 déc, 1862, *Nouveaux Lundis*, 13 vols. (Paris: Michel Lévy Frères, 1865), 4:82. All translations mine except where otherwise noted. This article as well as all the other articles which comprise the dossier of the controversy is reproduced in the appendix to the Club de l'Honnête Homme edition of *Salammbô*, p. 436. All further references to this edition will be indicated by the abbreviation CHH. Cf. CHH, pp. 384 and 408–409.

2. Gustave Flaubert, *Salammbô: A Story of Ancient Carthage*, p. 382. All references to the English text are drawn from the Brentano edition.

3. I am alluding here to a remark by R. J. Sherrington in *Three Novels by Flaubert:* "One may doubt the validity of this statement, and even Flaubert's sincerity in making it" (p. 215).

4. *Correspondance*, 2:343, as quoted by Jean-Pierre Richard in *Littérature et sensation*, p. 196.

5. Jacques Neefs, "*Salammbô*, textes critiques," p. 56.

6. Gustave Flaubert, letter of October 1857 to Charles Edmond, in *Extraits de la Correspondance, ou Préface à la vie d'écrivain*, p. 197.

7. CHH, p. 437. Cf. Froehner's judgment: "Salammbô is not a daughter of the earth; she is an extra-natural being, too highly placed to *interest* readers here below" (CHH, p. 379; emphasis added).

One could write a study about the critical response to Salammbô, a character who is always taken to task in one way or another for not "animating" the novel! Thus Dussolier writes: "There is a moment when one thinks that Salammbô, Hamilcar's daughter, who lives—no she does not live, she nods hieratically between her stupid nurse and a python snake—will become animated and at the same time animate the novel. It is when she goes to find Mâtho in his tent and following the example of Judith in the Bible, gives herself to him to take back the Zaïmph. Wrong! Nothing moves, nothing musses the stiff folds of the novel" (CHH, p. 407). As we will see below this opinion is not based on a very attentive reading of the novel.

8. Jacques Derrida, *La vérité en peinture*, p. 66.

9. Gustave Flaubert, *Salammbô* (Garnier-Flammarion), p. 207. All references to the French text of the novel are drawn from this edition.

10. Victor Brombert, *Flaubert par lui-même*, p. 82.

11. "I want to make something *purple*" ("je veux faire quelque chose de *pourpre*")—remark attributed to Flaubert by Jules and Edmond de Goncourt in the March 17 entry of their *Journal*, 4:167. Cf. Roland Barthes, *The Pleasure of*

6. Salammbô Bound

the Text, p. 31 for the negative connotations of the color purple under modernism.

12. E. H. Gombrich, *The Sense of Order: A Study of the Psychology of Decorative Art*, p. 116. All quotations refer to this edition.

13. The evenly poised attention of the spectator of the decorative arts is comparable in particular to the "wandering viewpoint" of the reader in Wolfgang Iser's poetics of reading; see *The Act of Reading: A Theory of Aesthetic Response*.

14. Roland Barthes, *Camera Lucida: Reflections on Photography*, p. 27. There are interesting divergencies and uncanny covergencies between my approach to the detail and Barthes' (which I discuss at greater length in my "Sublime Details: From Reynolds to Barthes"). Divergencies: Barthes recognizes that he is finally interested only in the detail that "is not, or at least not strictly intentional" (p. 47), a sort of "found detail" that the photographer cannot help but reproduce. Now, for obvious reasons, this type of referential detail does not exist in literature. There are, of course, textual details which escape the author's conscious intentions, but they are not necessarily, if at all, imposed on the text by mimetic determinations. Convergencies: à propos of the photograph entitled "Family Portrait" by the black photographer James Van der Zee, Barthes writes: "Reading Van der Zee's photograph, I thought I had discerned what moved me: the strapped pumps of the black woman in her Sunday best; but this photograph has *worked* within me, and later on I realized that the real *punctum* was the necklace she was wearing; for (no doubt) it was this same necklace (a slender ribbon of braided gold) which I had seen worn by someone in my own family" (p. 53). What makes this coincidence uncanny is that Barthes' book had not yet appeared when I stumbled over my gold chainlet. *Could it be that the gold chainlet is the detail of details?*

15. Ananda K. Coomaraswamy, *Figures of Speech or Figures of Thought: Collected Essays on the Traditional or 'Normal' Views of Art*, p. 86.

16. Jean Rousset, "Positions, distances, perspectives dans 'Salammbô,' " *Poétique* (1971), 6:154. One might object that all that Flaubert occults in the scene under the tent (ch. 11), is exposed in the scene where Salammbô makes love with the serpent. One need only superimpose one scene on the other to dispell the mystery and remove the censorship. I would respond by saying that what matters on the contrary is the strategy deployed by Flaubert to escape censorship, in a word, *différance*. Flaubert's *captatio benevolentia* produces a series of aftereffects that precipitate events into uncertainty.

17. Jacques Derrida, *Dissemination*, pp. 212–213.

18. *Ibid.*, p. 216.

19. Sigmund Freud, "Fetishism," *The Standard Edition of the Complete Psychological Works*, 21:154.

20. *Ibid.*, p. 152.

21. Guy Rosolato, "Le Fétichisme dont se 'dérobe' l'objet," p. 36. Let us note in passing the relationship Rosolato establishes between the fetish and perspective, which is of more than passing interest to us (see p. 38).

22. Cf. Flaubert, *Madame Bovary*, p. 38. If we superimpose this passage from

6. Salammbô Bound

Salammbô on the famous description of Charles' cap, the fetishistic network linking the glans/gland/gold, and the brilliant stands out very clearly.

23. Julia Kristeva, *About Chinese Women*, p. 83.
24. Jean Baudrillard, *Pour une critique de l'économie politique du signe*, p. 104.
25. Coomaraswamy, *Figures of Speech*, p. 64. The gold chain reappears in the description of the Queen of Saba in *La Tentation de Saint Antoine,* but displaced upwards along the vertical axis: "A flat golden chain passing under her chin runs up along her cheeks, spirals around the blue-powdered hair, and then dropping down grazes past her shoulder and clinches over her chest on to a diamond scorpion, which sticks out its tongue between her breasts" ("Une chaîne d'or plate, lui passant sous le menton, monte le long de ses joues, s'enroule en spirale autour de sa coiffure, poudrée de poudre bleue, puis, redescendant, lui effleure les épaules et vient s'attacher sur sa poitrine à un scorpion de diamant, qui allonge la langue entre ses seins"). Flaubert, *The Temptation of Saint Anthony* (Cornell University Press), p. 84, and *La Tentation de Saint Antoine* (Garnier-Flammarion), p. 63.
26. Flaubert, *Correspondance*, 2:148.
27. As quoted by Vincent Descombes in *Modern French Philosophy*, p. 189.

7. GERMINIE LACERTEUX: NATURALIZING WOMAN

As a paper *"Germinie Lacerteux:* Naturalizing Woman" was read at the 1982 meeting of NEMLA in a session organized by Sandy Petrey, whose close readings and constructive criticism of several of these texts I am pleased to acknowledge.

1. Roland Barthes, *S/Z*, pp. 172–173.
2. Edmond and Jules de Goncourt, *Journal,* as quoted by Hubert Juin in the preface to *Germinie Lacerteux,* p. 9. Translation mine. All references to the French text are to Union Générale edition.
3. Edmond and Jules de Goncourt, *Germinie*, p. 9. All future references to the English text are to the Weidenfeld and Nicolson edition.
4. Hélène Cixous, in Catherine Clément and Hélène Cixous, *La jeune née*, p. 276.
5. Emile Zola, *Nana* (Penguin), p. 459; and *Nana*, p. 430.

8. UNWRITING LAMIEL

"Unwriting *Lamiel,*" published here for the first time, was read at the Eighth Annual Colloquium in Nineteenth-Century French Studies held at Harvard, 1983. My thanks to Susan Suleiman and Laurie Edson for having invited me to participate.

1. Nancy Miller, *The Heroine's Text*, p. x.
2. Michael Riffaterre, "Flaubert's Presuppositions," in *Flaubert and Postmodernism*, pp. 177–191.
3. Gustave Flaubert, *Madame Bovary,* (Norton), p. 63; and *Madame Bovary* (Garnier-Flammarion), pp. 122–123. Emphasis added.

8. *Unwriting* Lamiel

4. I am referring here to Richard Bolster, *Stendhal, Balzac et le féminisme romantique*, p. 102, and F. W. J. Hemmings, *Stendhal: A Study of his Novels*, p. 206. By far the most frequent intertext invoked in criticism on *Lamiel* is Marivaux's *La Vie de Marianne*. The anachronistic impulse in *Lamiel* criticism is not, I hasten to add, solely retrospective; it is prospective as well. When Lamiel is not being compared to an eighteenth-century heroine, she is read as a modern woman, assimilated to whatever the dominant image of the "new woman" happens to be: "nor, do I suspect," writes the translator of the 1929 American edition of *Lamiel*, one Jacques le Clercq, "is there a scarcity of Lamiels among the sisterhood we call, for want of a better name, flappers," *Lamiel*, p. xi. More recently, updating the code, Gita May has, in an article that places great emphasis on Stendhal's debt to eighteenth-century representations of woman, imagined that in our turbulent times Lamiel "would have become the prototype of the urban guerilla ready to immolate herself in her rebellion against the arbitrary and oppressive powers of an unjust society," in "Le féminisme de Stendhal et 'Lamiel,' " p. 201. Whether Lamiel is viewed as a reincarnation of an eighteenth-century heroine (Juliette, Marianne, Mme de Merteuil, Mme Roland) or a precursor of a twentieth-century liberated woman, there is a clear consensus among her readers that she is not of her time, nor, as we shall see below (n. 6), of her sex.

5. Stendhal, *Lamiel,* Victor Del Litto, ed. (Cercle du Bibliophile). All translations mine except where otherwise noted. All references in French are to this edition.

6. See for example, Henri Martineau, *L'Œuvre de Stendhal: Histoire de ses livres et de sa pensée*, p. 507: "une sorte de Julien femelle"; or, Casimir Stryienski, *Lamiel*, p. v: "petite cousine de Julien Sorel"; or most recently, Anne-Marie Meininger, Introduction to *Lamiel* p. 8: "ce Julien Sorel féminin."

7. Dennis Porter, *"Lamiel:* The Wild Child and the Ugly Men," p. 21.

8. As Anne-Marie Meininger remarks: "Depuis l'arrêt du texte initial, le 3 décembre 1839, jusqu'au 19 mars 1841, la création a constamment évolué dans le même sens: l'effacement de Lamiel" (p. 18). This observation is not, however, followed up by anything which might be described, however loosely, as a feminist reading. Rather, as her contribution to the speculations on the reasons for *Lamiel's* incompletion, and basing herself on the identification of Lamiel with one of Stendhal's great unhappy love's, Mélanie Guilbert, Meininger arrives at the astounding conclusion that Stendhal stopped writing when he came to the realization that Mélanie-Lamiel was a lesbian (p. 29).

9. Simone de Beauvoir, *The Second Sex,* p. 242. In French, the word for Stendhal's preferred heroines is "prisonnières," a word rich in Proustian resonances. At the close of the Stendhal chapter of *Histoires d'amour,* Julia Kristeva chides de Beauvoir (and other first-stage feminist readers of Stendhal) for failing to probe the sexual fantasies underlying the novelist's memorable portrayals of bold and brilliant emancipated women, regressive fantasies of women as archaic maternal deities vested with mortiferous powers (pp. 338–340). While I agree with Kristeva that Stendhal's feminism is ambiguous in ways de Beauvoir does not choose to explore, for me what matters are the contradictions not between a

reformist ideology and an archaic private sexual theater, but rather between that ideology and a historically determined scriptural economy.

10. On woman in nineteenth-century France, see Jean-Paul Aron, ed., *Misérable et glorieuse: La femme du XIXe siècle,* and Michel Foucault, *The History of Sexuality;* on "Realism and the fear of desire" see the chapter by that title in Leo Bersani, *A Future for Astyanax: Character and Desire in Literature,* pp. 51–88. Finally, on the impact of the discovery of the second law of thermodynamics (1852) on fiction, the fundamental works are Michel Serres, *Hermès III: La Traduction* and *Feux et Signaux de Brume: Zola.* In an article entitled, "Details and Decadence: End-troping in *Madame Bovary,*" *SubStance* (1980); 26:27–35, I examine what I term an end-trope, the longest metaphor in *Madame Bovary,* looking at the ways in which the death of woman's desire produces a kind of figural aberration. For the proper functioning of the realist text, woman's desire can be allowed neither to die nor to run free. Significantly, Emma's waning fantasies about Léon are described in terms of a dying fire somewhere in the steppes of Siberia.

11. On the subject of pedagogy and literature, see Barbara Johnson, ed., *The Pedagogical Imperative: Teaching as a Literary Genre.*

12. Genette, *Palimpsestes: La Littérature au second degré,* p. 194.

13. Jacques Laurent, *La fin de Lamiel* in Stendhal, *Lamiel* suivi de *La fin de Lamiel,* p. 247.

14. See Honoré de Balzac, *Etudes sur M. Beyle: Analyse de 'La Chartreuse de Parme,'* and Georg Lukács, *Studies in European Realism,* pp. 65–84.

9. FEMALE PARANOIA: THE CASE FOR PSYCHOANALYTIC FEMINIST CRITICISM

An early version of this text was presented at a discussion session organized by Carolyn Greenstein Burke at the 1979 MLA; subsequently, a revised version appeared in the Special Feminist Issue of *Yale French Studies* (1981), no. 62, entitled "French Texts/American Contexts," edited by the Dartmouth Feminist Collective, whose sound editorial recommendations are gratefully acknowledged.

1. Sigmund Freud, *The Standard Edition of the Complete Psychological Works,* ed. James Strachey and trans. James Strachey et al., 24 vols. (London: Hogarth Press, 1953–74), 12:79.

2. Freud, *S.E.* 23: 268.

3. Freud, *S.E.* 17: 261.

4. Phyllis Chesler, *Women and Madness,* pp. 42–43, and 50.

5. Ruth Mack Brunswick, "The Analysis of a Case of Paranoia (Delusion of Jealousy)," p. 170.

6. Freud, *Collected Papers,* 2:150. All future references will be included in the body of the text.

7. For an illuminating Lacanian reading of this text and this scene in particular, see Guy Rosolato, "Paranoia et Scène Primitive," in *Essais sur le symbolique,* pp. 199–241.

9. Female Paranoia

8. *Ibid.*, p. 233. All translations mine except where otherwise noted.

9. Julia Kristeva, *Polylogue* (Paris: Seuil, 1977), p. 14. I wish to thank Alice Jardine for sharing with me her expertise in translating Kristeva's texts.

10. Kristeva, *Desire in Language: A Semiotic Approach to Literature and Art*, p. 240.

11. Kristeva, *Polylogue*, p. 79.

12. See Kristeva, "Féminité et écriture. En réponse à deux questions sur *Polylogue*," especially p. 500, and "Héréthique de l'amour," in particular pp. 45–46.

13. Rosolato, p. 223.

14. Kristeva, *Polylogue*, p. 269; the quotations are from Hegel's *Phenomenology of Spirit*.

15. See, for example, in Kristeva, *About Chinese Women*, p. 30; Carolyn Greenstein Burke, "Report from Paris: Women's Writing and Women's Movement," p. 852, no. 18.

16. Eugénie Lemoine-Luccioni, *Partage des femmes*, p. 101.

17. *Feminine Sexuality: Jacques Lacan and the 'école freudienne,'* p. 147. On the preceding page Lacan makes it quite clear that he is concerned exclusively with vaginal jouissance: "Petty considerations about clitoral orgasm or the *jouissance* designated as best one can, the other one precisely, which I am trying to get you to along the path of logic, since, to date, there is no other" (pp. 145–146).

18. Bonaparte and Lacan as quoted by Jacques Derrida in "The Purveyor of Truth," p. 68.

19. Derrida, p. 69.

20. *Ibid.* Bonaparte's attention to the detail of the knob-clitoris should be read in the light of the amazing pages she devotes to the clitoris in her book, *Female Sexuality*. Basing herself on the three developmental paths Freud charts for women, Bonaparte divides women into three categories: the *acceptative* (normal, vaginal women), the *renunciatory* (Virginal), and the *claimant* (homosexual and/or clitoridal). In the section entitled "Evolutionary Perspectives," she focuses on strategies the "clitoridals" resort to in their adaptation to the environment, in particular a bizarre surgical procedure, the so-called Halban-Narjani operation, which involves repositioning the clitoris closer to the urethral passage. According to Bonaparte's biographer, Celia Bertin, Narjani was the pseudonym Bonaparte adopted to write about female frigidity and to promote the therapeutic virtues of Halban's operation. In despair over her own persistent frigidity, in 1927, "she let Halban sever her external clitoris from its position and move it closer to the opening of the vagina. She always referred to the procedure by the code name 'Narjani,' her pseudonym. The operation, performed in the presence of Ruth Mack under local anesthesia, took only twenty-two minutes." *Marie Bonaparte: A Life*, p. 170. Despite Freud's disapproval of her resort to surgery, Bonaparte had herself operated on by Halban twice more, first in 1930 and then again in 1931, to no avail.

19. Derrida, p. 69.

21. Any attempt to link attention to all manner of details to a specifically feminist hermeneutics is bound to fail, for attention to details is characteristic of the post-Freudian textual approaches of Foucault, Barthes, and Derrida, to name only

the most spectacular self-styled contemporary *detailists*. For another example of the kind of clitoral reading I am proposing here, see my complementary text: "Female Fetishism: The Case of George Sand" (*Poetics Today*, forthcoming), where I focus on the detail of bizarre wounds inflicted on the female body in several of Sand's novels. The related question of the link between detailism and femininity is taken up more fully in my genealogy of the detail as aesthetic category, "Sublime Details: from Reynolds to Barthes."

22. Edgar Allan Poe, *The Complete Tales and Poems*, p. 222. All subsequent references will be included in the text.

23. The entire tale takes the form of a transposition of the facts of an actual crime which took place in New York City into a Parisian setting, and is made up for a large part of purported translations of French newspaper articles into English. Because this tale involves a de-naturalization, followed by a re-naturalization of American texts via a fictive Parisian setting, it is emblematic of the trans-Atlantic shuttle Franco-American scholars are perpetually engaged in.

24. Cf. Roman Jakobson's essay in *Fundamentals of Language* and Jacques Lacan, "The agency of the letter in the unconscious or reason since Freud," *Ecrits*, in particular pp. 156–157.

Bibliography

Aron, Jean-Paul, ed. *Misérable et glorieuse: la femme du XIXe siècle*. Paris: Fayard, 1980.

Auerbach, Nina. *Woman and the Demon: The Life of a Victorian Myth*. Cambridge: Harvard University Press, 1982.

Bachellier, Jean-Louis. "Sur-Nom." *Communications* (1972), 19:69–92.

Balzac, Honoré de. *Etudes sur M. Beyle: Analyse de "La Chartreuse de Parme."* Geneva: Skira, 1943.

Balzac, Honoré de. *Eugénie Grandet*. Marion Ayton Crawford, tr. Harmondsworth: Penguin, 1955.

Balzac, Honoré de. *Eugénie Grandet*. Paris: Garnier-Flammarion, 1964.

Balzac, Honoré de. *La peau de chagrin*. Paris: Garnier-Flammarion, 1971.

Balzac, Honoré de. *The Wild Ass's Skin*. Herbert J. Hunt, tr. Harmondsworth: Penguin, 1977.

Barthes, Roland. *S/Z*. Richard Miller, tr. New York: Hill & Wang, 1974.

Barthes, Roland. *The Pleasure of the Text*. Richard Miller, tr. New York: Hill & Wang, 1975.

Barthes, Roland. *Camera Lucida: Reflections on Photography*. Richard Howard, tr. New York: Hill & Wang, 1981.

Barthes, Roland. *A Barthes Reader*. Susan Sontag, ed. New York: Hill & Wang, 1982.

Baudelaire, Charles. *Œuvres complètes*. Paris: Bibliothèque de la Pléiade, 1961.

Baudrillard, Jean. *Pour une critique de l'économie politique du signe*. Paris: Gallimard, "Tel," 1972.

Beauvoir, Simone de. *The Second Sex*. H. M. Parshley, tr. New York: Knopf, 1971.

Berg, Elizabeth. "The Third Woman." *Diacritics* (Summer 1982), 12:11–20.

Berger, John. *Ways of Seeing*. Harmondsworth: Penguin, 1972.

Bersani, Leo. *A Future for Astyanax: Character and Desire in Literature*. Boston: Little, Brown, 1976.

Bibliography

Bersani, Leo. "The Subject of Power." *Diacritics* (Fall 1977), 7: 2–21.

Bertin, Celia. *Marie Bonaparte: A Life.* New York: Harcourt Brace Jovanovich, 1982.

Bolster, Richard. *Stendhal, Balzac et le féminisme romantique.* Paris: Lettres Modernes, Minard, 1970.

Bonaparte, Marie. *Female Sexuality.* New York: International Universities Press, 1953.

Borie, Jean. *Zola et les mythes.* Paris: Seuil, 1971.

Bremond, Claude. *Logique du récit.* Paris: Seuil, 1973.

Brombert, Victor. *Flaubert par lui-même.* Paris: Seuil, 1971.

Brunswick, Ruth Mack. "The Analysis of a Case of Paranoia (Delusion of Jealousy)." *Journal of Nervous and Mental Diseases* (1929), 70:1–22, 155–178.

Burke, Carolyn Greenstein. "Report from Paris: Women's Writing and Women's Movement." *Signs* (Summer 1978), 3:843–855.

Chesler, Phyllis. *Women and Madness.* New York: Avon Books, 1973.

Chodorow, Nancy. *The Reproduction of Mothering: Psychoanalysis and the Sociology of Gender.* Berkeley: University of California Press, 1978.

Cixous, Hélène. "The Laugh of the Medusa." Keith Cohen and Paula Cohen, trs. *Signs* (1976), 1: 875–893.

Clément, Catherine and Hélène Cixous, *La jeune née.* Paris: Union Générale d'Editions, 10/18, 1975.

Coomaraswamy, Ananda K. *Figures of Speech or Figures of Thought: Collected Essays on the Traditional or "Normal" Views of Art.* 2d series. London: Luzac, 1946.

Culler, Jonathan. *Structuralist Poetics.* Ithaca: Cornell University Press, 1976.

Danahy, Michael. "Le roman est-il chose femelle?" *Poétique* (1976), 25:85–106.

d'Aurevilly, Barbey. *Bewitched.* Louise Collier Willcox, tr. New York: Harper, 1928.

d'Aurevilly, Barbey. *Un Prêtre marié.* Paris: Livre de Poche, 1964.

d'Aurevilly, Barbey. *L'Ensorcelée.* Paris: Garnier-Flammarion, 1966.

d'Aurevilly, Barbey. *Les Diaboliques.* Paris: Garnier-Flammarion, 1967.

Debray-Genette, Raymonde. "Les Figures du récit dans *Un cœur simple.*" *Poétique* (1970), 3:348–364.

Deleuze, Gilles. *Proust et les signes.* Paris: P.U.F., 1971.

Deleuze, Gilles. *Logique du sens.* Paris: Union Générale d'Editions, 10/18, 1973.

Deleuze, Gilles. "Table ronde." *Cahiers Marcel Proust* (1975).

Derrida, Jacques. *Glas.* Paris: Galilée, 1974.

Bibliography

Derrida, Jacques. "The Purveyor of Truth." Willis Domingo et al. trs., *Yale French Studies* (1975), 52:31–114.

Derrida, Jacques. *Of Grammatology*. Gayatri Chakravorty Spivak, tr. Baltimore: Johns Hopkins University Press, 1976.

Derrida, Jacques. *La vérité en peinture*. Paris: Champs-Flammarion, 1978.

Derrida, Jacques. *Dissemination*. Barbara Johnson, tr. Chicago: University of Chicago Press, 1981.

Descombes, Vincent. *Modern French Philosophy*. L. Scott-Fox and J. M. Harding, trs. Cambridge: Cambridge University Press, 1979.

Dezalay, Auguste. "Les mystères de Zola." *Revue des sciences humaines* (1975), 160:475–487.

Duchet, Claude. "Romans et objets: L'Exemple de *Madame Bovary*." *Europe* (1969), 485–87:172–201.

Duchet, Claude. "Signifiance et insignifiance: Le discours italique de *Madame Bovary*." In Claudine Gothot-Mersch, ed., *La Production du sens chez Flaubert*. Paris: Union Générale d'Editions, 10/18, 1975.

Durand, Gilbert. *Les Structures anthropologiques de l'imaginaire*. Paris: Bordas, 1969.

Felman, Shoshana. "To Open the Question." *Yale French Studies* (1977), 55/56: 5–10.

Felman, Shoshana. *The Literary Speech Act: Don Juan with J. L. Austin, or Seduction in Two Languages*. Catherine Porter, tr. Ithaca: Cornell University Press, 1983.

Flaubert, Gustave. *Salammbô*. Dora Knowlton Ranous, ed. and tr. New York: Brentano's, 1919.

Flaubert, Gustave. *Extraits de la correspondance, ou Préface à la vie d'écrivain*. Geneviève Bollème, ed. Paris: Seuil, 1963.

Flaubert, Gustave. *Salammbô*. Paris: Garnier-Flammarion, 1964.

Flaubert, Gustave. *Madame Bovary*. Paul de Man, tr. New York: Norton, 1965.

Flaubert, Gustave. *Madame Bovary*. Paris: Garnier-Flammarion, 1966.

Flaubert, Gustave. *La Tentation de Saint Antoine*. Paris: Garnier-Flammarion, 1967.

Flaubert, Gustave. *Salammbô*. Paris: Club de l'Honnête Homme, 1971.

Flaubert, Gustave. *Sentimental Education*. Robert Baldick, tr. London: Penguin, 1978.

Flaubert, Gustave. *The Temptation of Saint Anthony*. Kitty Mrosovsky, tr. Ithaca: Cornell University Press, 1980.

Foucault, Michel. *The History of Sexuality*. Robert Hurley, tr. New York: Random House, 1978.

Freud, Sigmund. *The Standard Edition of the Complete Psychological Works*.

Bibliography

24 vols. James Strachey, ed.; James Strachey, Anna Freud, Alix Strachey, and Alan Tyson, trs. London: Hogarth Press, 1953–1974.

Freud, Sigmund. *Collected Papers.* 6 vols. Joan Rivière, tr. London: Hogarth Press, 1933.

Gale, John. " 'Sleeping Beauty' as Ironic Model for *Eugénie Grandet.*" *Nineteenth-Century French Studies* (Fall–Winter 1981–1982), 10:28–36.

Gallop, Jane. *Feminism and Psychoanalysis: The Daughter's Seduction.* London: Macmillan, 1982.

Gallop, Jane. "Beyond the Jouissance Principle." *Representations* (1984), 7:110–115.

Gautier, Théophile. *Works of Gautier.* 12 vols. F. C. Sumichrast, tr. Boston: C. T. Brainard, 1900–1903.

Genette, Gérard. *Figures.* Paris: Seuil, 1966.

Genette, Gérard. *Figures II.* Paris: Seuil, 1969.

Genette, Gérard. *Figures III.* Paris: Seuil, 1972.

Genette Gérard. "Table ronde." *Cahiers Marcel Proust* (1975), 7: 91–92.

Genette, Gérard. *Mimologiques: Voyages en Cratylie.* Paris: Seuil, 1976.

Genette, Gérard. *Palimpsestes: La littérature au second degré.* Paris: Seuil, 1982.

Gilbert, Sandra and Susan Gubar. *The Madwoman in the Attic: The Woman Writer and the Nineteenth-Century Literary Imagination.* New Haven: Yale University Press, 1979.

Girard, René. *Deceit, Desire, and the Novel.* Yvonne Freccero, tr. Baltimore: Johns Hopkins University Press, 1965.

Girard, René. *Violence and the Sacred.* Patrick Gregory, tr. Baltimore: Johns Hopkins University Press, 1977.

Girard, René. *Des Choses cachées depuis la fondation du monde.* Paris: Grasset, 1978.

Girard, René. Interview. "Special Issue on the Works of René Girard." *Diacritics* (Spring 1978), 8: 31–54.

Gombrich, E. H. *The Sense of Order: A Study of the Psychology of Decorative Art.* Ithaca: Cornell University Press, 1979.

Goncourt, Edmond and Jules de. *Germinie.* Introduction by Martin Turnell. London: Weidenfeld and Nicolson, 1955.

Goncourt, Edmond and Jules de. *Germinie Lacerteux.* Paris: Union Générale d'Editions, 10/18, 1979.

Goncourt, Edmond and Jules de. *Journal: Memoires de la vie.* 22 vols. Robert Ricatte, ed. Monaco: Les éditions de l'imprimerie nationale de Monaco, Fasquelle et Flammarion, 1956.

Granoff, Wladimir. *La pensée et le féminin.* Paris: Editions de Minuit, 1976.

Bibliography

Green, André. "Un, Autre, Neutre: Valeurs Narcissiques du Même." *Narcisses, Nouvelle Revue de Psychanalyse* (1976), 13:37–79.

Hamon, Philippe. "Zola, romancier de la transparence." *Europe* (1968), 468–469: 385–391.

Hamon, Philippe. "Un discours contraint." *Poétique* (1973), 16:411–445.

Hamon, Philippe. "Du savoir dans le texte." *Revue des sciences humaines* (1975), 160:489–499.

Hamon, Philippe. "Pour un statut sémiotique du personnage." In *Poétique du récit.* Paris: Points, 1977.

Hamon, Philippe. *Le Personnel du roman: Le système des personnages dans les Rougon-Macquart d'Emile Zola.* Geneva: Droz, 1983.

Hemmings, F. W. J. *Stendhal: A Study of his Novels.* Oxford: Clarendon Press, 1964.

Irigaray, Luce. *Speculum de l'autre femme.* Paris: Editions de Minuit, 1974.

Irigaray, Luce. *Ce Sexe qui n'en est pas un.* Paris: Editions de Minuit, 1977.

Iser, Wolfgang. *The Act of Reading: A Theory of Aesthetic Response.* Baltimore: Johns Hopkins University Press, 1978.

Jakobson, Roman. *Fundamentals of Language.* The Hague: Mouton, 1956.

Johnson, Barbara, ed. *The Pedagogical Imperative: Teaching as a Literary Genre.* A Special Issue of *Yale French Studies* (1982), vol. 63.

Kamuf, Peggy. *Fictions of Feminine Desire.* Lincoln: University of Nebraska Press, 1982.

Kofman, Sarah. *L'Enigme de la femme: La Femme dans les textes de Freud.* Paris: Galilée, 1980.

Kolodny, Annette. "Dancing Through the Minefield: Some Observations on the Theory, Practice, and Politics of a Feminist Literary Criticism." *Feminist Studies* (Spring 1980), 6:1–25.

Kristeva, Julia. *About Chinese Women.* Anita Barrows, tr. New York: Urizen Books, 1977.

Kristeva, Julia. "Héréthique de l'amour." *Tel Quel* (Winter 1977), 74:30–49.

Kristeva, Julia. *Polylogue.* Paris: Seuil, 1977.

Kristeva, Julia. "Féminité et écriture. En réponse à deux questions sur *Polylogue.*" *Revue des Sciences Humaines* (1977), 168:495–501.

Kristeva, Julia. *Desire in Language: A Semiotic Approach to Literature and Art.* Leon Roudiez, ed.; Leon Roudiez, Tom Gora, and Alice Jardine, trs. New York: Columbia University Press, 1980.

Kristeva, Julia. *Histoires d'amour.* Paris: Denoël, 1983.

Lacan, Jacques. *Ecrits.* Paris: Seuil, 1966.

Lacan, Jacques. *Ecrits: A Selection.* Alan Sheridan, tr. New York: Norton, 1977.

Bibliography

Lacan, Jacques. *The Four Fundamental Concepts of Psycho-Analysis*. Jacques-Alain Miller, ed.; Alan Sheridan, tr. New York: Norton, 1978.

Lacan, Jacques. *Feminine Sexuality: Jacques Lacan and the 'école freudienne.'* Juliet Mitchell and Jacqueline Rose, eds.; Jacqueline Rose, tr. New York: Norton, 1982.

Laclos, Choderlos de. *Dangerous Acquaintances: Les liaisons dangereuses.* Richard Aldington, tr. London: Routledge & Kegan Paul, 1979.

Laplanche, Jean and J.-B. Pontalis. *The Language of Psychoanalysis*. Donald Nicholson-Smith, ed.; introduction by Daniel Lagache. New York: Norton, 1973.

Laurent, Jacques. *La fin de Lamiel*. In *Lamiel* followed by *La fin de Lamiel*. Paris: Union Générale d'Editions, 10/18, 1966.

Le Huenen and Paul Perron. *Balzac. Sémiotique du personnage romanesque: L'Exemple de "Eugénie Grandet."* Montreal: Les Presses de l'Université de Montréal, Didier Edition, 1980.

Lemoine-Luccioni, Eugénie. *Partage des femmes*. Paris: Seuil, 1976.

Lévi-Strauss, Claude. *Structural Anthropology*. Claire Jacobson and Brooke Grundfest Shoepf, trs. Garden City, N.Y.: Anchor Books, 1967.

Lubbock, Percy. *The Craft of Fiction*. New York: Viking, 1957.

Lukács, Georg. *Studies in European Realism*. New York: Grosset and Dunlap, 1964.

Martineau, Henri. *L'œuvre de Stendhal: Histoire de ses livres et de sa pensée*. Paris: Le Divan, 1945.

Maupassant, Guy de. *Complete Works of Guy de Maupassant*. 9 vols. Alfred de Sumichrast et al., trs. Boston: C. T. Brainard, 1910.

Maupassant, Guy de. *Correspondance inédite de Guy de Maupassant*. Paris: Editions Dominique Wapler, 1951.

Maupassant, Guy de. *A Woman's Life*. H. N. P. Sloman, tr. Baltimore: Penguin, 1965.

Maupassant, Guy de. *Une Vie*. Paris: Livre de Poche, 1971.

Maupassant, Guy de. *Notre Cœur*. Paris: Livre de Poche, 1972.

Maupassant, Guy de. *Pierre et Jean*. Paris: Livre de Poche, 1973.

Maupassant, Guy de. *Mont-Oriol*. Paris: Bibliothèque Marabout, 1975.

May, Gita. "Le féminisme de Stendhal et 'Lamiel.' " *Stendhal Club* (1978), 78:191–203.

Mehlman, Jeffrey. *A Structural Study of Autobiography*. Ithaca: Cornell University Press, 1974.

Miller, Nancy. *The Heroine's Text*. New York: Columbia University Press, 1980.

Miller, Nancy. "Novels of Innocence: Fictions of Loss." *Eighteenth-Century Studies* (Spring 1978):325–339.

Bibliography

Miller, Nancy. "Emphasis Added: Plots and Plausibilities in Women's Fiction." *PMLA* (January 1981), 96:325–339.

Mitchell, Juliet. *Psychoanalysis and Feminism*. New York: Vintage Books, 1974.

Mitchell, Juliet and Jacqueline Rose, eds. *Feminine Sexuality: Jacques Lacan and the 'école freudienne.'* Jacqueline Rose, tr. New York: Norton, 1982.

Modleski, Tania. "The Search for Tomorrow in Today's Soap Operas: Notes on a Feminine Narrative." *Film Quarterly* (1975), 5:12–21.

Moi, Toril. "The Missing Mother: The Oedipal Rivalries of René Girard." *Diacritics* (1982) 12:21–31.

Montrelay, Michèle. *L'Ombre et le nom: Sur la féminité*. Paris: Editions de Minuit, 1977.

Muller, Marcel. *Les Voix narratives dans "La recherche du temps perdu."* Geneva: Droz, 1965.

Neefs, Jacques. "La figuration réaliste." *Poétique* (1973), 16:466–476.

Neefs, Jacques. "*Salammbô*, textes critiques." *Littérature* (1974), 15:52–64.

Paris, Jean. *Le Point aveugle*. Paris: Seuil, 1975.

Poe, Edgar Allan. *The Complete Tales and Poems*. New York: Random House, 1938.

Porter, Dennis. "*Lamiel*: The Wild Child and the Ugly Men." *Novel* (Fall 1978), 12:21–32.

Rank, Otto. *The Trauma of Birth*. New York: Harper, 1973.

Richard, Jean-Pierre. *Littérature et Sensation*. Paris: Seuil, 1954.

Richard, Jean-Pierre. *Proust et le monde sensible*. Paris: Seuil, 1974.

Richard, Jean-Pierre. "Céline et Marguerite." *Critique* (October 1976), 353:919–935.

Riffaterre, Michael. "Flaubert's Presuppositions." In Naomi Schor and Henry F. Majewski, eds., *Flaubert and Postmodernism*. Lincoln: University of Nebraska Press, 1984.

Rosolato, Guy. *Essais sur le symbolique*. Paris: Gallimard, 1969.

Rosolato, Guy. "Le fétichisme dont se 'dérobe' l'objet." *Nouvelle Revue de Psychanalyse* (1970), 2: 31–39.

Sainte-Beuve. *Nouveaux Lundis*. 13 vols. Paris: Michel Lévy, 1864.

Sartre, Jean-Paul. *L'Idiot de la famille*. 3 vols. Paris: Gallimard, 1971.

Schor, Naomi. *Zola's Crowds*. Baltimore: Johns Hopkins University Press, 1978.

Schor, Naomi. "La pèrodie: superposition dans *Lorenzaccio*." *Michigan Romance Studies* (1982), 2:73–86.

Bibliography

Schor, Naomi and Henry F. Majewski, eds. *Flaubert and Postmodernism*. Lincoln: University of Nebraska Press, 1984.

Schor, Naomi. "Female Fetishism: The Case of George Sand." *Poetics Today,* forthcoming.

Serres, Michel. *Feux et signaux de brume: Zola*. Paris: Grasset, 1975.

Serres, Michel. *Hermès III: La Traduction*. Paris: Editions de Minuit, 1974.

Serres, Michel. *Hermès IV: La Distribution*. Paris: Editions de Minuit, 1977.

Sherrington, R. J. *Three Novels by Flaubert*. Oxford: Oxford University Press, 1970.

Stendhal. *Lamiel*. Casimir Stryienski, ed. Paris: Librairie Moderne, 1889.

Stendhal. *Lamiel*. Jacques le Clercq, tr. New York: Brentano's, 1929.

Stendhal. *Lamiel*. Victor del Litto, ed. Geneva: Cercle du Bibliophile, 1971.

Stendhal. *Lamiel*. Anne-Marie Meininger, ed. Paris: Folio, 1983.

Tanner, Tony. *Adultery in the Novel*. Baltimore: Johns Hopkins University Press, 1979.

Todorov, Tzvetan. *The Poetics of Prose*. Richard Howard, tr. Ithaca: Cornell University Press, 1977.

Vial, André. *Guy de Maupassant et l'art du roman*. Paris: Nizet, 1954.

Wetherill, P. M. "*Madame Bovary*'s Blind Man: Symbolism in Flaubert." *Romanic Review* (1970), 61:35–42.

Wilson, Angus. *Emile Zola*. London: Mercury Books, 1965.

Zola, Emile. *A Page of Love*. 2 vols. T. F. Rogerson, tr. Philadelphia: George Barrie, 1897.

Zola, Emile. *Œuvres complètes*. 15 vols. Henri Mitterand, ed. Paris: Cercle du Livre Précieux, 1962–1969.

Zola, Emile. *Les Rougon-Macquart*. 5 vols. Henri Mitterand, ed. Paris: Bibliothèque de la Pléiade, 1963–1967.

Zola, Emile. *Nana*. Paris: Garnier-Flammarion, 1968.

Zola, Emile. *Nana*. George Holden, tr. Harmondsworth: Penguin, 1972.

Zola, Emile. *Zest for Life*. Jean Stewart, tr. Bloomington: Indiana University Press, 1956.

Index

Accessory, 114-15

Actaeon, 89

Adams, Parveen, 165*n*31

Aesthetics, 112-13, 129-30; Kant's, 114; modernist, 115-16; Parnassian, 115

Albouy, Pierre, "Le Mythe de l'androgyne dans *Mademoiselle de Maupin*," 167*n*6

Allegory, 45, 105, 133

Analepsis, 128

Androgyny, 5, 28, 30-31

Ariadne, 3-5, 164*n*11

Aron, Jean-Paul, *Misérable et glorieuse: La Femme du XIXe siècle*, 182*n*10

Artaud, Antonin, 155

Artemis, 97

Asmodeus, 36, 37

Asyndeton, 20

Atropos, 105

Auerbach, Nina, *Woman and the Demon*, xi

Autobiography, 90, 171*n*23

Axis, 130; of algomania, 101; castration, 12; of class difference, 128; of communication, 7, 14; of consummation, 58; diachronic, 145; of eroticism, 58; of profitability, 58; of reproduction, 58; semantic, 58; of sexual difference, 101, 128; speech, 7, 9; of substitution, 174*n*14; synecdochic, x; vertical, xi, 9, 180*n*25

Bachelard, Gaston, 3

Bachellier, Jean-Louis, "Sur-Nom," 171*n*28

Balzac, Honoré de, xii, 30, 32, 45, 91, 93-94, 99, 101, 127, 136-37, 146, 177*n*23; *La Cousine Bette*, 97; *Etudes sur M. Beyle: Analyse de "La Chartreuse de Parme*,"

145, 182*n*14; *Eugénie Grandet*, xiii, 91-107 passim, 136, 137, 176*nn*14, 18, 177*nn*23, 24; *Illusions perdues*, 106; *La Peau de Chagrin*, 44-46, 94; *Père Goriot*, 97, 176*n*18; *La Recherche de l'absolu*, 97; *Splendeurs et misères des courtisanes*, 106

Bardèche, Maurice, 113-14, 115, 117-18

Barthes, Roland, 3-4, 20, 33, 116, 127-28, 135, 141-42, 145, 157, 179*n*14, 184*n*21; *Camera Lucida: Reflections on Photography*, 179*n*14; "Flaubert and the Sentence," *A Barthes Reader*, 166*n*35; Hermeneutic Code, xii-xiii, 33, 43-44, 46, 167-68*n*18; *Image-Music-Text*, 165*n*31; *Le Plaisir du texte (Pleasure of the Text)*, 29, 50, 165*n*31, 178-79*n*11; *S/Z*, xiv, 127, 165*n*22, 167*n*6

Baudelaire, Charles, 5, 6, 28, 159

Baudrillard, Jean, 123

Beauvoir, Simone de, *The Second Sex*, 142, 181*n*9

Berg, Elizabeth, "The Third Woman," 177*n*26

Berger, John, *Ways of Seeing*, 96

Bernini, Gian Lorenzo, 158

Bersani, Leo, 107, 142; *A Future for Astyanax: Character and Desire in Literature*, 182*n*10

Bertin, Celia, *Marie Bonaparte: A Life*, 183*n*20

Bildungsroman, 90

Bloom, Harold, xii

Body, 29, 39, 156; and clitoris, 156; desirable, 55; diseased, 55; female, x, 50, 57, 114, 142, 146, 155, 169*n*9, 184*n*21; and female paranoia, 156; and female theorizing, 154, 156; fetishization of, 146; and jouissance, 157; knowledge of,

Index

Index

Index

Index

Index

Index